MYTHBREAKER

MYTHBREAKER

*Kiran Mazumdar-Shaw and the
Story of Indian Biotech*

Seema Singh

COLLINS
BUSINESS

First published in hardback in India in 2016 by Collins Business
An imprint of HarperCollins *Publishers* India

Copyright © Seema Singh 2016

P-ISBN: 978-93-5177-839-4
E-ISBN: 978-93-5177-840-0

2 4 6 8 10 9 7 5 3 1

Seema Singh asserts the moral right to be identified
as the author of this work.

The views and opinions expressed in this book are the author's own
and the facts are as reported by her, and the publishers are
not in any way liable for the same.

All rights reserved. No part of this publication may be reproduced,
stored in a retrieval system, or transmitted, in any
form or by any means, electronic, mechanical,
photocopying, recording or otherwise,
without the prior permission
of the publishers.

HarperCollins *Publishers*

A-75, Sector 57, Noida, Uttar Pradesh 201301, India
1 London Bridge Street, London, SE1 9GF, United Kingdom
Hazelton Lanes, 55 Avenue Road, Suite 2900, Toronto, Ontario M5R 3L2
and 1995 Markham Road, Scarborough, Ontario M1B 5M8, Canada
25 Ryde Road, Pymble, Sydney, NSW 2073, Australia
195 Broadway, New York, NY 10007, USA

Typeset in 11.5/14.5 Minion Pro at
SÜRYA, New Delhi

Printed and bound at
Thomson Press (India) Ltd.

For Mum and Dad

CONTENTS

	Prologue	1
1.	Brewing a Business	6
2.	A Decade with Unilever	38
3.	Birth of a Cluster	71
4.	Transformation: From Enzymes to Drugs	99
5.	Diversification: Closing the Life Sciences Loop	129
6.	Start-up Becomes a Corporate	161
7.	Big, Hairy Bets	204
8.	The Start-up Industry	229
9.	Public Life	264
10.	The Road Ahead	281
	Epilogue	300
	Notes and References	305
	Index	317
	Acknowledgements	323
	About the Author	324

PROLOGUE

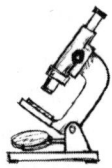

'She is pushing sixty and still at it,' I said to Leslie Auchincloss.

'I am eighty-two and I am also at it,' he shot back seriously, going on to admit that he was gobsmacked at what Kiran Mazumdar-Shaw had done with her garage start-up in thirty-seven years, one that he had helped start and grow. He marvelled at how, in her entrepreneurial journey, she has managed to break the kind of myths that abound in the Indian scenario – a tech start-up seeded nearly four decades ago in life sciences and *not* information or communication technology, by a woman who was *not* an engineer and who did *not* come from a business family.

As one of India's earliest technology start-ups (the other being Patni Computers, founded in 1976), Biocon today stands solitary among its peers. No life science business of scale has come up in nearly fifteen years. When Biocon went public in 2004, many believed it would pave the way for other biotechnology companies to follow suit. Not a single firm did. If anything, the second company – though only tangentially biotech – to list in July 2015 was Syngene, also from the Biocon stable. In early 2016, Strand Life Sciences opted to go to Nasdaq, in a reverse merger with an American diagnostics company. Raising growth capital in clinical genomics was proving to be daunting in India.

Economic Darwinism and reverent isolationism of Indian academics have ensured that biotech companies remain small. It's unfortunate, because this is the age of biology, just as the twentieth century was the age of physics. All global metrics point towards more real tech innovations happening in life sciences or at its intersection with other disciplines.

Still, Kiran Mazumdar-Shaw managed multiple risks to build business within business, consistently ratcheting her company's scientific capability and, no less importantly, her own public profile. Much like evolution, but on a shorter time frame. A brewer who did not understand what a joint venture meant, today makes a deal almost every quarter. As I learnt, much of her selection, like in nature, has been based on random mutation.

Biotech companies have traditionally started with science. She started with technology, and added science at the back end, and then kept adding to it. A good part of that thrust had to do with her early team of chemical engineers, almost all of them from the Indian Institute of Technology (IIT), a brand that fuelled Silicon Valley's start-up engine as well. It was not by design, she says. 'All those who understood biotech in those days gravitated towards me. At that time, it made a lot more sense to get engineers who would help me deliver products, it was never about science.'

Over time she became a brand ambassador, not just of a fledgling industry but of innovation-led business in general. By interacting with the funding and regulatory agencies and the political system, she gave a face to the industry. 'It would have been difficult to build the industry without a face. In the vaccine industry, there were some very credible and visible people, but she emerged as a stronger face of tough entrepreneurship,' says Maharaj Kishan Bhan, former secretary, Department of Biotechnology.

Pursuing life sciences is expensive. One of India's foremost chemists, Gautam Desiraju, once told me that India has done well in chemistry, and he was referring to the success of generics companies, because 'chemistry is cheap'. Of course, he was lamenting the resources available for science in India but the point he made explains why the chemistry-based pharmaceutical industry grew faster and became bigger than biotech in India in the same span of time. Given the similar talent pool both sectors tap into, comparisons are inevitable. In fact, in the course of writing this book, some pharmaceutical executives asked me why I was not writing instead about Dilip Shanghvi, founder of Sun Pharmaceuticals, which after numerous acquisitions had emerged as the biggest pharma company in India and the fifth largest generics company in the world. Another pharma chief vexedly said, 'Biotech entrepreneurs complain too much.'

Like in business, in science too the methods of chemistry and biology are competitive. As this famous 1936 conversation between the American electrical genius Charles Steinmetz and Nobel Prize-winning chemist Carl Bosch, then head of the German chemical company IG Farben, goes: 'Bosch, I know you can make indigo cheaper than God, some day you may make rubber cheaper than God, but you will never make cellulose cheaper than God.' That was before the Second World War, before biologists and engineers had been introduced to the power of biotechnology.

That power unleashed a Janus-faced tool in the hands of tech tinkerers, but countries like India dragged their feet in regulatory overhaul. Policy often lags behind innovation but to lag behind by more than a decade is hara-kiri.

In August 2001, when former US president George Bush announced that only sixty-four stem cell lines could be used for doing research using federal money in the United States, ten of those cell lines being from two Indian laboratories, I had just returned from a journalism fellowship programme at the Massachusetts Institute of Technology (MIT). Programme director and former science editor at the *New York Times*, Boyce Rensberger, said I had a 'bonanza' waiting for me back home since I could write 'so many stories on stem cells from India'. I did write a few, but they were more about their runaway commercial use in the absence of any regulation, not on any breakthroughs. India, unfortunately, had become notorious for snake oil treatments.

Fifteen years later, with Stempeutics winning a patent in Japan and regulatory approval for orphan drug indication in the European Union for its stem cells product, the industry stands partly exonerated. But remember, it took the Bengaluru company eight years to get here.

Regulatory hoops impact the speed and scale of biotech business, which then impact how often a biotech entrepreneur hits the headlines, how 'cool' or 'uncool' she is in public perception. In 2011, a reporter from *India Today*'s Delhi office visited XCyton, a molecular diagnostics company in Bengaluru, and spent two days understanding the multiplex technology and the Bio Safety Level-3 lab that the company runs. Then he made an error – he missed the decimal in the revenue figure – and was heard pleading with his editor for his story to live. The story was eventually killed. For the magazine, the marker for success was a certain revenue cut-off; the brand new technology did not matter.

Some of these Ph.D holders and scientists don't make your typical entrepreneur. They do not build companies for scale or exit, but is it a cause or an effect that the famous Saxenian 'brain circulation' phenomenon has not occured in biotech? Founders still cannot find science-minded business executives as their replacements. In 2005, when Janakiraman Ramachandran was raising the second round of funding in India for Gangagen, which he founded after retiring from AstraZeneca India Research Centre, an Indian fund almost ready to invest was dissuaded by a veteran investor because 'the founder was seventy'! Ramachandran returned to the Bay Area in San Francisco and since then has raised $28 million. Gangagen's novel molecule, anti-Staph recombinant polypeptide, is designed and developed in Bengaluru, produced at Syngene, and it recently completed phase-two clinical trials in Singapore.

A decade later, sentiments are a bit different. De novo biotechs are finally being born, though still countable on your fingers. And a functional cluster is finally emerging in Bengaluru – followed by Hyderabad, Pune and Delhi – in which Biocon and Kiran seem to have played anchoring roles. Cluster development is not easy; there is no formulaic process to do it. Japan and parts of Europe have tried building them without success. The true biotech clusters of the United States were not built by design, in the top-down manner that Singapore has tried with Biopolis. However, to the successful clusters of Boston, Bay Area and San Diego, there's been a new addition – Cambridge, in the United Kingdom, which has been a long time in the making.

Clusters are also not made through policy alone – it's a mix of people, academics and industry, even media. In Bengaluru, a large number of engineering and aerospace public sector units provided the working-class culture, similar to what the defence industry offered in San Diego. 'It is part circumstance, part climate,' says the current biotech secretary K. VijayRaghavan, 'and part distance from Delhi.'

I came to this story as a journalist; I did not intend to write a definitive history of Indian biotechnology. I was interested in the 'whatness' of Kiran's story, to borrow a term from late *Washington Post* editor Benjamin Bradlee, than the 'rightness' or 'wrongness'. If this book falls short of narrating this 'whatness', the fault lies with me.

As for a book on Dilip Shanghvi's incredible journey, I am sure someone someday will write it but any comparison between the two entrepreneurs is neither necessary, nor fair. Endocrinologist Harold Lebovitz at the State University of New York, a clinical advisor to Biocon who has also conducted various programmes for Sun and other Indian drug companies, puts it correctly: 'These two are like apple and orange. Biocon is a research company that is running a number of programmes to bring new drugs to change the course of the disease. Sun is a fabulous company that is good at introducing products to people to treat them. But both are different.'

Finally, *Mythbreaker* is not a commissioned book, though many have flung this question at me: 'Is this your book or Kiran's?' She agreed to cooperate on reading a short note, as did publisher Karthika V.K. at HarperCollins India. I am grateful to both for not asking more at that time.

1

BREWING A BUSINESS

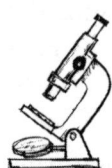

THE RELUCTANT ENTREPRENEUR

Baroda can get muggy and hot in late March. On 25 March 1978, Kiran Mazumdar woke up to a whirring fan, a mix of anticipation and unease, and a phone call. Later in the day, she was leaving for Delhi from where she would fly to Scotland to begin work at a malting company, on her 'voyage to a new land'. On the other side of the phone line she heard: 'Hi, this is Les Auchincloss. Can we meet today?' Kiran had received a telegram from him that he was reaching Baroda and would like to meet her.

The meeting was fixed for forenoon; her train, the Rajdhani Express, was in the evening. After a few weeks of experimentation with some enzymes at Barmalt Malting Limited in Gurgaon (a far cry from the urban sprawl and corporate powerhouse that it is today), she would join Moray Firth Maltings in Scotland. Three years earlier, she had returned from Australia with a degree in brewing which did not get her a job; she figured that being a woman brewmaster was not acceptable in India. It was not safe for the employers.

At Express Hotel, the only upscale hotel in Baroda in the late 1970s, Auchincloss told her about his business which dealt with enzymes and process improvement formulations for the brewing industry. Until then, Biocon Biochemicals in Ireland had been sourcing some raw materials from India but now Auchincloss wanted to set up a local company. He had come to Baroda in search of a partner who would start and run Biocon India.

A few minutes into the meeting that day, he asked Kiran to be his partner.

'You must be joking,' she told him. She was in Baroda helping her father wind up his business. After retiring as the chief brewmaster at United Breweries (UB) in Bengaluru, Rasendra Mazumdar had started a malting company in Baroda. It wasn't quite successful and the Mazumdars had lost a good part of their post-retirement savings. ('I want to forget it like a bad dream,' says his wife Yamini Mazumdar, decades later.) Kiran had watched her father piece together his self-esteem and build on a consulting life, amidst which Auchincloss landed with his proposal. It meant giving up a new job overseas to start a new venture in India. It was a ballsy bet all right.

Auchincloss wasn't ready to give up easily. He said he would be in Delhi for a few more days and would like to meet her again even as she continued to intern at Barmalt.

To deflect Auchincloss's attention, Kiran decided to introduce him to Puran Chand, founder of Barmalt, a successful business and one of the top four companies in the Indian malting industry. Auchincloss had by then contracted diarrhoea but still came to Puran Chand's guest house for a discussion.

The next day, Auchincloss asked Puran Chand if he would mind if he met Kiran separately for dinner. At Imperial Hotel, where he was staying, Auchincloss said: 'Thanks for introducing me to Puran Chand but I don't really want a business partnership with him. I want an entrepreneur and I want you to be that entrepreneur.' She would not need the money she thought she needed, he assured her, nor would she need any business expertise. He would mentor her. He even offered to call Oliver Griffin, managing director of Moray Firth Maltings, to tell him that she had changed her mind.

As the two crossed the bar at the hotel, they found Rasendra Mazumdar with his drink. He was returning from Kolkata and had a business halt in Delhi before proceeding to Baroda. Auchincloss walked up to him and said he needed help in convincing his daughter to join him. That night, Mazumdar Sr chose to have dinner with the two potential partners but made sure he did not influence his daughter one way or the other. The decision was hers to make.

At around 9 p.m., Auchincloss finally pried Kiran loose from her Scottish employer by promising her that if she did not enjoy the work after a year, he would make sure she got the same job, or some other, in the brewing industry in the United Kingdom. Kiran took the bait. She informed Puran Chand that she was accompanying Auchincloss the next morning to the Horlicks plant in Nabha near Chandigarh and would no longer intern at Barmalt.

The Horlicks plant was run by John Buchanan, a Scotsman who told her she was welcome to do trials with Biocon's enzymes in the plant. Besides, Auchincloss had some enzymes and $3,000 cash with him which he gave to Kiran, instructing her to get started on setting up Biocon India. They had agreed it would be located in Bengaluru, a city she grew up in and where, thanks to her father's network in the brewing industry, getting early customers would be easy. Two months later, she set off for Ireland, where, for the next few months, she would develop processes for isinglass and papain, two products for which India was particularly suited to supply raw materials – collagen from dried swim bladders of a certain marine fish and a proteolytic enzyme from the tropical fruit, papaya.

THE COMPULSIVE ENTREPRENEUR

There are entrepreneurs, and then there are entrepreneurs' entrepreneurs. Most often, the entrepreneurs start a venture by taking a calculated step or by acting randomly, the latter by placing their faith in people – they don't just incubate their own ideas but push and pull people along the way to hatch their ideas. And thus, a whole tree of ideas takes root. Leslie Auchincloss belonged to the latter category. He would pick his team members from different geographies, select people who could work together and innovate collectively. (By mid-2015, when he was eighty-two, he had started thirty-seven companies of which three had failed miserably. One of the fiascos was a start-up in yacht building; another was mobile dry-cleaning, certainly an idea ahead of its time.)

After graduating from Glasgow University in 1955, Auchincloss had gone to Canada as a brewmaster to Canadian Breweries Limited. Eight years later, when he returned to Ireland, it was to 'clean up' the breweries his company was buying. The Canadians had better brewing technology and he was responsible for setting those standards in Irish plants. After twelve years of service at the Canadian company, he exited to join BioCel which was started by an ex-colleague, and did a variety of things, all of which were consolidated to form Biocon. A few years later, in 1969, Auchincloss branched out to run his own business.

The branching out was geographic as well. Very quickly, he had Biocon subsidiaries set up in Edinburgh, Spain and Australia, the latter two with the help of a Kurd in Edinburgh who was a victim of German prosecution and had 'all sorts of contacts' overseas. Every time Auchincloss flew to Australia, he would stop at Mumbai and visit a few breweries. 'They would all universally say, "Oh yes, we will buy your enzymes" and shake their heads. But, of course, we never got any business,' he remembers.

On one such trip to Australia, he once said to Colin Dowzer, who was heading Biocon Australia, that he was going nowhere in India and they needed to find someone with 'passion'. Dowzer suggested Kiran's name as he knew her from the brewing course at Ballarat University whose students would visit the breweries he had worked at. He didn't know what Kiran was up to those days but he did know she was in Baroda.

In 1978, when Auchincloss met Kiran, Biocon Ireland was five years old with a laboratory in Cork, in south-western Ireland, where he had spent a lot of time working on enzymatic extraction of cereals. After much experimentation, he had come up with a blend which would allow distilleries to make more liquor. Around that time, he had also begun to test the American market and landed on the east coast to visit one of Seagram's distilleries. He covered more ground in the US, all the while 'living like a hostage', and eventually got an order for a container of enzymes. But the products he was showcasing in the US were made from enzymes originating in Japan and Biocon did not have enough supplies. The Irish start-up was buying most of its enzymes from Japan and blending them to make formulations. Somehow, they managed to deliver the American order of a container-full but Auchincloss understood it was time to have their own manufacturing facility. He bought some old fermenters to start the submerged fermentation facility in Cork. Over the years, visiting old equipment farms to scrounge for a good deal would become the norm as Auchincloss brought more people like himself on board to tinker with new ideas.

'In Biocon, we'd look at the idea, smell it and say: Give it a go, give it a lush. More often than not, we would get it right,' says Declan MacFadden, who started as a general manager of the Cork facility.

Auchincloss would often get ideas on flights, where, by some strange coincidence, he frequently met interesting people. 'They were not always the greatest ideas, but they were new ideas. You had to sift,' says Joe Dunne. Hired as a technical director in 1976,

Dunne came to know Auchincloss after he sold one of his flagship products, invertase, an enzyme that was used in the production of soft-centred chocolate and had a long market life in the After-Eight mint chocolate that Rowntree produced. (Nestle now makes thin mints after it acquired Rowntree in 1988.)

One day, Auchincloss came to Dunne and said that while returning from London, he had met a guy who had a mink farm in Canterbury on the south-west coast of Ireland. He took out a crumpled piece of paper from his pocket and, reading from it, said the farm owner had '57,000 kilos of mink bodies every year and it was free material which the guy wanted someone to take away'.

When Dunne asked what he would do with mink bodies, Auchincloss said he wanted to 'extract enzymes out of it'.

Which enzymes? Dunne asked, befuddled. Auchincloss looked at him as if he had asked a seriously stupid question. 'That's your job, Joe. That's what I hired you for.'

Hiring, according to Auchincloss, was the key ingredient in his entrepreneurial recipe. He almost obsessed over it, to the extent that he had a handwriting reader in Cork whose analyses he greatly relied upon. However prized the candidate may be, if the lady did not rank him or her high on integrity – based on the handwriting analysis – he would not hire the person. Once, after he fell out with a senior hire who quit after some acrimony, he confided in Colin Dowzer, his manager in Australia: 'I knew it, the guy ranked only seven in the integrity index.' (A good hire had to score eight and above.) So, when he went back to Ireland after meeting Kiran, he described her in detail to his colleagues: 'A fantastic, enthusiastic, ass-kicking woman who is aggressive, demanding, and would make a great partner for Biocon.'

Soon the Ireland team would meet her when she arrived for an orientation and training programme in June 1978. One day, during that period, she was in the lab, learning how to make cheese colour from annatto seeds that grow on the tropical shrub *Bixa orellana*. The colour, which ranges from yellow to orange, is on the outer coat of the seed but when Dunne entered the lab, it was splashed all over the walls. He offered to help her but she said she would do it herself. 'That was the beginning of our relationship,' Dunne remembers, a relationship that would take a new colour years later when they together knocked at investors' doors.

AUSTRALIA TO IRELAND

Medicine for girls, engineering for guys – those were the stereotypical career options for students in India in the early 1970s. When Kiran did not qualify for the medical entrance test, that conventional path was ruled out. Her father refused to pay the capitation fee that many medical colleges charged in India. 'He said he'd rather keep that money in my bank account than give it as capitation fee,' Kiran remembers. She took to zoology rather seriously though. When students at Central College – hardly the most stimulating of intellectual places in Bengaluru – would be 'watching Hindi movies on K.G. Road, she would be studying hard', says Pratima Rao, a childhood friend. 'Kiran was different from us,' she recalls. 'As teenagers, many of us were dissenters, questioning our parents, sporting that I-don't-care attitude but she was not a rebel; she was very sensitive about her parents.'

Upon graduating with a Bachelor of Science degree in zoology, she began to explore the options that lay in store for her. At United Breweries, her father had sent a few people from his company to pursue a course in brewing at Ballarat College of Advanced Education at Ballarat University in Australia. He himself had trained at the Brewing School at Heriot-Watt University in Edinburgh in 1946 and had returned to become the first-ever Indian brewmaster.

He encouraged her, eldest of his three children, to pursue the one-year course. Brewing was, after all, the oldest kind of biotechnology and it suited her aptitude for applied science. At Ballarat, Kiran was the only woman in the class of 1975. In fact, the brewing course did not have a woman for many more years after that. In 2015, the university named a road in its Mt Helen campus as Mazumdar Drive.

*

In 1975, when Kiran returned to Baroda, the family was at the airport to receive her. She came out and lit a cigarette. If Mazumdar Sr was surprised to see her non-smoker daughter take a drag, he did not show it; instead, he asked her if he could borrow one. Brother Ravi Mazumdar, who smoked in front of his father – he even had a friend coming over to their house to smoke – has vivid memories of that arrival. 'When she came back, she was a completely changed person. She had become a person who wanted to lead … she was no longer a person who would simply submit and accept things.'

Two years younger than her, Ravi was then studying at IIT Powai in Mumbai, and would see her only during vacations. 'When she left for Australia she was my parents' daughter; when she returned, she was, in a way, the main person in the family.' He believed that during her stay at Ballarat, she came to realize she was intellectually superior to her classmates. As she was learning the process of brewing, she had begun to understand the science behind it. 'She took a different tack on brewing than the brewers around her,' Ravi says.

But here she was in Baroda, a back-of-beyond place from where she was expected to eke out her career. No brewery in the country was willing to 'risk' its plant by having a woman brewmaster, not even United Breweries from where her father had just retired. Dismayed at how potential employers treated her – with such blatant gender discrimination – she worked as a technical manager at her father's company, Standard Maltings, in Baroda for a while, but that was not the life she wanted. The city offered a cramped and conservative lifestyle. To beat the boredom, she began to learn music – classical Hindustani vocal from Ghulam Rasool Khan, nephew of noted vocalist Ustad Faiyaz Khan of the Agra gharana.

In two years, she became reasonably good at singing but her father's business worsened and it had to be wound up. Although a successful and well-known brewmaster in Bengaluru, his failing business in Gujarat had taken a toll on his self-esteem. The family had sold its house on Cunningham Road in Bengaluru to invest in the business which, after twenty-seven years of service at United Breweries, was meant to keep him engaged as well as generate income. Eager to get back on his feet again, he decided to take up a consulting job at Jupiter Breweries in Kolkata and Kiran joined him as a technical consultant.

On her trips to the city, she wasn't content sitting in the hotel room after office hours. She would go and work at the plant late in the night, even asking the workers to get on with incomplete jobs. Kolkata in the 1970s was a hotbed of political unrest and labour trouble. Many workers did not like her being at the plant at that hour, particularly one worker who had his arm blown off in a violent incident. Kiran wasn't bothered. 'By going to Australia, she got mental emancipation in the true Western sense – that she could do everything. She continued to be that way, but was not satisfied,' rues Ravi Mazumdar.

In 1977, Ravi graduated from Mumbai and went to Imperial College of Science in London to pursue his master's degree. It was then that Kiran made the decision to seek a job overseas.

Starting Up

In September 1978, Kiran returned from Ireland after learning all about making two products – papain and isinglass. 'It was very low-tech stuff and I had a nice buy-back arrangement with Ireland,' she says. Her father had taken up a job in Delhi, so it was easier for her to stay with him and begin the process of getting government approvals for starting Biocon India, as a 70:30 joint venture with Biocon Ireland. Politically, it was not the best of times for 'foreigners' to do business in India. Under the Janata Party, India had sent IBM and Coca-Cola packing the previous year and did not allow multinationals to own more than 30 per cent in an Indian company.

The following two-and-a-half months were spent trekking to and from Udyog Bhawan in Delhi. Nirmal Biswas, head of the Directorate General of Trade Development (DGID) under the Ministry of Commerce, the ministry in charge of approving any foreign investment or joint venture, advised her that the only way to get approval would be to have either import substitution or an export element explicitly listed in the project report. If both could be listed, chances would be higher.

'For someone who did not even know what a joint venture was, getting import–export data in those pre-Internet days was daunting,' she says. As she went around the corridors of Udyog Bhawan, touts followed her. 'Madamji, you give it to us, we'll make the project report and get the approval. You will not have to do anything,' they would tell her in Hindi. They asked for a bribe of ₹10,000. 'That was a lot of money in those days. Besides, I only had ₹10,000 in my bank to start the company,' she recounts, sounding indignant even after thirty-seven years. As weeks passed, she began to get worried. The touts would rub it in every time she waited on the corridor benches: 'You keep sitting here, nothing will move.'

One day, she told Biswas what those touts said to her and asked him to tell her frankly if she would ever be able to file a project report and get approval. 'I did not know whom to bribe, how to bribe, when to bribe. So I asked him if it was even worth starting the business.' Biswas then got serious and assured her that he would help her with the application and she would get the approval without paying any bribe to anyone.

Biswas gave her a handful of ministry of commerce publications which had data on what they were importing, and with some extrapolation, she figured out what her company could substitute for these. On exports, she was clear about what and how much she would be able to export to Ireland. Since he could not do much about the brokers floating all over the building, Biswas lent her a desk in a corner of his office and suggested she work there to avoid snooping characters in the corridors. She managed to make a simple project report. There were a few rounds of corrections. Her mother doubled as a driver during the day and a typist at night, incorporating all the changes that Biswas wanted on her Remington typewriter. By the end of October, Kiran had submitted her application.

By mid-November, she received a letter from Biswas saying that her application had been approved; the ministry intimated her by a telegram. This was fast even by today's standards when it takes at least ninety days to start any venture. She wasted no time in applying to the registrar of companies, and Biocon India was incorporated on 29 November 1978.

A tin-roofed shed in Koramangala at a monthly rental of ₹3,000, constituted the office; the laboratory and the manufacturing space were carved out at the back. She placed the order for equipment and began looking for people to work with her. She was twenty-five years old and starting up in a garage of sorts. Prospective employees and colleagues were not willing to risk their future. Somebody in her social circle, always a thriving and ever-expanding entity in her life, recommended two men – Gangappa and Nazir Ahmad – who were in their fifties and about to retire from a tractor factory.

Once the two retired men were on board, she taught them the initial processing of the enzymes and the raw material and with a few daily wage workers, Biocon India got off the mark. 'Even before the first shipments went out, I was keen on everything looking good and hi-tech. I designed uniforms for the workers and promised free food and education for their children,' she recalls. (These employee benefits continued.) Since the India unit had a buy-back arrangement with Biocon Ireland, she was assured of revenue once she started shipping products. Auchincloss had given her an advance payment of £10,000 (which amounted to about ₹1,50,000) against which she was seeking bank credit of ₹3,00,000.

The first call was to Vijaya Bank where she had a current account and knew the branch manager well. The bank asked for collaterals like land or a house; she had neither registered in her name. For the bank, her personal guarantee as the managing director of the company was not enough. They suggested she get her father as a guarantor. After making her 'dance around for two weeks', they refused. 'I was angry but I couldn't do anything. Beggars can't be choosers,' she recalls.

During that time, at a wedding in Hotel Ashok, a former classmate from Ballarat who was now at United Breweries, Devendra Kumar, introduced her to Dinesh Nayak, a manager at Canara Bank. When she complained to him that banks were being unfair to her, he called her to his office and agreed to offer a credit line against a demand draft. Subsequently, she closed her Vijaya Bank account and vowed to never bank with them. (Till today, Biocon India has avoided banking with them even though they tried to make amends later. Canara Bank in Vasanthnagar remained the principal branch until the mid-1990s, when the bank moved Biocon's account to its international branch.)

*

The first professional hire was Subodh Mukherji, a junior brewer from United Breweries. He was being transferred by UB to another city, but he wanted to stay in Bengaluru for his children's education. Once he joined Biocon as factory manager, Kiran was free to focus on marketing and business development. If being a woman brewmaster in Indian breweries was difficult, selling brewing products to those breweries was anything but. Because of her father, who was well respected in the industry, customer doors opened for her; once she had a foothold, she stood her ground on technical competence. Starting with UB, she sold enzymes to many other breweries around the country, including Mohan Meakin, Skol Breweries (now SABMiller) and Associated Breweries. She sold to Barmalt too, Puran Chand's company in Gurgaon, where she had planned to intern.

In the first year, Auchincloss and Kiran hired a station wagon and went around some coastal towns, securing fish maw supplies. In Delhi, her mother would source it from the fish market near Jama Masjid. She would go there once in ten days, chat up the sellers so they would accept a cheque, and buy a few hundred kilos of fish maws. She would then take it to the Patel Roadways' office nearby – with the smelly cart following her rickshaw – and ship the stocks to Bengaluru.

On the company's milestone list, the year 1979 is marked as the year Biocon India became the first Indian company to manufacture and export food processing enzymes to the United States and Europe – symbolic, surely, of her ambition to produce quality products from India, no matter how small.

'She constantly feels that as Indians we have to run faster to stay in the same place. It's all about self-worth; it's not nationalism,' says Ravi Mazumdar.

In late 1979, she came across an advertisement in a local daily, the *Deccan Herald*, about a distress sale of a twenty-acre plot. The first year's sale at Bicon India was ₹8,00,000, with about ₹1,00,000 in profits. The two partners were keen to expand manufacturing in Bengaluru. From a 3,000 sq. ft shed to a twenty-acre plot was like a wild dream, but she discussed it with Auchincloss nonetheless. He had thought of expanding manufacturing in Ireland but it was expensive. So when he looked at a cost estimate of '€168,000 for a 15,000 sq. ft facility in Bengaluru', he found it 'very cheap'. He agreed to release advance payments for buying the piece of land.

'My Irish partners were really great,' Kiran says, with a touch of nostalgia. 'Without them I would not have done half the things I have done. I am really indebted to Les.'

The land was acquired in 1980 for ₹6,00,000. It was now up to her to plan and build a factory. 'When I applied to Karnataka State Finance Corporation for a loan, Chairman S.K. Warrier first made sure I was not a proxy for a male entrepreneur. Then they suggested I apply under a quota for the disabled, Scheduled Castes and Scheduled Tribe, and women entrepreneurs. It was mortifying. On principle, I would not apply against any quota,' she said. Eventually, they approved ₹14 lakh.

During the early 1980s, the construction industry was in overdrive as India prepared for the Asian Games of 1984 and many raw materials – steel and cement in particular – were in short supply. Ironically, a lot of it ended up in the black market. Biocon India's first office and factory premises, the '20th KM Campus' – which today looks more like an institutional campus than a gleaming modern-day corporate head office – took three years to take shape. Every time Kiran would approach the industry secretary Gokul Ram, he would sanction release of cement and steel, but one hundred bags of cement and ten tonnes of steel could go only so far.

Once, relenting to Mukherji's request to procure materials from the black market at a premium of ₹10, she agreed to buy cement. But an overzealous quality division, which was just getting set up, found the cement to be adulterated. That was the end of their purchase history from the black market. The campus was finally inaugurated in November 1983.

Biocon soon began to tie up all the loose ends on company formation and government approvals. In those days, Kiran had a financial consultant on the company board of directors. A chartered accountant who filed tax returns for Vitthal Mallya and other United Breweries executives, H.N. Chandrashekar was introduced to Kiran by her father. A man well versed with finance and company laws, Chandrashekar became the troubleshooter for Biocon India in its first two years. He had lent his garage on Palace Road to expand the Biocon office. Sometime in late 1980, when Karnataka State Finance Corporation Chairman S.K. Warrier and Praful Daftary, then managing director of Skol Breweries and her father's friend, were inducted as directors, Kiran thanked Chandrashekar for his help and guidance and asked him to step down from the board. The company needed to induct a few more directors, she told him.

'Fine, I'll resign,' he said curtly. Kiran and Auchincloss left for Mumbai soon after to meet some customers. When she returned to Bengaluru two days later, her driver handed her a handwritten note from Chandrashekar: 'I would like you to meet me urgently. I am taking some very serious steps since I have been very grossly insulted by you and I will see how you run Biocon. I can expose you and show all the fraud you have committed.'

Shocked, she was clueless how to react. 'I did not know what fraud I had done; he was the one handling every financial transaction,' she recalls.

Chandrashekar, the authorized signatory of the account, had also sent her a copy of the letter he had written to Canara Bank. It said he was withdrawing his guarantee and would like to bring to the bank's notice that there were serious financial frauds being carried out in Biocon and he would like the bank to 'freeze the account'.

At that point, Kiran couldn't turn to anyone for advice. Her accountant was too nervous to even think of a way forward. When she went to the bank, she indeed found her account frozen, even though she had not figured what fraud she 'had been accused of'.

After meeting some senior bank managers and showing them the handwritten note that Chandrashekar had sent to her, Canara Bank allowed her to open a second account, gave her a line of credit and allowed her to transact.

It soon became clear that Chandrashekar wanted to drag her to court. He soon filed a case in which he said she had 'used him' and unfairly dismissed him from the board after committing fraud. Finally, when she went to his house to meet him, with bloodshot eyes and a glass of whiskey in hand he taunted her. 'You wanted to get rid of me. Now you see ... I'll teach you and Auchincloss a lesson.'

Rasendra Mazumdar felt miserable for having introduced Chandrashekar to his daughter. He pleaded on her behalf because her name was being sullied for something she had not done. They all came to an agreement finally: Kiran would pay Chandrashekar ₹3,000 per month for ten years; he would retain Biocon shares which he had received as a board member, and he would be dutifully given annual reports.

In later years when he visited Biocon, Kiran and other staff, particularly finance chief Murali Krishnan, would resort to theatrical dodging, agreeing to his demands to cut his visits short. A few years before the public offering, he sold his shares back to Biocon. Financial distress and illness did him in.

The Core Team

Just at the time Kiran was extracting herself from the financial and legal mess that Chandrashekar had heaped upon her, in May 1981, the accountant at Biocon brought part-time assistance in the form of Murali Krishnan who would come into work in the afternoon for a few hours. Krishnan worked at a small accounting firm which audited Biocon. Within six months of part-time work at Biocon, he moved in as full-time accountant when his predecessor accepted a better offer at Ashok Leyland, a much bigger automotive company.

Krishnan was pursuing a chartered accountancy course and hoped to find a banking job which his mother so dearly wished for him. He stayed on for twenty-five years and never completed his formal accountancy studies.

It was an unexpectedly demanding operation that Krishnan came to. The salary of ₹1,100 was nearly five times higher than what he was getting at the previous firm, but the challenges were equally amplified. His was a one-man show in finance – from writing vouchers to balancing the books. The revenue had grown to ₹80 lakhs in 1981 but due to limited capacity and the agreement with Biocon Ireland, which mandated 80 per cent products for exports and 20 per cent for the local market, the road from ₹1 crore to ₹10 crore in revenue turned out to be an unexpectedly long one.

Around the same time, in mid-1981, an undergraduate student from IIT Chennai visited Kiran. He needed some enzymes for his final-year chemical engineering project on immobilized enzymes, the kind of enzymes that had a wide range of commercial uses. When he met her in the Biocon office at Cunningham Road in central Bengaluru, he mistook her for the managing director's secretary and then he disappointed her. Kiran was hoping to make a sale of ₹1,500 for 100 grams of enzymes that Shrikumar Suryanarayanan needed for this undergraduate project. On hearing the price, he tried to bargain and said his allowance was only ₹250 and that he would have to pay out of his pocket. 'Let me think about it,' Kiran told him.

Three weeks later, Suryanarayanan, known as Shri to all, was at the cafeteria in Chennai when a green-blue box arrived. It carried small enzyme-filled bottles, with a little note from the sender: 'Since you said you would pay for it from your pocket, I decided I would give it to you for free,' Kiran had written. Shri wrote a nice thank-you letter saying he would do research, publish it and acknowledge Biocon's assistance. 'You know how students think of their work. I wrote, it'll be great for you and all that,' he chortles.

After graduating, he went to meet her and showed her the project report. Even though he had a few scholarships from universities in the US, he chose to pursue his master's at IIT Delhi. They decided to stay in touch. One day, in December 1983, she landed at IIT Delhi with Auchincloss. As they drove, sitting on the back seat, Shri spoke animatedly about his work, showing off occasionally but never sensing that Auchincloss was quietly assessing him as a potential hire. Soon after, Kiran asked him if he was still thinking of a Ph.D abroad. 'I want to start my research and development division; why don't you join me? I don't have a Ph.D but I don't consider myself any less without it,' she said to him.

A few months later, while visiting his parents in Bengaluru, Shri met Kiran again. She took him in her white Ambassador to the new campus being built on Hosur Road, a complete wilderness then unlike today's technology suburb dotted with glass, chrome and nickel architecture. She took him to the quality assurance lab where she lost her temper at a mason for not placing the tiles, soothing aquamarine in colour, properly. He figured the lab meant a lot to her. For most companies in those days, research and development was symbolic; an excuse to get tax breaks. A fresh master's degree in hand, Shri was looking for real industrial research opportunities, not symbolism. On their way back to the city, he said yes to her offer.

The offer letter came with the designation, chief R&D chemist. 'I told her, my parents won't agree,' he says. She said he could take whatever designation he wanted; he settled for manager, R&D. The middle-class hang-ups persisted. He wrote her a long acceptance letter asking for various allowances. Shri remembers Kiran writing back to him: 'You know, all that doesn't matter. Why don't you just join and we'll figure out the rest.'

He joined in 1984 and the first thing they had to figure out was how to design and build a pilot-scale solid state fermentation plant. On his first day at work, Kiran handed him a test tube and a process description from Ireland. The Bengaluru team was to develop the solid state fermentation process and she wanted to know the stuff they needed for this. There was no accompanying data, nor had Ireland collected any.

Shri's chemical engineering training at IIT was poking holes in the handed-down process details. There was no data on how much heat evolved during the process, how much cooling was required, what the optimal humidity was, how to measure and control that humidity, what the inoculum ratio was and so on. The whole of Biocon Ireland at that time had no chemical engineer. Shri got down to brass tacks: building a pilot plant out of a wooden packing crate.

No other Biocon subsidiary – and there were more than a dozen by then – was engaged in any R&D. None was manufacturing enzymes; they were trading outfits of the parent company.

After R&D was in place, Biocon needed to beef up its sales. In 1986, she got a letter from Ajay Bharadwaj, a chemical engineer from IIT Delhi who was working at Max India. Ranbaxy Laboratories founder Bhai Mohan Singh had co-founded Max India with his youngest son Analjit Singh in 1982 to explore biotechnology. Max would use the enzymatic route to make a key drug intermediate of penicillin; family pharmaceutical company Ranbaxy would be the buyer.

After completing his master's at Louisiana State University, Bharadwaj had a Ph.D position offer in Florida but he did not see himself as a 'bench researcher'. At Max, he worked with Analjit Singh and would call him by his first name when the rest called him 'Sir' and 'stood up when he entered the room'. Naturally, they found Bharadwaj pompous, a US-returned guy who was 'full of himself'. That culture was not for him. So when he read a story about Kiran in *Businessworld* magazine, he was 'impressed' and wrote her a letter. She responded saying she would soon be in Delhi with Auchincloss and suggested they meet up then.

At Hotel Taj Palace, when the three met, Bharadwaj found her 'refreshingly different – modern and self-made and just a few years older' than him. They were looking for somebody to drive sales and, even though he had no training as a salesman, he accepted the job, took a pay cut and joined Biocon. When they were leaving the hotel that day, Auchincloss took out a piece of paper and asked Bharadwaj to write something. (What exactly, nobody remembers.)

The scribbled note at the hotel was for Auchincloss's famous personality assessment tool – handwriting analysis by a psychic in Ireland who weighed in particularly on the integrity quotient of a potential hire.

(Both Shri and Bharadwaj received a copy of the analysis after they joined. When I asked Auchincloss what his handwriting expert had said about Kiran, he replied: 'That she has a strong personality, very open … you know all that stuff,' he chuckled.)

Bharadwaj stayed in Delhi for a year. Working from home, he managed to develop some customers because until then no one had done systematic sales in India; most of what was produced was sold to Ireland.

As an entrepreneur, Auchincloss did not like to pay taxes; he looked for ways to increase tax efficiency in his ventures. Even in a tax haven like Ireland, where even today the effective corporate and capital gains tax rates remain the lowest, though they are set to be fully phased out by 2020, he had struck a deal with the Irish government under which for twenty years he did not have to pay taxes for starting new businesses. He also convinced Kiran to keep the markup price of Indian products low, to sell at a mere 10 per cent premium. In return, he promised to give Biocon India money to invest in R&D. That money came in various forms, some tangible, the rest intangible.

Although Bharadwaj had no marketing experience or knowledge of costing and pricing, once he began serious business development, he shifted to Bengaluru with his family.

A few years later, in June 1990, Kiran was invited to a dinner hosted by Mani Sabharwal, head of Brooke Bond India, where she met Ashok Ganguly and Sushim Mukul Dutta, chairman and vice-chairman of Hindustan Unilever Limited (HUL), respectively. During the conversation, she mentioned she had met an engineer graduate from Massachusetts Institute of Technology whose father worked with them and that she had offered him a job. The two gentlemen from Hindustan Unilever wrecked her hopes. Arun Chandavarkar, they said, had also been interviewed by their research centre in Mumbai; he had been offered a job with a considerable salary of ₹6,500 a month which she would never be able to match. She forgot about Chandavarkar altogether. She had offered him ₹4,500 when she herself was drawing ₹3,000 a month.

Suddenly, in September, she received a letter from Chandavarkar saying he had never heard from her. He had defended his Ph.D thesis at MIT, he was ready to move to India, and he was interested in joining Biocon. 'I said, I thought you are not interested in joining because I can't offer you more than ₹4,500. I hurriedly typed the offer letter and sent it to him,' Kiran remembers.

Chandavarkar joined as head of operations. Right from his chemical engineering days at IIT Powai in Mumbai, he had wanted to do biotechnology. So after a master's at MIT, he had chosen to do his doctorate in proteins and protein purification. Because of his father, Suresh Chandavarkar, an HUL lifer, he knew all the top management in the conglomerate where biotech opportunities were growing. HUL's parent company, Unilever, had created Quest International to consolidate a handful of new biotech acquisitions it had made in the late 1980s. Nonetheless, he opted to join Biocon. He wasn't particularly interested in working for pharmaceutical or biotech companies in the US where he had multiple offers. He was seeking professional satisfaction. On his visit to Biocon, he had met Bharadwaj, Shri and Krishnan and had wanted to come back after his Ph.D, 'no matter what salary or benefits Kiran gave' him. When most of his classmates were joining big brands, he says, it was a big risk joining Biocon, which was a small company, and Kiran, who in spite of winning the Padma Shri in 1989, 'was not a magnate'.

'I see myself as entrepreneurial and as much of a risk taker as Kiran. I joined her when Biocon was small and no one had heard about her [globally],' he says. 'There was no initial public offering, not even an inkling of it, in 1990, or for that matter, even in 2000, that Biocon would go public. It was the ethos of the company that I liked.'

Later that year, when he joined, Shri was working on the first solid state plant, BioChemizyme and Chandavarkar plunged into its commissioning.

While building her team, Kiran did not hire prima donnas; none of them came from particularly privileged backgrounds. She had learnt from Auchincloss to hire people who could work together. They did, indeed, for over twenty years. Equipped with technical degrees from premier institutes, they could have had their pick in the global job market at that time when most IIT graduates sought to build their careers in the US. Instead, they chose to take a risk. They felt they 'should make a difference'. It was not about 'differentiated' products, a business and marketing philosophy that Kiran coined later.

'We built a culture,' says Bharadwaj. 'Kiran let us be intrapreneurs.'

The Outlier

For the first few years, Biocon India supplied papain and isinglass to the parent company in Ireland. Then Kiran had an epiphany – she did not want to make papain all her life. In Cork, Biocon used bacteria to make enzymes; she wanted to work with other micro-organisms, like fungi and yeast, and use solid state fermentation, a technique which was different from the submerged liquid fermentation that Biocon Ireland was using. The former uses a solid substrate to ferment; the latter, more widely adopted then, uses liquid. Think fermentation of dough for making bread – naan or kulcha in the Indian bread basket – versus fermentation of milk for making curd.

In Cork, laboratories primarily made new formulations for different applications. They would buy enzymes from Danish, French, Japanese and other manufacturers and try out different combinations for new uses; these were types of experimentation that enzyme manufacturers were loath to undertake themselves. Over time, Biocon understood that the enzymes from Japan, which were made using Koji technology, had a variety of salient features which proved very useful in making new enzymatic blends and formulations.

Kiran had visited Japanese suppliers and was reasonably confident that solid state fermentation could be done in Bengaluru. That was her chance to do real biotechnology. Submerged fermentation requires sophisticated equipment and would have been an expensive affair. Merely trading, she knew, was not going to sustain her interest in business. She found the whole lark of maturing, whether in science or manufacturing technology, overrated. It was also one of the 'side activities' of having a committed partner in Ireland. For her, then and even now, common sense has its place and purpose.

At that time, Auchincloss was paying a steep price for Japanese enzymes but could not think of starting solid state fermentation in Cork because it was very labour intensive. Always open to experimentation, he readily agreed to Kiran's proposal; it made a lot of sense to reduce his reliance on Japan. That would also add value to his India bet, he thought, since more finished products could be exported and Biocon could also address the growing brewing market in India.

*

Koji is a culture made by growing different fungi on solid substrates like cooked grains or legumes. A fermentation process using Koji requires small-size bioreactors, less water, less energy; it does not produce liquid waste, and downstream processing is easy and cheap – all attributes which made Biocon choose it over submerged fermentation.

Starting with the wooden crate and the same trays that were used for drying papain, Shri and his team built two pilot plants, collected all the data and then designed a solid state fermentation plant. In some ways, it was reinventing the wheel; the Japanese had mastered this technology but would not share it.

Still, with some hard work, Biocon India came up to speed and on par with the state-of-the-art in the domain; other than the Japanese, nobody else was working in that field. The rest of the world had moved to submerged fermentation since it was easily scalable. The Danish enzyme maker, the Novo Group, got the solid state fermentation system when it bought Schweizerische Ferment AG (SFAG) in 1968, and later, its competitor Dr Schubert AG (SAG) in 1978. The group had two plants running until 1988 when one of them shut down, and then in 1996, the second one in Switzerland closed as well. There was a widespread belief within the company that submerged fermentation was more predictable and economical than surface fermentation. The complex Swiss labour laws did not help labour-intensive industries either.

Biocon had its own share of labour pains. When it moved into the new premises on Hosur Road, Kiran wanted to promote local employment. Scores of people, mostly uneducated, were hired and they lost no time in forming a union. They shot off a letter to the management asking to be acknowledged as a labour union, without stating any problem that needed to be resolved. One morning, as employees walked in for work, it was shutters down; all local hires were sitting on dharna. They had joined a communist labour union. Thankfully, the rest of the employees ensured that the operations continued uninterrupted.

'The symbolism was, if we can't do this job, we shouldn't be running the organization,' says Krishnan. Nothing stopped, even for a day, but the lesson they learnt was not to hire uneducated employees; at least that ensured one did not have a blocked communication channel. Kiran retaliated by automating the plant; the strikers, by burning her effigies. The strike, which lasted four months, prevented Biocon from servicing its Karnataka State Financial Corporation (KSFC) loan and it was soon declared a defaulter. The financier advertised in newspapers that Biocon's assets would be auctioned.

Once the solid state fermentation plant BioChemizyme was designed, Biocon needed money to build it. It approached KSFC again for a loan. However, when the powers that be learnt that the technology was locally developed and not 'imported', they developed cold feet. Not confident it would work, they brought accounting and management firm A.F. Ferguson to evaluate the project. For technical evaluation, they called senior scientist N.G. Karanth from Central Food Technological Research Institute (CFTRI) in Mysore. Karanth couldn't guarantee the technology would work unless Biocon gave him the micro-organisms and he tested the enzyme-making processes in his lab.

In fermentation, as in many biotechnology processes, strains of micro-organisms, or living cells, are the key raw materials and are often painstakingly developed. Biocon, therefore, wasn't willing to share its proprietary strains, which it had developed by random mutagenesis, subjecting the micro-organisms to gamma radiation at Kidwai Cancer Hospital – employing the same technology used to develop improved wheat varieties.

After much song and dance, KSFC said it did not understand the technology and would not lend money. Around that time, the chairman of the Industrial Credit and Investment Corporation of India, more popularly known as ICICI Bank, Narayanan Vaghul, was on a local technology development crusade. He had pooled in ₹100 crore from ICICI and created the Technology Development

Information Company of India (TDICI) to 'increase the technological base of the country and to disseminate information across the investor community'. 'Those were the two missing links,' he recalls.

He visited many research institutions, giving talks and trying to understand what inhibited new technology development in the country, meeting the who's who of the Indian research community. At the Indian Institute of Science (IISc) in Bengaluru, C.N.R. Rao, who was awarded the Bharat Ratna in 2013, was the director. He hustled up twenty-odd faculty members before Vaghul to discuss challenging issues in technology commercialization. At the Defence Research Development Organization (DRDO), its chief, A.P.J. Abdul Kalam, who later became the president of India, organized a 'big meeting' and spoke about defence 'inventions' which could be commercialized. Vaghul remembers meeting defence minister, Sharad Pawar, and floating the idea of dividing DRDO into one-part defence research and one-part technology commercialization. When Vaghul met the Indian Space Research Organization's (ISRO) then chairman U.R. Rao, he learnt that ISRO did have some space technologies with commercial applications.

All told, the illustrious institution's heads responded to Vaghul's missionary appeal but none sent any proposal for funding. This went on for two to three years, after which ICICI president S.S. Nadkarni called Vaghul and said they were going nowhere with the fund since no Indian institution had sent any proposal for funding; a few that did apply were entrepreneurial set-ups. So they converted TDICI into a regular venture fund called ICICI Ventures.

It was during those 'technology obsession' days of Vaghul that Kiran approached him. Her project proposal was evaluated by a professional team which found it had 'enough attractive features to carry a bet'. Vaghul wasn't new to betting on people. When he met her, he was 'impressed by her passion and commitment'. 'It was not me taking a risk, it was Kiran wanting to take a risk. There were very few entrepreneurs who wanted to develop technology, and the environment was not supportive of her. Her proposal was like an oasis to me,' recounts Vaghul, who is now retired and serves on the board of many companies.

Kiran was seeking a loan but Vaghul recommended she offer equity as Biocon did not have enough revenues and repaying a loan would end up draining the company. 'That much I knew that time [about venture capital],' he says. Kiran had no experience of company valuation, nor did she understand it well, so she held on to Vaghul's hand. In 1989, TDICI took 20 per cent stake in BioChemizyme for ₹1.15 crore. Later, Exim Bank joined TDICI and they shared the investment in a ratio of 70:30.

After ICICI Ventures formally came into existence, Vaghul travelled to the US to meet some venture capitalists, including Vinod Khosla, founder of Khosla Ventures, to understand the philosophy and intricacies of venture and private equity funding. 'The ICICI fund participated in future rounds in Biocon and had a series of successes,' Vaghul recalls fondly. (Or maybe not, it did miss out on the big one later.) 'Kiran had by then become a seasoned entrepreneur.'

Pangs and Perks of the First Plant

BioChemizyme was built with the TDICI money. It had three Koji rooms to process 1.5 tonne of biomass each. When the plant was being commissioned, batch after batch failed. More than 2 tonnes of wheat bran were going down the drain. It was normal to have four or five batches of contaminated products during a lab process scale-up. Everyone knew this in theory, but watching the batches go waste was not for the faint-hearted. Kiran would come by every few hours and ask why it was failing. At one point, Shri, whose public spats with Kiran are part of Biocon folklore, shouted back at her: 'I don't care who you are, let me do my job.' He knew what was happening and was trying to troubleshoot systematically.

Kiran went up to Bharadwaj, asking why Shri was talking to her like that. Shri remembers Bharadwaj coming to him and asking him to cool down. 'She was perhaps panicking. I can now imagine what she was going through,' Shri recalls.

When Chandavarkar joined Biocon the plant was functional. His MIT learning in microfiltration helped as he got down to adding downstream processes to the plant. Those days Shri had 'smuggled' a hollow fibre filtration membrane into Bengaluru while returning from Ireland. According to customs law then, one could carry goods worth only $125 but the membrane cost $1,100. Add $300 for customs duty and it was beyond Shri's R&D budget. Rolled up as a 3–4-ft bazooka, he brought it through the customs check, posing as a student carrying the stuff for his engineering project. He had even written down a project report. The customs personnel examined the papers, clearly not fathoming much of the fermentation jargon, and then looked at the man, who, with his characteristic boyish charm, looked every bit the student he was pretending to be, and let him pass. Chandavarkar figured out a way to use the membrane and get the product quality that they needed.

Slipping laboratory chemicals and small instruments into the luggage of people travelling to and from Ireland was common all through the 1980s. It was like Christmas shopping in Cork. Chemicals ordered there came overnight, but when ordered from Bengaluru, they would take three to four months. There was no X-ray baggage screening at Indian airports. 'The guy would look at your face and decide whether you were carrying any undeclared goods,' says Shri.

At one point, he brought 120 strains of microbes and all twenty amino acids neatly stacked at the bottom of his bag. The X-ray machine at Cork blinked but he managed to clear all airport checks by spinning his usual boyish spiel. Even today, he savours the matter-of-fact magic of enzymes; ask him more about that close shave and he loses twenty years when he narrates the episode.

Local, inventive R&D, coupled with the manufacturing capability in BioChemizyme, helped Biocon get into pectinases, the class of enzymes that the Japanese suppliers had dominated in. Ireland also made pectinases using submerged liquid fermentation but they would never match the Japanese enzymes which were more 'all-rounded', not just 'specialists'. They worked particularly well in fruit juices.

Developing pectinases soon became the core focus for Biocon India. It was a move that would fetch Biocon a fortune nearly two decades later.

Fungi or microbes that are grown in solid matrices have to actually develop abilities to break down these matrices in natural materials, say, barley or fruit juices, which are all complex materials. It's somewhat like the human world – the rigours of life make one a well-rounded person. In submerged fermentation, specialized nutrients are added to the medium, which not only curb the expression of a full spectrum of properties in enzymes but also make the process expensive.

The teams in Bengaluru and Cork began mixing the two types of pectinases – solid and liquid fermentation – and produced formulations that few companies in the world could offer. They were improvising on the go. Once they needed a rotary sterilizer, a special cooker where they could put the wheat bran, and tumble, steam and sterilize it. Kiran wanted to have it built in the United Kingdom but Auchincloss got 'ridiculous quotations', even from Japan. However, on one of his visits to the south-eastern part of Spain, he saw extractors that were made of stainless steel. He found there a father and son team that manufactured high precision parts for atomic submarines. Losing no time, he conveyed to Kiran that he had found a set-up which could get the rotary made. Shri worked on the design and the rather special piece of equipment was made in Spain.

GROWING THE PIE

Within a year of joining, Bharadwaj went to Ireland. At the end of his second day there, a Friday, Auchincloss invited him and three others for a drink. (He had a full-fledged bar in the office.) Pouring a large whiskey with little water, he said, 'This is how we drink in Ireland. Let's see what you have learnt in Biocon.'

Bharadwaj could see where it would lead to; he drank some and slickly threw some away. At the end of a long evening, when others were drunk, he remained sober. A surprised Auchincloss remarked: 'This Indian *can* hold his drink.' He would later understand that 'this Indian' also knew how to do business.

Enzymes was a good business to be in. Major companies like Novozymes and Genzyme were making 25–30 per cent margins and it was as close to industrial biotech as one could get in those days. 'You could make much better margins on a truckload of enzymes than on a truckload of corn starch,' jokes Dunne.

In India, the first business breakthrough for Bharadwaj came when he bagged an order worth ₹8,00,000 from Himachal Pradesh Horticultural Produce Marketing and Processing Corporation. He had been camping at their office and running trials, assuring them that if the products did not work, it would be his responsibility. The company later floated a tender. Some overseas manufacturers were also contenders, but Biocon participated aggressively in every bid.

Gradually, the brewery business took off. United Breweries was the first customer. 'My father's reputation in the industry opened doors for me. Of course, they were patronizing,' she concedes, 'but I could talk in a technical language with them.' Biocon had built a complete suite of products for the beer industry and established its products in the breweries' portfolio by replacing the imported enzymes and formulations slowly but surely.

Kiran travelled widely within the country. Her first visit to Jagatjit Industries, a malting company in Jalandhar which became an important customer over time, is particularly memorable.

While boarding the train in Bengaluru, the compartment door was blocked by passengers and she had to be pushed inside the bogie through the window. On her onward journey, a bus ride from Delhi to Jalandhar, she was the only woman passenger and the driver was so taken up with this fact that he insisted on taking a detour and stopping the bus at the gate of Jagatjit Industries. 'He waited till I got inside the gate safely,' she fondly recounts.

When Bharadwaj arrived, he began to take some load off her. The son of migrant parents from Pakistan, he had survival and competitive instincts in his genes. He started to look around for any loopholes in the ongoing processes. As promised by Auchincloss, a lot of research requirements were fulfilled by Ireland. Overall, the R&D team valued this enormously because it took them many years to mature and begin contributing to the products. For a long time it was blending, trading and working with formulations which were all developed in Ireland. They would not charge any royalty and Bengaluru's products would go as reasonably marked-up products. Still, the India business was in the red. Senior management would often take their salaries late; sometimes, the delay would stretch for months.

No one complained though. 'We knew that we were all in it together. It was *our* company. Watching Kiran I learnt what makes people tick; that itself was a big motivator,' says Bharadwaj, adding in the same breadth that had he known it was a loss-making company he wouldn't have joined. 'In those days, no one looked at numbers and balance sheets before joining.'

While casting the revenue net wider, he also looked to plug income leaks and he found one in the return gifts to Shri's team coming from Ireland. In practical terms, it was very difficult to measure those favours to R&D from Ireland. He understood Kiran was obligated to Auchincloss and would not bring this up with him. So he and Krishnan decided to take the axe. They increased the price of products shipped from Bengaluru to Ireland. This stabilized Biocon to some extent. But Auchincloss was furious when he learnt that the raw material price had not increased but Biocon India had raised its mark-up. 'He gave me hell. There was a big push back from them but I'm not someone who gives in so easily. They had to lump it and accept it,' says Bharadwaj.

More than twenty-five years later, Auchincloss hasn't forgotten the incident; he still nurses a grudge. For him, keeping the tax burden low came from habit, rather out of post-war history. When Biocon was started in 1969, the Government of Ireland had introduced a scheme whereby anyone exporting anything received tax benefits. That government policy was meant to correct the trade imbalance which was a direct fallout of being neutral in the Second World War in which Ireland was neither with the Allied Forces nor with the Germans.

During the war, America was pouring military hardware and munitions into the UK. Famously fond of alcohol, British prime minister Winston Churchill could think of shipping back only whiskey. But to grow that industry, Churchill decreed that anyone working in farms producing barley (which was made into malt) for malting and the distillery business was excused from war service. That decision led to a big spurt in whiskey production. So, as part of returning the American favour, all sea vessels going back to America were loaded with Scotch whiskey. 'That is how Scotch whiskey in America became a huge brand,' says Auchincloss.

But while Scotland had 135 distilleries in those days, Ireland had just a handful. No one went to Ireland to collect the stock for shipping to the US and the Irish liquor industry slowly found itself stunted. After the war, Scotch liquor dominated the region. Tax breaks from the Irish government were one of the ways to tide over this difficult situation.

2

A DECADE WITH UNILEVER

THE COOKIE CRUMBLES IN CORK

Throughout the 1980s, Biocon Ireland grew rapidly; it became a micro-multinational with operations in twenty-one countries. Most of its managers were imports from big companies with a latent yearning for autonomy. Auchincloss would leave them alone as long as they were running the business and earning profits. This was very attractive to people and it fostered a collegial atmosphere.

'If Les perceived you were not doing your job, soon enough, he'd send you a letter or a note, "Go Ya", which meant "Get off your asses". That would also be if you were not working well with somebody else,' says Roland Cocker, who had worked in fermentation in England and had come from Glaxo to scale up submerged fermentation at Biocon Ireland. Cocker, like others, understood why Auchincloss was so customer-focused – he had struggled to sell in his initial days. Owing to his experiential learning, he insisted on forging a technical connection with customers and, as a result, top executives at the Irish beer maker Guinness were on first-name terms with everyone at Biocon laboratories.

Auchincloss had started Biocon with only £1,200; so keeping the cash flow steady was a perennial challenge. All managers were under pressure to have a decent profit-and-loss account; bank borrowings were not easy since bankers viewed them with scepticism. At one point, remembers Declan MacFadden, Auchincloss asked all senior managers to invest in the group. Many of them mortgaged their houses and brought in money with zero assurance that it would be paid back or that the new idea would work out.

Adventurism ran in their veins. In Peru, where they were selling their products to the brewing industry, they wanted to set up a business for natural colours too. At that time, inflation was hitting the roof at 4,000 per cent. Auchincloss couldn't get his money out. He had also set up a company in Venezuela, which was dealing in fish maws. Once, he set out with his colleagues from Caracas, the Venezuela capital, to head to Lima in Peru to try get his money out. But they ended up in neighbouring Ecuador because the guerrillas were shelling the airport in Lima. Unable to proceed to Lima, they requested KLM Airlines to let them sleep in one of their planes at Ecuador's airport in Quito.

Initially, Biocon was not successful in producing natural colours because the seeds were produced in Peru. The idea was that if the group could get those seeds, they could get their money out by trading them. Resourceful as ever, Auchincloss found somebody working on annatto seeds in the university there. Four days later, they founded Biocon Peru and began producing annatto seeds themselves.

It was almost as if they were a bunch of 'cowboys' on a wild ride, having fun. 'We loved a bit of rough and tumble,' MacFadden reminisces. Maybe more 'buccaneer' than 'cowboys', counters Cocker. As a lateral thinker, he believes that Auchincloss was an extreme example of the breed. If you have ten ideas and nine fail, the tenth is permanent and the nine were your – often minor – investments to get there.

'We had all kinds of activities in all kinds of places,' admits Auchincloss, stressing that it was never a lack of ideas or opportunities, but a lack of funds that forced him to do what he did: sell the Biocon Group. He had sworn to his managers that he would never sell. His dream was to build a big fermentation plant – be it a major producer or marketer. But the company was growing so fast that he could not keep up with it.

First, a Finnish company wanted to buy it out in the late 1980s. Auchincloss declined. Then, in 1989, he met a director at Quest International, a Unilever business which was created in 1987 by merging its proprietary perfume and flavours business with Naarden International NV, a similar enterprise in the Netherlands which Unilever had then bought. In his meeting with Quest, Auchincloss learnt that they had paid millions of dollars for acquiring a microbiology technology to produce flavour compounds for the food and beverages industry but it remained unused because Quest was not able to scale it up for commercial use.

The Biocon team began working on the processes at Cork and was soon successful in producing the desired yield. (Later, Unilever's fragrance division in the Netherlands would send a lot of technologies to Cork for scaling up; they would all become functional.) This brought the creatively adventurous team under spotlight within Quest, which unsurprisingly showed interest in acquiring Biocon. It was a time when the Biocon Group was making money on paper but most of it was locked up with debtors and creditors.

Everybody was unhappy with the news of selling out, so much so that Dunne and Kiran, acting as ringleaders, decided to confront Auchincloss and demanded an opportunity to create a management buyout group that would compete with Unilever's bid. This group went to London and New York, raising money. They got the best offer in New York from a financier whom Parag

Saxena, then at Chancellor Capital Management, had connected them with. Saxena knew Kiran through her brother who was his classmate at IIT Powai in Mumbai. The offer that Kiran and Dunne got in New York was, they thought, a good price for all the assets and potential Biocon Group possessed. But Unilever was prepared to pay over the odds.

Auchincloss owned more than 70 per cent of the Biocon Group and he decided to cash out, for £35 million. All the managers were called to Ireland when Unilever tried to organize a management buyout. Auchincloss wasn't opposed to it at all but the cookie crumbled ten minutes before signing the deal when Unilever found that Biocon India was missing from the final documents. Auchincloss explained to Unilever that he was a minority stakeholder in Biocon India and it was not part of the deal. In any case, it would go bankrupt in a few months, he told them. (The revenue of Biocon India then was ₹2 crore.)

'I wanted to keep Kiran out of it. But unfortunately I could not; finally, I had to agree since it was a minority holding – 30 per cent – and that they could keep it,' Auchincloss said. Incidentally, he had managed to keep Biocon Spain out of the Unilever deal, and later, Biocon Japan, with financial help from him, was able to buy back its share from Unilever and become independent.

BENGALURU BULKS UP

Life for people in Bengaluru changed, for the better and for worse. Kiran and Dunne talked about the buyout later – they might have succeeded in raising £35 million but they might never have got their money back; they would have been saddled with significant debt.For the most part, in its association with Ireland, the Bengaluru team had shown ingenuity, particularly in developing applications until big-time manufacturing took off with the BioChemizyme plant.

One day, in 1986, Jyothi Kamath, who had returned with a

degree in microbial and food technology from the Massachusetts Institute of Technology, called Kiran and said she was interested in working for Biocon. (As was the practice those days, people came to know of Biocon through hearsay and would call Kiran or other senior executives directly to check if there was any job opening. This continued until 1996 when the company released the first official advertisement for candidates.)

Kamath joined Shri's two-year-old fledgling R&D team. Systematically, she began developing a variety of pectinases, enzymes that the Japanese were very good at. A principled professional, Kamath would roam the world – from Israel to Argentina – with the marketing team as the technical expert. At meetings, she would carefully list new opportunities or any complaints or scope for improvement. Cocker remembers she would go out to dinner with them, braving the cold Irish nights in her sarees, sporting a 'bare midriff'. All persuasion to make her wear a cardigan would fall flat. 'She was proud of her Indian dressing. But it was cold; she had no fat, no in-built insulation,' recalls Cocker, still sounding a bit baffled.

The pectinases based on solid state fermentation that Kamath worked on differentiated Biocon India, first, within the Biocon Group and then globally, making them just the third or fourth manufacturer of high-quality pectinases. These are enzymes which hydrolyse pectin, a complex polysaccharide found in fruits, and are responsible for the haze and precipitate formation in juice. Fruit juice producers use them to clarify juice and increase yield during production.

Biocon's first big break came from the American juice producer Ocean Spray, the largest cranberry juice producer in the world. This enzyme was so critical to the company that it did a comparative study of all pectinases it was sourcing from around the world and ranked the Biocon product as the best. Biocon's enzymes worked at low pH, which meant Ocean Spray did not have to adjust the pH in the juice. This saved them time and money. The Biocon Group ended up with a lucrative contract from Ocean Spray.

'All this while, Ireland did not disclose that the enzyme was sourced from India. It feared losing business,' Kiran reveals. In any case, they were blending solid state fermented pectinases from Bengaluru with liquid fermentation pectinases from Ireland before shipping to customers. Then one day, Ocean Spray decided to have a research programme in Massachusetts, US, to improve the enzymes. Kamath and a few others from the Ireland research division attended the programme. Kamath knew pectinases inside out; she impressed everyone with her knowledge and, of course, her Indian-style dress.

Once Ocean Spray tested the unblended Bengaluru pectinases, it said it wanted only the Indian product. 'That was one "Aha" moment for me. What made me proud was that they wanted only the Made-in-India product. They even came to Bengaluru to see our processes,' Kiran says. Until 2007, when Biocon divested its enzyme business, Ocean Spray remained one of the biggest buyers of pectinases. These enzymes also brought Biocon India its first set of patents.

Meanwhile, the business team had diversified into other industries and baking was taking off swiftly with alpha amylase and amyloglucosidase. Auchincloss had hired a consultant baker, Arthur Emory, who had graduated from the best baking school in England, at Chorleywood, and sent him to Bengaluru to help the team. Armed with a discerning sense of aesthetics, Emory set about building a baking lab in Biocon, showing them how baking was a pursuit for precision. He would turn out such amazing breads that most of the staff would take their home supplies from the lab.

In her usual hands-on style, Kamath, along with Emory, conducted baking trials at all possible places – the retail bakery Nilgiris (which was acquired by the Future Group in 2014), the old Bengaluru restaurant, Koshy's, and the confectionary major,

Britannia. Emory was particularly friendly with Kiran's friends and gleefully traded gossip with them. To Kiran, he was like a caregiver, pampering her with freshly baked snacks when she returned home in the evening. 'He taught us a lot ... almost behaved like a wife with me,' Kiran says, laughing.

New Beginnings, New Challenges

When Unilever acquired the Biocon Group to merge with Quest International, the latter did not have an identifiable culture. It had been in existence for just two years and its two constituents, Naarden and Unilever's own proprietary perfume and flavour business, had not spawned a shared culture. In contrast, the Biocon Group had a very distinct entrepreneurial spirit running through it, and it was like nothing the two merged divisions of Quest had ever experienced. Metaphorically speaking, says Mike Powell, Biocon was adopted by two parents who did not have the best of relationships. Powell was a vice-president of finance at Unilever who had a ringside view of both the corporate and the foods divisions. He retired in 2000.

For many years after the Quest incorporation in 1987, people from the two groups moved around with their respective tags – Naarden and Unilever, the former smarting from the takeover which it believed was unfriendly. They never could become a fully integrated team despite visibly superb efforts by Charles Miller-Smith, former finance director of Unilever and the first chairman of Quest.

Being part of such an organization, structurally complex and culturally conflicted, was not going to be easy either; neither for the Biocon Group, or for Biocon India.

Kiran did not have a particularly velvety start herself. In July 1990, she was going to meet the senior management at Quest. The meeting was organized in The Hague. At Amsterdam station, as she waited for Bharadwaj to get their tickets, guarding his pilot briefcase, someone tapped her right shoulder, asking change for a ten-dollar bill. When she turned, another person snatched her Gucci bag and sped away. Bharadwaj heard her scream and saw a guy running with the bag. In what could easily have been a scene out of a Bollywood film, Bharadwaj, who was working out those days and had the confidence of an athlete, chased the bag snatcher but the guy ran on to a platform and jumped into a train. As the door of the speeding train closed, he even waved at Bharadwaj with a victorious smile.

Standing at the Amsterdam railway station platform, Kiran sobbed 'like a little girl'; her entire presentation for the Quest meeting was gone with the bag. They went to the police but were advised to lodge a complaint in The Hague. At the hotel in The Hague, the evening prior to the big Quest meeting, the mood was glum. Kiran was in her room, sulking. Suddenly, Joe Dunne, who headed the North America business of Quest, after the acquisition, rang her room and said: 'Guess what, someone found your fuckin' bag. Now cheer up and come down for a drink.'

A local locksmith had found her Gucci bag lying at the railway line and since the presentation – the overhead transparencies of the pre-digital age – had her and the hotel's name on it, he had brought it to the hotel. The junkies had taken the cash and thrown the bag with everything else intact, including her imitation jewellery.

'Kiran didn't need those transparencies to give her presentation. She presented her facts with incredible courage and positivity and knowledge. We never doubted them and she never shied away from attacking some fool in that sceptical audience,' says MacFadden, chuckling at the memories. Her preparedness allowed her to settle in during the first few years; the tug of war would begin later.

At the time of acquisition, Shri and his team had built the BioChemizyme plant with frugal resources and were about to run trial productions. Soon after the dust settled on the Biocon–Unilever deal, Shri got a long telex message from Ireland with elaborate specifications on the processes and the products. He could see how his former counterparts in Cork were now taking instructions from Quest. Biocon, the entire group, was quite unsophisticated when it came to manufacturing standards, especially in relation to a global trendsetter and stickler for quality like Unilever.

The Bengaluru team had designed the plant prudently. Unilever made them redo the plant quite substantially, down to the conveyor system which was changed from mesh to stainless steel. After its inauguration in 1989, it went back into revamp mode, pushing full-scale production back by nearly two years. What was built to be a cash cow became a white elephant for some time. Not happy to be a minority owner with 30 per cent holding, which came to it through the Biocon Group acquisition, Unilever wanted to acquire the 20 per cent stake that TDICI held. And they did. In less than a year TDICI had its breakout moment, with four times the return on its investment. The plant picked up steam in 1992, because the pectinases coming out of it were good and competitively priced.

Kiran would take new ideas and with help from the late Liam Horgan, the R&D manager responsible for transferring technology from Cork to Bengaluru, quickly develop processes and sell on the market with 'amazing speed'. 'She was the only one moving fast in the group. That can-do attitude permeated everything she and her team did. She had incredibly good people – people who came from humble backgrounds, had amazing intellect and fire in their belly to make things happen,' remembers MacFadden, who went to Holland as vice-president of the bio-products division of Quest which handled colours and ingredients.

During the mid-1990s, Quest was contracting R&D work to Bengaluru. Every year there would be arguments about increasing the research funding and volume commitments. Those annual negotiations were unforgettable. 'It was not easy to come to a deal,' remembers Mike Woulfe, who had joined the Biocon Group in 1984 as a process development chemist and then moved into managerial roles at Quest. 'Kiran is a tough negotiator and her team members were also similarly indoctrinated.'

Biocon India was supplying its products to Quest, which also promoted them around the world through its network. That meant managing the tenuous business relationships that were evolving in the motley group of managers, some of whom remember Kiran as a 'tough, tough lady to deal with'.

'In the negotiations over supply agreements between Quest and Biocon India, while all other subsidiaries wanted to make profits, Kiran would be unwilling to give in and would often piss off people. In negotiations, sometimes, there has to be a give and take; Kiran was not willing to give much,' recalls MacFadden.

In all the financial dealings between Biocon, Unilever and Quest, Powell was an important link. Though Quest consisted of two legs – fragrances and foods – and they shared some locations around the world, for all practical purposes, they were separate businesses. Results were monitored separately and there was always a high level of competition between the two divisions.

The two group vice-presidents presided over their divisions, and the person heading the foods division, executive Sergio Lecchini, was central to the knotty plot that unfolded for Biocon before and after the acquisition. His colleagues say that 'he was a visionary like Kiran and was sympathetic to her later on' when the relationship between Unilever and Biocon India started fraying.

Lecchini wanted to make Quest and its foods business unique in the industry. He wished to offer clients 'total solutions' rather than individual products. To do that, he needed to extend the basket of food ingredients and cover the entire range – flavour, texture, appearance, aroma and nutritional value. With this in mind, Unilever had made a slew of acquisitions in the US and Europe, the Biocon Group being the last biotech bastion to be brought under the conglomerate.

Like the warring satraps of a lumbering empire, the regional managers – and all the way down to the product managers – would have never-ending disputes. In addition to corporate-versus-food disputes, there would be serious disagreements within the foods division itself. When it came to profits, they were measured down to the bottom line and this inevitably involved apportionment of divisional, Quest Corporate and Unilever overheads to regions and product groups, says Powell. 'Of course, everybody felt they were being charged too much and this led to endless discussions and arguments which did not add a cent to the company's bottom line. Instead, it took much time which could have been devoted to discussing proper issues.'

Face-off

When Unilever bought the Biocon Group, it perhaps did not do enough 'due diligence' on the Indian operation. Initially, Bengaluru's activities seemed minor and the minority holding was a lame asset for a company where many saw the Biocon Group acquisition itself as an unwelcome and unnecessary complication. Apart from Ireland, India, Peru and to some extent the Philippines were important locations for the Biocon Group. It took little time for Unilever's seasoned executives to map the opportunity and the company began to manoeuvre and take control of the Indian business.

Every few weeks, some senior executive would descend on Bengaluru. 'It would start off well but would often end with – "What would you want from Unilever?"' says Bharadwaj. Unilever was beginning to understand that Kiran had scant intention of ceding control. On her part, she knew that as long as they were a minority partner, she could call the shots.

After almost eighteen months of trying to convince Kiran to dilute her stakes, a large delegation, which included the global head of R&D at Unilever and his team, came to Bengaluru. In the opening meeting, Kiran gave a presentation, and her first slide, memorable to many, declared that there were three types of companies:

Companies which make things happen
Companies which watch things happen
Companies which wonder what happened

Biocon India, she said, was the first type of company and Unilever was the third type.

That in-your-face presentation left everyone stunned. 'We didn't know where to look. There were board members, some senior managers and the head of Hindustan Unilever. Those days we did not have [smart] phones to fiddle with, we just went red in the face,' recalls Bharadwaj.

If egos were bruised, nobody showed it. Back in Europe, Biocon as a group was having a hard time assimilating itself within the Quest and Unilever family. It was seen as a 'mafia' or a 'Band of Brothers and Sisters' by many. When Kiran visited Naarden, she would often go first, informally, to Powell's office in order to 'check the temperature' at senior Food and Corporate levels. 'Mutual trust is a very strong force in business, as in all walks of life,' notes Powell.

With each passing year, the relationship soured some more. In the meetings, in early years, Unilever members would extend 'warm, loving attention' which increasingly became antagonistic. As a former Biocon Group manager recalls, it would often be like, '"We've had enough of this. We know what's best. You little company, you start obeying our rules." It would get rather nasty.'

COG IN THE CONGLOMERATE

To say that Biocon managers got a culture shock when they came to Unilever would be an understatement. Getting into a structured, disciplined, slow-moving and slow-decision-making organization was just the opposite of what they had practised in Ireland and elsewhere. At Unilever, they learnt that managers hardly made a decisions. That slowed things down; people did not show the courage to experiment. If the Biocon way of designing a new manufacturing process meant looking at the theory, figuring out a sense of how it would work and then getting the old, run-down equipment to implement the design, the Unilever way was going out and buying everything that was most expensive and hygienic. 'Money was slow [to come] but when you got the money, you got to do the best possible plant, not the cheapest possible plant,' says Mike Woulfe, vice-president (enzymes) at Kerry Group in Ireland.

Process hygiene was a big deal in Unilever. Hygienic design principles were also critical for people's safety because enzymes can cause allergies and had been a recurring problem earlier at Biocon Ireland. After Unilever improved the processes, allergic reactions stopped. Cocker, who had earlier worked in global companies like Glaxo, said the scientific design principles of Unilever were very special worldwide; even Glaxo was no match for it.

Unilever designed manufacturing and other processes in a way that they did not get dirty easily – the type of material and design used had the least number of crevices and couplings – and if they got dirty they would get cleaned, drained and sterilized quickly, using minimum water, energy and chemicals, at minimum environmental cost. It's an almost Zen-like approach to design, based on experimental results from science and it was new to the Biocon Group.

'If you take a lot of biotech plants from big pharma companies, you'll find they use couplings and valves which are very common; they wouldn't pass the process cleanability test,' says Cocker, who now runs Cocker Consulting, which specializes in hygiene design principles and does food safety and quality audits for the National Sanitary Foundation in the US.

In Biocon India, people quickly absorbed the supply chain quality culture. The company spruced up its financial reporting as well. Internal financial reporting in Unilever is rigorous, frequent, detailed and very structured. 'It must have taken a major effort for Bengaluru to get that organized because when I arrived in the first quarter in 1991, it was running absolutely perfectly,' says Powell.

Around that time, Unilever had asked its businesses to qualify for the International Organization for Standardization (ISO) certification. For all her fiercely guarded independence, Kiran was ready to 'toe the line' when it came to conforming to their processes to benchmark her company against global standards. Biocon India grabbed the opportunity and became the first business within the Unilever Group, and only the third company in India (the two others being Bosch-Mico and Widia, both mechanical engineering companies), to get ISO 9001 certification from the German authority RWTUV.

'I was passionate about building credibility for an Indian company. I wanted the Made-in-India label to be of high quality,' she remembers, even though it meant writing their own quality manuals and fumbling along the way.

In 1994, when Biocon India wanted to expand its export-oriented BioChemizyme capacity fourfold, Unilever wanted a 50 per cent share. So they decided to set up a new plant called Biocon-Quest. By then, the Indian market was opening up, following the economic reforms of 1991. There was an attractive Export Promotion Capital Goods (EPCG) scheme which let companies pay a reduced import duty of a mere 5 per cent and sell their products wherever they wanted on the condition that they would have to export seven times the worth of goods they imported.

The investment in Biocon-Quest amounted to ₹12 crore, of which the two partners would pay ₹2 crore each and the rest would come from Deutsche Bank, an old lender for Unilever. Since the amount was over the authorized limit of Quest management, the proposal had to go to a special committee for approval within the Unilever Group. It could take six months or more, Bengaluru was told.

'I was ready to start, like, tomorrow. I couldn't wait. I was short on capacity because pectinases were doing very well. I wanted to complete the plant in one year, so I didn't wait for their approval. I put in my money and the borrowing, and I started,' says Kiran. On the day of the plant inauguration in 1995, Victor Rensing, chief executive of Quest, gave her the cheque and complimented her for 'fast execution', but it came packaged with some flak 'for violating the norms of a multinational'. (For a while, there was an internal joke at Biocon about who Con-Quested whom.)

After Biocon-Quest started, Unilever began to put pressure on Kiran. Biocon was supplying a lot of food enzymes to Unilever's global food business; it had become strategically important. Keki Dadiseth, chief executive of HUL, would convey 'messages' from Unilever and say, 'It would augur well if you gave control of Biocon India to Unilever by some way, we wouldn't mind if it came even through HUL. Why don't you give 1 per cent to Hindustan Unilever? That way we'll be able to do a lot more for you – invest more, get more business.'

When Kiran, avoiding getting caught in bureaucracy and certainly with no intention of forfeiting her freedom, kept ignoring those messages, Dadiseth said she was sending the 'wrong signals'. At one point, Kiran told him, 'You keep telling me I'm sending wrong signals, but what assurance are you giving that you will stay invested in biotechnology? Can you ensure 1 per cent will translate into a guarantee that you will not sell the biotech [division]?' 'If anything,' she added in half jest, 'I'd like to buy back your share.'

Dadiseth hushed it: 'Don't even say such things.'

BUILDING PLATFORM TECHNOLOGIES

While the ownership tussle went on with Unilever, the engineers focused on foundational technologies. When Arun Chandavarkar joined in 1990, BioChemizyme was ready to be commissioned. The design of the facility was such that no one could benchmark it against any facility in the world. Solid state fermentation technology was known only in Japan. 'We had to pretty much guess what to do and scale it up. It took time, but within a year, we shipped our first truckload of pectinases to Ireland,' says Chandavarkar.

By the mid-1990s, Bharadwaj and his team had expanded into selling digestive enzymes. In the R&D team, one person had taken a special liking for business intelligence. Everybody called him 'Mr Novozymes'. He would scour the databases and published literature to figure out what Novozymes was doing. He could even tell who worked where in Novozymes, and deduce details in the Dutch company's formulation for stonewashing denim, one of the biggest opportunities for enzymes in those days when denim manufacturers were moving from pumice stone to enzymes to get the famed faded look.

In digestive enzymes, Novozymes would often trigger a free fall in prices. They made those enzymes by submerged fermentation where one specific activity, starch hydrolysis, was very high. Pharmaceutical products are usually sold on a single activity of the ingredient, so competitors' products did well. Biocon's enzymes were from solid state fermentation and could break down the entire food, not just starch. Its proteolytic activity was more beneficial but the drug makers were hardly impressed. On pricing grounds, the Indian pharmaceutical industry was hyper-competitive even then.

It was the time when Bharadwaj, having acquired a toehold in the pharma industry, would have discussions, sometimes even leading to squabbles, with Kiran and Shri on paying more attention to pharmaceuticals. 'My argument was that we are first a fermentation company which happens to be in enzymes and can get into pharmaceuticals,' he said.

Fortuitously, Rakesh Bamzai, a key executive in rival Advanced Biochemicals, whom Bharadwaj had been trying to hire for sometime, joined Biocon in 1995. Advanced Biochemicals was the same size as Biocon and its close competitor in the enzymes business, and Bamzai was doing well there. One day, Bharadwaj called him and asked him a few questions without disclosing who he was. Satisfied with the answers, he called him a second time, and this time he offered Bamzai a job at Biocon. The latter recalls how, even though the two companies were similar, Biocon had a 'better image and Kiran had a good name'. 'At the end of the day, you work for people,' he says. He said yes to Bharadwaj, thinking he would 'just check out Biocon for a few years'. He stayed on for nineteen years.

At first, he helped Biocon get some enzyme accounts which it had lost, like Ratlam, Bharat Starch and others, and then, gradually, added serious pharma flavour to the business which, by the turn of the decade, would change the direction of the company.

By 1996, Biocon India had augmented its fermentation foundation by developing production technology for a variety of host organisms – bacteria, fungi and yeast. Animal cell culture would be added later when Biocon would get into antibodies.

One of the growing areas in enzymes was textiles where, like pharmaceuticals, the side activity of enzymes matters less. Biocon could see the limitations of solid state fermentation. The business team began sourcing cellulases from overseas and selling them in the Indian market. One of the two companies worldwide that was producing this enzyme for stonewashing jeans was Dyadic International, based in Jupiter, Florida. Its founder, Mark Emalfarb, was a self-taught biotechnologist. After founding Dyadic in 1979, he made money selling stonewashing ingredients to denim companies, including pumice stones, and later, with help from university collaborations, developed cellulases that became indispensable to the textile industry.

Emalfarb was frustrated by the trade barrier of high import duty, 70 per cent in those days, that he had to pay in India. So Dyadic and Biocon decided to form a 50:50 joint venture; the latter would build two 30,000-litre fermenters and Dyadic would provide micro-organism strains and the processing technology. The idea was that they would avoid duties and dominate Indian and other markets. It made perfect business sense except that Kiran, always keen to sweat her manufacturing assets, had planned to produce pharmaceuticals alongside, and that idea backfired.

Globally prevalent Current Good Manufacturing Practices, a regulatory norm in pharmaceuticals, wouldn't allow her to produce industrial goods in one fermenter and pharmaceuticals in the other. The two partners then decided to call off the agreement and the joint venture was dissolved 'in the best interests of all', says Emalfarb. He was disappointed about the lost opportunity, but for Biocon there was a bigger challenge looming – what would the fermenters produce if not cellulases?

An awful lot was riding on those fermenters. Shri, Chandavarkar and a few others would get together and joke: 'If this damn thing bombs, we'll end up in jobs in a hotel somewhere, doing the dishes.'

'We were too young to know the extent of the risk we were taking,' says Shri.

By then Kiran had learnt to punt on capacity building. If you had capability, you could somehow find opportunities, she thought. 'Looking back, I think I was so naive, even idiotic, to think that if nothing worked, I could make digestive enzymes.' She pauses and adds: 'Today, that plant makes insulin.' (The submerged fermentation plant was first retrofitted to make statins and further retrofitted to make insulin.)

The plant construction continued. The business team was engaged with a Japanese company, Shin Nihon, for enzymes but it also had a popular product, serratiopeptidase, which was derived from bacterial enzymes and was used to make anti-inflammatory drugs. Shin Nihon had a proprietary technology to make serratiopeptidase but under Japanese law and good manufacturing practices, it could not make both products. Biocon licensed the technology.

This fit Bharadwaj's strategy, which was to outsource products, sell them to test the market and create a brand name before Biocon's own R&D came up to speed to produce them in-house. The Shin Nihon deal gave them a breather.

Unlike enzymes, a sector in which Biocon Ireland and later Unilever provided captive buyers as well as channels for distribution, the pharmaceuticals business needed to be hatched and grown independently, both in India and overseas. Shri needed to reskill his team and hire fresh pharma people. Forget having a vision, nobody had a clear idea which products would be the big revenue earners even though everyone knew pharmaceuticals were going to be money-spinners.

But that was not where Unilever wanted to be. It already had a gigantic geographic spread and product range; it might have been 'boring' but at least it was 'safe'. 'There were so many checks and balances that it was never easy for a true entrepreneur to flourish,' says Powell.

Within Quest, the management was having a hard time implementing Lecchini's strategy, the catch being the sales force: it was not educated to sell a huge variety of products as a 'total solution'. In that situation, the last thing the MNC wanted to hear was a proposal for yet another diversification. Kiran was learning through some hard knocks. 'She was not a wilting lily by any chance. I'm glad she fought the battles that needed to be fought along the way to chart her own course. Unilever did not see the benefits of Biocon India expanding into pharmaceuticals. It was what the Bains and the McKinseys of the world were then advising – stick to your core. But that was never her philosophy,' says a former Biocon manager who worked in Unilever until the earlier part of the 2010s.

To wing its way, Biocon formed a separate pharma company called Helix in the mid-1990s in the name of Bharadwaj, Krishnan, Chandavarkar and Shri on a separate half-acre plot. Helix began to do research and development and then built a mock clean room. When a US Food and Drug Administration consultant came to inspect, he said Helix would fail the inspection. Clean room walls were not supposed to have 90-degree angles on the grooves, they had to be slanting so that dust slipped. He demonstrated how the actual inspection was done – put out the light, close the door and look around. Even a speck or a crack somewhere would allow some light to stream in.

Thankfully, by then Biocon had had a clear change of goals. It was doing well in enzymes but the opportunities were limited; the global market itself was under $1 billion, growing in single digits. More than two decades later, the enzymes industry was expected to reach $7 billion by 2017. Even getting an ambitious 10 per cent share of the global market meant a $700 million opportunity. On the other hand, the market for biopharmaceuticals – products that are derived directly or indirectly from live organisms or their components like cells, proteins, gene sequences, and so on – was expected to grow to more than twenty-five times the enzymes market in the same period.

Plafractor

With the lucrative pharmaceutical business in sight, Biocon had to enhance its team with pharmacy professionals. One of the most sought after campuses those days was the University Department of Chemical Technology, more widely known as UDCT, under the University of Mumbai. After Chandavarkar shortlisted a few candidates in 1997, Kiran came in for the final interview. All five shortlisted students already had job offers in hand. The interview lasted forty-five minutes, of which Kiran spoke for forty. She spoke about why she wanted to enter pharmaceuticals and how she wanted the company to grow.

That 'campus-placement experience' was different for Shreehas Tambe. 'My offer was from Lupin; I don't think D.B. Gupta [founder and chairman of Lupin] gave a damn about who was joining the company. A general manager had come from Tarapur and we were all very happy because the salary was nice,' says Tambe, a hefty man with a sense of humour. On hearing Kiran out, he was impressed that the 'chairperson' of the company was explaining to a fresher what the vision was. At twenty-three, the idea of working in a pub city wasn't bad even though leaving Mumbai was not in his scheme of things. 'I thought it'd be fun to check out the city for two to three years and then come back to Mumbai,' he remembers thinking.

Kiran said she had spoken to his placement manager; she knew his salary and would match it. She insisted that he say yes to the offer right then. Tambe was anxious. He had not submitted his master's thesis and his supervisor, J.B. Joshi, generally decided where his students would go, which often was Reliance Industries. Surprisingly, after some intimidating remarks like 'how could you attend the campus interview without asking me', Joshi encouraged him to join Biocon. He did not conceal his cautionary advice though: 'Come back after two years, finish your Ph.D and then we'll see.'

Tambe did go back to his university – which was granted a deemed university status in 2008 and renamed Institute of Chemical Technology – several years later, when he got nominated to its advisory board by Kiran. He sat on the same committee as Joshi, who went on to become the director of the institute. Biocon had a long association with the institute because it had an evolved food technology department and it allowed the R&D in Bengaluru to use its equipment and laboratories.

In Bengaluru, Tambe started as a line manager responsible for protein purification operations. His day job was at the plant and during the night, when he was 'loaned' by Chandavarkar to Shri, he would work on the design of a new contained bioreactor which Shri had brought up to version three, graduating from plastic prototypes to steel frames.

As a chemical engineer, Shri knew tray-based solid state fermentation in Koji rooms was not the best way to do it – the problems of heat generation, heat removal and drying up of the substrate needed better solutions. There were days when certain organisms sporulated. You could enter the Koji room on any fine day to find it filled with an orange, green or pink cloud. It was a nightmare, particularly because the company had hopes of entering pharmaceuticals. Shri therefore floated the idea of building a new fermentation system which would be fully contained and automated, doing away with all the manual handling of tray-based fermentation.

He had been at it for a few years, and when Tambe joined, they were struggling to break the algorithms to mix the material and allow the system to extract the product. Tambe was briefed to see if he could crack the code. The fermenter was called Plafractor. The name was a play on its looks – it resembled a plate and frame in the way it was assembled as well as in its operating philosophy. The alternating trays performed similar functions, just like in a plate-and-frame press.

'Shri called me and said, "I want you to take up this very exciting project. It'll make you rich – in knowledge"', recalls Tambe. It was a good concept but not easy to scale. The delay was hurting the company because in the very first product portfolio it wanted to try had an immunosuppressant – a potent, toxic substance whose manual handling in the fermenters could prove harmful to the operators.

When Tambe began working on the prototype, views were divided. Many thought it was a lost cause. Shri had already had a few public rows with the marketing team which wanted more money to invest in its team and brand building. Tambe would also have disagreements with Kamath who had herself worked on some concepts and did not quite agree on the Plafractor design and the principle that they were pursuing.

Meanwhile, in 1997, Kiran had convinced the board to sanction ₹4 crore for the project. She also made a key contribution to the design. Owing to the legacy of the tray system, the team was just stacking up the square frames although mixing in a square frame on a central axis was proving to be difficult. She suggested making the frames round. It worked. It was common sense but it somehow hadn't occurred to the team for a long time.

Tambe and Shri worked on it for nearly two years. It was a side project for Tambe, who after plant hours spent on enzymes, would come to R&D and then the two would work till late in the night. Shri, who had a company hatchback, the Maruti 800, would drop him halfway, from where he would take an autorickshaw. On days Shri left early, he would leave his car behind. Tambe would then drop the car at Shri's house, go home, sleep for a few hours and take the office pick-up van in the morning.

One day, during lunch in the cafeteria, Kiran inquired how the Plafractor work was going on. When Tambe described how it was all worked out in shifts, she asked him how he commuted. A few minutes later, when lunch was over, she asked Tambe to have 'a word with Krishnan'.

When Tambe went to Krishnan, the finance head blurted: 'Why did you have to go to Kiran for all this?'

Surprised, Tambe said, 'I didn't go to her for anything.'

Looking at his computer, Krishnan said, 'Which car do you want?'

'I can't afford a car,' Tambe said.

'That I can see; we will give you a Maruti 800,' Krishnan said.

Tambe didn't like that car; he had set his heart on the Zen, a snazzy hatchback from the same company, for whenever his pocket would allow.

Before Tambe could fully grasp what was happening, the next day, he was at Sagar Automobiles, a Maruti dealer, negotiating a Zen price along with his father, Krishnan and another finance executive from Biocon. Tambe had to pay back the car loan to Biocon at zero interest and he could decide his equated monthly instalments.

'It was a fantastic gesture,' says Tambe. 'A free car would have made it look very different. This was a car I owned but it was not a burden on me. I did not feel obligated.' Since then Tambe has had quite a ride. He now drives a BMW-320d, and as a senior vice-president also heads the global insulins business and capital projects.

Around the same time, Anindya Sircar, who had joined as a scientist but was soon moved to set up the intellectual property cell, one day walked up to Kiran in stubborn resolve: 'It's not working out. I'm married now and have more responsibilities.' She asked if he had found another job and pulled out his salary details, expressed surprise at how little he got and then called Krishnan. The finance head feigned ignorance. 'What can I say, his boss should know better.' Kiran threw a number at Sircar, who accepted the raise and walked away, glowing that he had managed a good bargain. Next month, when the salary was credited to his account, the hike was more than twice what Kiran had promised him that day.

*

After nearly eight years of work, Plafractor was ready for commercial production in 2000. During these years, many within the company, including some board members, had felt the project was 'going nowhere'; some secretly sneered at it. But Kiran kept the faith. She believed the idea would work, and against all odds, in 1997 she had earmarked ₹4 crore for its development when the company was merely grossing ₹25 crore.

When it first became operational in 2000, it was modelled for cyclosporine, an immunosuppressant derived from a fungus which was first approved by the US Food and Drug Administration (FDA) in 1983 to prevent organ transplant rejection. But Biocon never made production batches of cyclosporine for commercial sale. It was a difficult product to make because any culture that produces cyclosporine produces twenty or more types of cyclosporine. With minute differences in structure – which led to even tinier differences in properties – it would have required high expertise in large-scale chromatography to make a high-quality product. Biocon found it more practical to switch to mycophenolate mofetil, another fungus-derived immunosuppressant. Plafractor thus seeded this new API portfolio, which for some years was a niche product made in a few hundred kilograms and was not a high-volume bulk drug.

Eventually, a sum of ₹40 crore was kept aside to make nine units of Plafractor. However, as the business grew, the limitation of solid state technology surfaced again and the company had to move its immunosuppressant production to liquid fermentation. In 2004, a separate plant for this category was built and, by 2006, when the cost and quality of the new plant caught up with Plafractor's, the latter was decommissioned. Biocon had outgrown its baby.

Although its life was short, Plafractor certainly brought some glory to Biocon. The story of the US patent being granted on her birthday in 2001 may be slowly disappearing from public memory but some old-timers within the company still cherish it. The sentimental value is priceless: Kiran broke down in front of her colleagues.

The steel frame of the fermenter has long since become an exhibition at Biocon. It's also part of the Visvesvaraya Technological and Industrial Museum in Bengaluru. Now, it's going to be part of a bigger exhibition at the World Science Gallery in London – the hulking steel drum – representing the history of evolution of biotech in Bengaluru.

Learn, Earn, Burn

As for its own evolution, the kitchen-and-sink operation at Biocon continued for some time. Everyone groped and learnt from mistakes. In September 1987, Tara Jayaram, a biochemist who had worked for thirteen years in public health engineering in Zambia, rang up Kiran, who had been her junior in Central College. Jayaram had relocated to Bengaluru and was looking for work. A few days later, Kiran called her to say she had an opening in Quality, but quickly added that Quality jobs were often considered boring. 'Why don't you try for a week and if you don't like the work, we can say bye-bye to each other?' she told Jayaram.

In three days, Jayaram confirmed that she would like to stay on. As the forty-ninth employee, she began to build quality systems. It was called Quality Assurance then, and as the name suggested, analysis was done and recorded after the products were despatched so that in case of any complaint, they could trace the batch. The quality systems grew as products grew – from beer to leather to textile industry.

However, it was the quality head in Cork, Ann Francis – she came to Bengaluru twice a year to audit and help improve the general quality standards – who truly taught the team international quality practices. 'We were so naive that we did the work but never recorded or even calibrated things like automatic pipettes and balances,' recalled Jayaram. People would dread Francis's visits so much that they would 'pray that she fell sick before her travel to India'.

Learning was a scramble, as were resources. Even something like parafilm was a luxury that someone travelling to Ireland would have to bring back to Bengaluru. At Heathrow in London, airport staff would be puzzled at the stocks of automatic pipettes, parafilm rolls, reagents and similar stuff that the staff would carry with them. The photosensitive assays in the lab used to be covered by aluminium foil. There was a lab assistant who would straighten those foils for the next use. 'We did not get it in India; so we'd be very frugal with the one roll we'd have. Cut a bit and then stretch it as much as possible,' says Nirupa Bareja.

Bareja, a biologist from Bangalore University, first joined the quality team, then moved to head production, and eventually became the human resource manager. Like Jayaram, who wrote her quality manuals – since none existed for the biotech or process industry when ISO 9000 certification was sought – Bareja wrote the human resource manuals that were relevant for a biotech manufacturing company.

In the early 1990s, the company bought a few second-hand Bajaj matadors to ferry people. They were branded with the slogan 'Working with Nature', a tagline that was later discontinued because people would call Kiran to complain if the van was spotted speeding. Around the same time, Biocon took loans from HDFC to buy a few flats for the senior team, which would be given to them after they completed ten to fifteen years of service. Sometime in the late 1990s, the flats were given to Bharadwaj, Shri, Krishnan and Chandavarkar.

A generous gesture or a natty business strategy, it helped the team remain cohesive when the business was choppy and tempers ran high. Employees, other than the suave Bharadwaj who avoided getting into slanging matches, would often get into arguments which sometimes could be heard beyond the Biocon premises. 'It'd never be in closed rooms. Many times, something in the cafeteria would kick off and the next thing people would hear was a cacophony of high-pitched notes. They knew Kiran was the boss, we were employees and that tomorrow we would be history,' recounts Krishnan, though he hardly looks like the high-decibel, argumentative finance head that he describes himself as.

Next day, it would be business as usual.

Parting

It was not so at Unilever. Within six months of having that conversation with Dadiseth during which Kiran sought assurance on Unilever's commitment to biotechnology, the conglomerate did a massive strategic review and decided that biotech was not their thing. Just then, London's Imperial Chemical Industries (ICI), decided to rebrand and move away from the bulk chemicals business which was under pressure due to disappointing results. It wanted to get rid of the 'bulk' label and become a 'speciality' chemicals company. ICI bought Unilever's speciality business, where all its biotech businesses were bundled, in one whale of a deal, for £8 billion.

Joe Dunne still remembers it with some amount of bitterness: 'We were one of the top speciality companies in the world, inching towards number one, and they sold us to a paint company. ICI knew nothing about the business.' As it turned out for many Biocon executives, Dunne 'got sold three times' before he decided to strike out on his own. He founded Westgate Biologicals in Ireland, and consults for a host of food ingredient, nutrition and health companies, and government organizations.

Unilever announced the decision and sought a stamp of consilience from Kiran. 'They sent me a piece of paper asking to sign what was supposedly my no-objection to their selling away to ICI. Fortunately, my earlier agreement with them had a clause that gave me the first right of refusal, so I said I'd like to exercise my rights,' she says. Their share had gone a little beyond 30 per cent because of their investment in BioChemizyme.

Unilever's announcement came soon after Kiran and John Shaw, then managing director of Madura Coats in India, had decided to tie the knot. After leaving Scotland in 1970, Shaw had lived and worked all over the world and had a rich experience of working in global businesses. He would tell her, 'Look, multinationals have a very keen sense of their interests. They are also clever at portraying things and they will try to do what they want to do. Don't take them at their face value.' Those words would ring true, not just in the following months, but many years later too.

Around that time, Kiran had met Kunal Kashyap, who had just

set up the south India practice for the Chicago-based accounting firm, Arthur Andersen. It turned out she knew his mother and she hired him without letting him present his pitch. 'I believe I can trust you, and for me that is more important,' she said. When Unilever divested, she called Kashyap and said, 'I want you for an assignment which is life changing for me', and asked him to negotiate on Biocon's behalf. Unilever–ICI being a global deal, there was no specific price for the Indian business, and the parties had to arrive at a mutual price.

When ICI became the successor partner to Unilever, they, even more than Unilever, did not want to get involved in the pharma business. ICI had been in the big pharma sector and had earlier spun off the division, Zeneca, to Swedish drug company Astra. Together, they became AstraZeneca, one of the largest pharma companies in Europe.

With ICI, Biocon continued with the old supply agreement but soon the new partner began to come under pressure because the Unilever deal had not proven successful. ICI began to sell in bits and pieces. It was then that Kiran sat down with ICI for a fresh deal through Kashyap. But Kashyap figured there was a conflict of interest – while he, from the south India practice of Andersen was handling Biocon, Andersen's north India practice was handling ICI – one firm with two different offices working on one deal! 'Lecchini used his offices and they had no objection to my handling Biocon as long as there was a Chinese wall between the two offices. They were actually happy that there was someone who knew the lady,' says Kashyap. 'Unilever was helpful; if they had got legal and nasty about it, I don't think Biocon would have made it. To Unilever, it would not have mattered, but, for Biocon, it would have taken a lot out of the system.'

Kashyap negotiated a buyout of ICI's holding in Biocon India for $2.2 million. But there was no money. Serendipitously, John Shaw was planning to sell his London house soon after his wedding, which he did. 'So, instead of ICI becoming Kiran's shareholding partner, I became her partner,' says Shaw. Unilever had put Biocon shares in a special purpose vehicle in Rotterdam. Since he had stayed in the Netherlands for a while earlier, it helped that he could carry the conversation with ICI on a social and personal level too.

Shaw, after staying in India for eight years as managing director of Madura Coats, had been transferred to Amsterdam in 1997. The sprawling textile multinational enterprise he had worked with for thirty years had begun to fall apart. When he got married to Kiran in 1998, he was nearly fifty and ready to retire from the textile world. He accepted Kiran's offer to become a board member. 'I left a sunset industry and joined a sunrise industry,' he says.

Far away in Ireland, Auchincloss continued to work in the sunrise industry. After selling Biocon Group, he 'sat at home for a few months but soon got bored' and started Marigot Limited in 1989 with £4 million, part of the sum he had earned from the Unilever deal. A typical Auchincloss venture, Marigot today produces natural ingredients, particularly marine multi-minerals, through twelve subsidiaries and production facilities in Iceland, England and Ireland. Eternally entrepreneurial, he is rather blasé about his own role: 'I've structured Marigot in such a way that nothing will be sold to pay death duties if I kick the bucket.'

Support System

On separating from Auchincloss and the party-loving boisterous gang in Ireland, many thought the fun quotient would dip in Bengaluru. Not really. In late March 1992, after returning from London, Kiran told her friends that she had met a guy named Alex Frater there and had fallen for him. Spinning around them a romantic story, she disclosed that he had proposed to her, and that she could not say no to him. Frater would be in Bengaluru the following Wednesday for the engagement, she told them. Most of them were delighted that she was finally settling down, but a few felt bad for Shaw, who was also seen as a potentially good match by then. Some fifty people were invited for the party. Vijay Mallya, United Breweries scion and childhood friend, who was infamous for never arriving on time, called off his late-evening meetings to attend the ceremony.

Incidentally, on the same day, Krishan Aurora, head of SmithKline Beecham India, was throwing a party for his visiting boss Jan Leschly, who would later become the chief executive of GlaxoSmithKline. Since there were many common guests, Aurora suggested Kiran and her guests come to his party after the ceremony. That evening, dressed in a gorgeous saree and holding a puja thali, she greeted everyone at the door. Everyone waited for Frater to arrive, for Kiran had told them her parents had gone to receive him at the airport. She kept them guessing until 7.30 p.m. when she declared, 'Guys, it's a joke', one of her annual April Fool jokes. The name of the imaginary fiancé came from a book she had just read – *Chasing the Monsoon* by Alexander Frater.

At first, the guests were angry but they soon decided to pretend they were not fooled, so that they could together fool some more at Aurora's party where he had planned to celebrate with a cake that said 'Congratulations Kiran and Alex'. When Leschly, who had just arrived, congratulated her, she told him the truth. Sportingly, the nine-time Wimbledon player said since that no one recognized him, he could pretend to be Alex if she wanted to fool some more folks, which she blithely did.

In reality though, Kiran was too busy to take marriage seriously. One day in 1991, Kiran threw a party at home for which her parents were also invited. Since Shaw, whom she had met that year at a party at Mallya's, showed up early, he spent some time with her father watching a cricket match on television. That night, when the Mazumdars went home, her father took out a bottle of beer from the fridge and had a long chat with his wife at the kitchen table, as he often did after dinner parties. He said to his wife, 'If ever Kiran decides to get married, she should marry someone like Shaw – both are managing directors, they like paintings and cricket, and play golf. There won't be any ego hassle and he doesn't carry any baggage.'

They never dared to bring this up with Kiran though, partly because she always made her own decisions, and partly because, as parents, they let their children 'make their own fate'. Unfortunately, Rasendra Mazumdar did not live to see the marriage he had so wistfully spoken about.

Kiran's relationship with Shaw evolved over eight years. In 1997, when he was transferred to Holland, it was the distance that brought them closer. They decided to get married in the coming year. 'It was very hard for her. In India, few men would accept the success of a woman and the fact that she played such a prominent role. John plays the background role and for that you've got to be secure. It's not easy, even in the Western context,' says Ravi Mazumdar.

After their wedding in April 1998, they managed their long-distance marriage for a year but it was very exacting. A year later, Shaw turned fifty and was eligible to take early retirement; he chose to make Bengaluru his permanent home. As a corporate executive, he was not exactly rooted anywhere, not even in Scotland, although his family lived there. 'So we thought he could drop anchor in Bengaluru. All he wanted was to build a Spanish hacienda-style home,' says Kiran, casting a warm eye around the poetic allure of the greenery at Glenmore. They shifted into their villa in 2000. Spread over seven acres, Glenmore is their 'oasis of sanity', away from the glossy glass and steel structures of the technology suburb less than five kilometres away.

Until the marriage, which was also the turning point in the business, as Biocon India extricated itself from Unilever that year, she was happy being small, non-complicated, and doing her own thing. 'In fact, we were beginning to get restless by the growth and size of the business. My friends from IIT were in big companies and doing well and here we were, stuck in a start-up. But marriage, in some sense, gave her the confidence to go into the big league,' says Bharadwaj.

When Shaw came to Biocon, it was still a small company with about 100 employees. He found it had a 'very good senior team' and he did not wish to interfere in the close relationship that Kiran had with them. 'I was a johnny-come-lately. I had seen this in some big companies and I did not want to get management relationships confused,' he said.

He would advise her to be 'adventurous in your science but be very conservative in your finance'. As a finance person, he would sit on management decisions but not interfere in any functional matters. He set up the monthly information system so that structured reports were generated in fixed formats and everybody was able to see the collections, borrowings, budgets and top-line numbers. An extremely private person, who recoils even at the thought of talking to the press, Shaw made a conscious choice to remain in the background.

'There is one star in the family and that is my wife; there is no room for two. I am the support system,' he says in a clipped Scottish tone.

3

BIRTH OF A CLUSTER

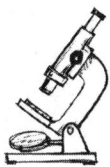

Modern Biology – Lifting the in vivo Veil

Pushpa Mittra Bhargava returned to India as a convert. He had left the country as a chemist and returned in 1957 as a biologist. During the four years that he spent at the University of Wisconsin and at the National Institute of Medical Research (NIMR) in London, he saw the scientific world embrace molecular biology while India remained steeped in classical biology. After resuming research at the Indian Institute of Chemical Technology (IICT) in Hyderabad, he wrote a proposal to Syed Hussain Zaheer, the then director general of the Council of Scientific and Industrial Research (CSIR), to start a new laboratory of modern biology, an emerging reductionist approach that studied the structure, function and synthesis of nucleic acids and proteins. Zaheer liked the idea, thinking it would be easy to gather converging opinion on the initiative, and pre-emptively bought 1,500 acres of land near Palampur in Punjab for the new laboratory. He planned to call it National Biological Laboratory (NBL).

Soon, a five-member committee of eminent biologists,

including botanist Panchanan Maheshwari, was set up to evaluate the proposal, which it shot down, suggesting instead a new institute for the 'extension of traditional biology'. In the end, no institute was set up. Bhargava continued to work at the biochemistry lab at the Indian Institute of Chemical Technology. He would often write and speak in forums – a practice he continues even in his eighties – and would posit that a time would come when it would be possible for scientists to put a nitrogen fixation gene in non-leguminous plants so that they would not need fertilizers; they would make their own from atmospheric carbon dioxide.

He would make these arguments not knowing how complex the nitrogen fixation system was. After some years, in 1974, the *British Medical Journal* carried an editorial espousing those very ideas – that genetic engineering can put nitrogen-fixation genes in non-leguminous plants. 'I took a copy of the editorial and sent it to the then director general of CSIR, Yelavarthy Nayudamma,' says Bhargava. Once again a committee was set up, but this time, fifteen years after the first proposal was rejected, it approved setting up India's first molecular biology centre. On 1 April 1977, the Centre for Cellular and Molecular Biology (CCMB) was formally started in Hyderabad, four years after Herbert W. Boyer and Stanley N. Cohen in the United States invented the recombinant DNA technology which became one of the few scientific advances in history that shaped public perception and spawned an industry with equal intensity.

The 1970s was a pivotal decade for biological sciences. Many groups were trying to establish the central dogma of molecular biology – that gene sequence information flows from DNA to RNA, which translates it into protein – and much of that research work was coming out in bacteria, especially *E. coli*. It was also the time when scientists and industry were evaluating uncertain commercial applications of recombinant DNA, cloning, stem cells and others amid loud and persistent activists and student protestors in the

Bay Area in California pressing for a new purpose in science. Life sciences looked socially responsive and healing. Elsewhere in the world too, particularly in King's College, Cambridge and London, Pasteur Institute in Paris, and the University of Tokyo, applications of bioscience had gripped researchers. But it was San Francisco that grew the fastest and went the farthest. Politicians in America were trying to create policies that would aid, sometimes even alter, the course of science and unleash brute entrepreneurial energies. The first biotech company, Cetus Corporation, was foundering by 1975; yet it did not discourage Boyer from pairing up with a young venture capitalist, Robert Swanson, to found Genentech in 1976.

Meanwhile, prospects of biology continued to soar. In the autumn of 1977, a Swedish science manager from the pharmaceutical company Astra, Ivan Ostholm, visited India, looking for some 'unique' research ideas that the drug company would be interested to fund in the future. One of the early outcomes of Ostholm's visit was Astra's investment in a pharmaceutical company in Bengaluru, which led to the joint venture Astra-IDL. But even after a few years, Ostholm had not found a research idea worthy enough to fund. He only had one year left for retirement. In June 1982, he visited research scientist S. Anand Kumar at the State University of New York in Albany because during his visits to India he had learnt that Kumar dreamt of building a biotechnology centre in Bengaluru and was waiting for his motley research projects to get over in the US before returning to India.

When Ostholm left Albany that summer, Kumar shook his hands and said: 'You have to promise me, Ivan, not to give up.' He did not. With Kumar's help he prepared a proposal, waded through traditional pharmaceuticals' legendary resistance to biotechnology, and presented it to Astra's board and to its chief executive Ulf Widengren, a marketing genius and an Indophile who could read Sanskrit. Kumar's proposal was visionary and he had also sold the prospect of having the Indian Institute of Science as a collaborator in developing biomedical applications for local use. By then, Govindarajan Padmanaban at the department of biochemistry was one of the few scientists in the country who had brought the tools of biotechnology from his visits to the University of Chicago and was cloning genes to figure out their DNA sequence.

Ostholm was hopeful. 'I don't manage scientists, I don't manage science; I help scientists build their dreams.' Ostholm's managerial compass at Astra had been consistent for twenty-four years. Once, he spotted a distraught person, possibly Swiss, at Basel airport. When he walked up to him, he learnt that the young man had failed in his job interview at a pharmaceutical company. The researcher had an idea of preventing acid secretion in the stomach by shutting down proton pumps. After Ostholm showed interest, right there at the airport, the man drew a diagram to explain the idea. Ostholm asked if he had a molecule in mind. Convinced by the man's reply, he instantly wrote him an offer letter and invited him to Stockholm. Astra was already working on anti-ulcers and the drug that Ostholm's offer letter propelled was the multi-billion-dollar anti-ulcer drug Omeprazole which turned around Astra's fortunes. If Ostholm sensed a scientist's passion, he would brook no barrier to his/her support. Another time, Arvid Carlsson, a pharmacologist, came to him and said he wanted to find out the cause of schizophrenia. Ostholm funded his research at the University of Gothenburg for twenty-two years. Carlsson returned the favour differently – by winning the Nobel Prize in 2000, five years before Ostholm died.

To Ostholm's telescopic eye, a biotechnology centre in Bengaluru looked both strategic and tactical. He brought Widengren to Bengaluru who became 'enthusiastic as soon as he had visited the Indian Institute of Science' in April 1983. In their subsequent meetings with Padmanaban, it became clear what was possible in terms of products and research ideas. In rare academic candour, Padmanaban shared his experience with them. He had found a toxin for a mysterious neurological disease in north India that caused a symptom called lathyrism from time to time. But it could not reach the patients because no one knew how to convert it into a diagnostic.

On his return to Sweden after that visit, Ostholm got the project approved, with $2.8 million as his budget to start a centre in Bengaluru for a trial period of three years. In October 1983, Astra submitted a formal application to the Indian government seeking permission for a research centre in Bengaluru.

The Gospel of Biotechnology

After submitting the application, S. Anand Kumar and Ostholm set off on a new mission – to look for a competent director and some enthusiastic researchers. They visited many cities in the United States and obtained informal acceptance from at least twenty researchers who were willing to return to India. The director's position was still open. Self-effacing Kumar had refused, saying he did not have the right administrative abilities to lead a competitive research centre that had the spirit of pharmaceutical R&D, though he had offered himself as a 'standby'. When Ostholm met Padmanaban, who was visiting Chicago in October 1983, and offered him the position, he too refused, politely. He could do more for the centre by being at the Indian Institute of Science, he explained.

In fact, Padmanaban had anticipated such an offer and had written down his response on paper before Ostholm and Kumar visited him at his flat near the university. It said: 'One has to realize that not all professors at the Institute are positively inclined towards research centres that have a connection with the industry. By staying back as a professor, I think, in the long run, I can influence other professors to see the positive side of this collaboration. We have to help each other to create something valuable for India.'

A year later, in October 1984, when written permission finally came from the government, Ostholm, who was by then living in Bengaluru with his wife, visited Delhi to meet officials at the Department of Science and Technology. A friend at the IISc gave him advice: 'Officially, it is the department that selects the representatives on the board. However, in reality, it is Professor Mambillikalathil Govind Kumar Menon who makes the decision, so I advise you to go and meet him.' Ostholm was beginning to understand the importance of good personal contacts in India and did as he was advised. Since Nobel laureate Sune Bergström had agreed to be on the board of the Astra Research Centre, and the drug company was starting the project at an even keel – half of the board members would be appointed by Astra, half by the Department of Science and Technology – Ostholm's visit set the right tone.

In any case, the Swedes were bending over backwards to make the Centre happen. They increased the project budget from $2.8 million to $3.5 million and assuaged all concerns of a brain drain by committing that commercialization of any technology or discovery made at the Centre would depend on the board; Astra would have the rights outside India. The Swedes also dropped a board seat which they intended to keep for an industrialist after the science and technology secretary said the department had bad experiences 'of having too close a contact between research and the industry'. 'Research in Indian industrial companies is most of the time development work; it is called research to avail of tax reduction which the government has given to support real research. We cannot accept an industrialist on the board,' Secretary S. Ramachandran said.

Meanwhile, one unit of Astra Research Centre was started in Padmanaban's biochemistry laboratory; six fresh Ph.Ds were hired. The company gave a sizeable grant to Padmanaban to start research and build new laboratories. But the mistrust of the industry was deep-rooted at the campus too; the chairman of the biological sciences division refused the grant. This was leaked and a local newspaper carried a front-page report headlined: Internal Brain Robbery. The article said Padmanaban was planning to move to the Centre with some top-notch scientists from the IISc.

Ostholm was busy managing scientific sentiments in Delhi and Bengaluru when Kumar wrote to him that he thought he had found the right person to head the Centre. While travelling to Buenos Aires for a conference, Ostholm met Janaki Ramachandran who had worked in the United States for over two decades; Ramachandran had also taught at the University of California in San Francisco for many years. When Ostholm called Ramachandran for a meeting, he was heading the protein chemistry research lab at Genentech, the most hip and happening biotech firm in the world at that time.

Before the meeting, Ostholm was very 'tense'. From what he had researched on the man, Ramachandran was indeed the right person to lead the Bengaluru centre but Ostholm could not build an alluring enough case to bring him back to India. Over lunch, they discussed the Centre when Ostholm's lurking fears were confirmed. A lot was going on in Ramachandran's career at Genentech, and returning to India was not even a remote possibility. Living in India for several months now and having interviewed dozens of researchers in America, Ostholm understood that family ties held a special place in every Indian's heart; it was his trump card. He told Ramachandran that in his old age he would need India more than America, after which the biochemist suddenly became serious and said: 'There *is* something in what you say. At the end of my career, I would indeed like to move back to India, but not just now.'

The next morning, Kumar and Ostholm ruminated on their luncheon meeting and concluded that maybe they were partly successful in convincing Ramachandran. In early 1985, Astra invited him to Stockholm to meet Bergström and deliver a few lectures at the Karolinska Institute.

'Sweden was very socialist. Astra was making 22 per cent profits those days and many felt that if that figure went up to 25 per cent, all hell would break loose. So they thought of doing some good. I felt kind of embarrassed. The Swedes were trying to do something in India and I was hesitating,' Ramachandran recalls. He told them what they were doing was fine, but he did not have expertise in infection – an area their Indian centre wanted to focus on – as he worked on signal transduction and cell surface receptors. The Swedes said they wanted him for his management skills and offered to 'make a deal with Genentech' where the US company would allow him to spend two months spread over a year in India.

'It was an unusual deal but they made it happen,' says Ramachandran. Between 1986 and 1988, he shuttled between California and Bengaluru, setting up the Centre. In January 1987, it was inaugurated by Prime Minister Rajiv Gandhi, who, two years ago, while meeting a delegation of fifteen eminent Indian-Americans in New York, had made an eloquent appeal to them to return. Ramachandran, in principle, had accepted the Astra offer but his American citizenship was holding up his appointment in Delhi. At the Indian embassy in New York that day, Gandhi ensured that the bureaucracy got the message.

Ostholm had already hired a few doctorates, one of whom was Banda Venkata Ravikumar, a psychiatrist who had trained at Christian Medical College in Vellore but had given up practice to pursue research in molecular biology. During his final year of Ph.D, Ostholm would often engage him in conversations over cups of tea. One day, when he learnt that Ravikumar had a postdoctoral fellowship from the Massachusetts Institute of Technology, Ostholm looked at the applications and found that Ravikumar had not applied to Astra Centre. He wrote the covering letter on his behalf and told him, 'You join Astra now and after one year I will send you to MIT.'

During the interview, the committee asked him what problems in tropical diseases the Centre should work on. Over ninety minutes, Ravikumar presented three ideas on leprosy, neurocysticercosis and Japanese encephalitis. Ostholm, who was in the committee, asked what Ravikumar would do after completing the MIT fellowship. 'Come back to India and work on two of these ideas,' he replied; he had already written to the Indian Council of Medical Research (ICMR) for grants.

'What would be your job description in India?' Ostholm inquired.

'Independent investigator,' he said.

'If I make you an independent investigator now, would you still need to go to MIT?' he asked. A trained physician who had lost his certificate in a bombing during the Second World War, Ostholm was a sensitive soul whose life's purpose was mentoring scientists.

Ravikumar froze; Ostholm was offering him a position where he could choose to work on any of the two projects and report to the director as long as he worked at that Centre. He could not refuse. 'Ostholm had done slow infection of the Astra job on me for over a year, even offering a fellowship at Carlsson's lab in Sweden before I got the MIT fellowship,' Ravikumar recalls.

At the Bangalore Centre, Ramachandran told all researchers that they must go out after five years and start a company. 'That was the need,' he assessed. As a generous and benevolent company, Astra had given him carte blanche to foster science in India. The initial group began with developing tools which they needed to isolate, characterize and manipulate parts of cells. Restriction enzymes, which cut DNA into smaller pieces, was one of them; it was also one of Kumar's pet projects. In 1989, Padmanabhan Babu left molecular biology at the Tata Institute of Fundamental Research (TIFR) in Mumbai to start the Bangalore Genei which would commercialize restriction enzymes and other technologies developed at Astra. Ramachandran housed the start-up for four years in the Centre, providing all kinds of support, including the crucial one: quality control.

By that time, Ramachandran had moved out of Genentech, where some people had begun objecting to his time in India, and joined a start-up called Neurex which had agreed to his spending more than two months in India. Over the next five years and across two time zones, Ramachandran built a venture-funded company in America and a non-profit research centre in Bengaluru.

Soon, in 1989, he was faced with a challenge. In Sweden, the new chief executive of Astra, Hakan Mogren, a forty-four-year-old chocolatier, was turning some of the company's programmes on its head. He asked his friend Charles Cooney, a professor at MIT, to visit the Bangalore Centre and figure out what it did and what it might do in future. Cooney had an affinity for India. In the mid-1970s, when he visited New Delhi for a conference, he and his family were invited to meet Prime Minister Indira Gandhi who served Coke to his thirteen-year-old son. 'It was a memorable visit because you don't get served Coke by the head of a government. It spoke of the very social fabric of India. For me that was a peek in the window,' Cooney reminisces.

When he came to Bengaluru in 1989 at Mogren's behest, he met Ramachandran whom he knew from his time at Genentech. Cooney met every researcher at the Centre, visited each lab and walked through 'every piece of infrastructure'. In his recommendation letter to Mogren, he said the Bangalore Centre could become an important asset for Astra. The model that Ramachandran had put together was unique: track the diaspora, approach the scientists who have been trained in the US and Europe and who for social reasons would want to come back to India, but could not because of gaping holes in life sciences infrastructure or the bureaucracy of getting lab consumables. Ramachandran had created a system that insulated scientists from those hassles. 'He had created this shell of an organization that would nurture an internal environment that would build upon human capital,' says Cooney. In his letter, however, Cooney added a caveat. He said the Centre would become an asset only if Astra invested in it and kept the communication channel open between Sweden and India.

Mogren paid heed to Cooney's counsel and also appointed him on the Centre's advisory board.

A year later, Cooney's student Arun Chandavarkar joined Biocon, and he would often invite him over. Like a duck taking to water, Kiran plugged herself into this academic and bigger stream of knowledge at the Centre. In the pre-Internet era, the Astra Centre, which Ramachandran ran like an American university, open and non-hierarchical, acted as a potent idea exchange. Four start-ups would come out of it subsequently.

If the Indian government's permission of 1985 allowing Texas Instruments to set up a development centre in Bengaluru – that directly transferred data to its headquarters in the US – was a trigger for information technology's outsourced service industry in India, its permission to Astra in 1984 was no less transformative for the biotech industry.

Spotlight on Biology, Finally

The first steps towards growing the biotechnology industry were taken at the Indian Science Congress in Mysore in January 1982. Prime Minister Indira Gandhi announced creating a National Biotechnology Board (NBB). Under the Department of Science and Technology, the NBB would promote biotechnology by creating manpower and infrastructure, and would also frame necessary regulations. It was the first time that biology got political capital. The science czars in Delhi – the troika of Homi Jehangir Bhabha, Shanti Swarup Bhatnagar and Prasanta Chandra Mahalanobis, which would later include Vikram Sarabhai and M.G.K. Menon – had somewhat ignored biology; they were advocates of mission-based science in atomic energy, space and electronics.

Biology suffered short shrift even earlier. After the Indian Institute of Science was set up in 1909, Sir Dorabji Tata wanted to establish an institute for medical research, on tropical diseases specifically. He had offered a corpus, similar to what Jamshedji Nusserwanji Tata gave for establishing the institute itself. The British director Morris W. Travers felt two research institutions for India would be redundant and refused to take the grant. (The Dorabji Tata Trust, more than eighty years later, fulfilled that wish when Govindarajan Padmanaban, as director, proposed such a centre at the institute.)

By the mid-1980s, the practical benefits of biotechnology were bursting on the international science skyline. Pushpa Mittra Bhargava wrote to Prime Minister Rajiv Gandhi stating that India needed an independent agency for biotechnology, an idea that had mutated from his earlier proposal for setting up a National Biological Laboratory in the late 1950s. Gandhi took notice. In 1986, the government converted the NBB into the Department of Biotechnology, an independent entity like other departments in space and atomic energy. In terms of status, if not budget, biology had come on par with other sciences. Bhargava was offered the leadership role, but the maverick scientist placed three conditions. 'I wanted the department to be located in Hyderabad. I also wanted to continue as the director of the Centre for Cellular and Molecular Biology because I had made a promise to the nation. My third condition was I would give a programme to the prime minister who would review and approve, but once approved, I would not be interrupted. I was summoned to Delhi but the government was not willing to accept my conditions,' recalls Bhargava.

Coincidentally, what Bhargava was seeking had a precedent. When the Electronics Commission was set up within the Department of Electronics in 1971, Vikram Sarabhai recommended a solid state physicist, M.G.K. Menon, at the Tata Institute of Fundamental Research in Mumbai to head it. Menon was reluctant to accept the assignment in Delhi and placed two conditions: he wanted to continue as the director of TIFR and wanted the Electronics Commission to be located in Mumbai. The Prime Minister's Office accepted both the conditions and the Electronics Commission operated from the Air India building in Nariman Point for many years.

*

So it was S. Ramachandran who became the first secretary of the Department of Biotechnology and he went full bore on training manpower and building general competence, an outlook that seemed genetically encoded because for several years, scarce attention was paid to converting research into applications. An agency that was meant to aid product development did what other, and older, government agencies did – give research grants and start institutions. Industry continued to be at an arm's length. Ramachandran's remark to Astra that the government did not want an industrialist on the board was reflective. Few could then fathom what would float the biotech boat in future.

Meanwhile, a fresh break from classical biology was taking place in Mumbai. Obaid Siddiqi, who was invited by Homi Bhabha to start a molecular biology unit at TIFR in the early 1960s, was associated with an elite group of scientists like Francis Crick, Sydney Brenner, and Seymour Benzer who studied the nature of gene and how it regulated life forms. Later on, along with his international collaborators, Siddiqi moved on to study neurogenetics to understand how the brain works. That pumped new energy into biology in the country as he built and brought tools to understand the organ. Until then, most labs, primarily in Bengaluru, Delhi and Kolkata, 'crushed' tissue to understand what happened in biochemistry. At places like the Indian Institute of Science, there was even antipathy to genetics. Many viewed it as 'all new nonsense'.

'That's unfortunately true. We were looked down upon,' rues H. Sharat Chandra, who, as a professor of microbiology at the

IISc, specialized in genetics. Classical genetics was practised in agricultural universities, even in animal husbandry, for breeding purposes. Higher yield of milk, egg-laying ability of poultry or better quality of meat are quantitative traits which are genetically selectable by breeding. However, the cytological and chromosomal aspects of genetics were largely confined to zoology and botany departments in universities. 'One option was to give up the Institute linkage and go out [to do human genetics research] but sufficient funding was not available,' Chandra says.

In Hyderabad too, Bhargava was struggling to get real molecular biology research off the ground. In the mid-1980s, he invited Lalji Singh, who was visiting the Banaras Hindu University with his colleagues from the University of Edinburgh, to give a seminar where Bhargava sprung a surprise on him. He offered him a position at Hyderabad. When Singh returned to Edinburgh, Bhargava remained persistent and made him a written offer. Singh's colleagues at the Institute of Animal Epigenetics discouraged him, so he put forth a number of conditions before Bhargava. One by one, Bhargava fulfilled them all, even appointing two of Singh's students at CCMB. 'I then had a moral obligation to come to Hyderabad. It was a rare gesture in a government laboratory those days,' recalls Singh. He joined in June 1987.

As Bhargava followed Singh's research, he knew that a part of his work on sex determination in snakes would lead to DNA fingerprinting technology. Singh had found some DNA sequence repeats that were highly conserved in humans, but he was reluctant to develop the technology. When Bhargava goaded him to move beyond 'arm-chair' research, Singh relented, but it took him more than a year to develop a probe from the DNA sequences isolated from a poisonous Indian female snake, banded krait. It was named the Bkm-derived probe, only the third DNA fingerprinting probe in the world then. After it was successfully presented as evidence in a case in the Kerala High Court, Singh found himself in a bind.

As first-generation technology, it was time-consuming, for which he had no support at CCMB after Bhargava retired. But the judges had found it so useful that they wrote to him to make it available, even offering to write to the Central government to rustle up resources for its development.

Clearly, someone had to commercialize DNA fingerprinting. But who would? During the mid-1980s and the early 1990s, DNA fingerprinting was a fairly new process. Prime Minister Rajiv Gandhi showed interest and Lalji Singh was called to Delhi. After he presented the idea of a new centre that would develop DNA applications, to the Ministry of Home Affairs, Secretary (Home) J.A. Kalyana Krishnan was dismissive in this infamous remark: 'We have to fight crime with danda (stick) in this country, we don't need sophisticated technology.'

A few years elapsed before the Department of Biotechnology provided support and the Centre for DNA Fingerprinting and Diagnostics (CDFD) was set up in 1995. Over the years, basic-research-minded scientists populated it and it began to look more like a 'mini CCMB' rather than an application development centre. Twenty years later, Singh, who had conceived this centre but gave up its leadership to become the director of CCMB in 1998, said: 'It's easy to fool people in basic research, but in applications, you either succeed or fail. So it's understandable why scientists in India shy away from applications.'

THE CLUBBY ENVIRONMENT

By the early 1990s, Bengaluru and a few other centres in Delhi and Kolkata were beginning to give priority to development of molecular diagnostic tools for infectious and chronic diseases. Due to Astra's generous budget, some of the essential consumables had become easy to procure. Earlier, a pack of Eppendorf tubes cost more than $100 to import. 'We would wash them and reuse them at the Indian Institute of Science,' recalls biophysicist Samir

K. Brahmachari. After the Astra Centre got teeming, Brahmachari went to Tarsons Products, the company that supplied imported Eppendorf tubes, and requested it to make the products locally. When the trader wasn't convinced about steady business, Brahmachari took him to Raman Roy at Astra who assured the manufacturer that if his products were of the same quality, his centre would stop importing. Brahmachari's biophysics lab at the institute became the test bed for Tarsons, which eventually became one of the largest suppliers in the country.

Making products was a learning experience for most, even in manoeuvring the corrosive corridors of bureaucracy in Delhi. Many public-funded research labs claimed to be developing kits, including G. Padmanaban's. 'A memorandum of understanding was signed with companies – mostly with a single person – for the development of diagnostic kits. But not a single kit ever reached the market. Scientists did not know what it took to bridge the lab-to-market distance and industry was only used to importing kits or assembling them from imported components and packaging it well,' G. Padmanaban wrote in *Current Science* in 1991. Later on, when some kits were indeed manufactured, the government possibly followed every anachronistic rule in its book to snuff out the locally developed ones.

By 1993, Ramachandran's start-up in the US had developed a novel painkiller, the first non-opiate drug for intractable pain, and had filed an Investigational New Drug application. It also went public. So he was ready to return to Bengaluru, also because Astra was pleased with the Bangalore Centre and had closed down its infection unit in Sweden, giving full responsibility to its India unit. Subsequently, preclinical, medicinal chemistry and the whole kit and caboodle of drug discovery research was set up.

Kiran was introduced to that buzzing place by Ravikumar when her researchers made a hyper-producing strain of the fungus *Aspergillus* by random mutation and wanted to know what they could do with it commercially. As one of the few industrial biotech companies doing some research, Biocon was known among academics who would send their students there for internship. Once when she was visiting Pune, Raghunath A. Mashelkar invited Kiran to give a 'hard-hitting' talk at the National Chemical Laboratory (NCL) and, as director, hurriedly pulled together a reasonable crowd of faculty and researchers. He wanted her to jolt them out from their cushy, future-proof academic environment. One person who was ready to leave that environment by late 1994 was Banda Venkata Ravikumar.

In nine years at Astra and working with the Indian Institute of Science, Ravikumar had developed a peptide-based ELISA kit to detect human immunodeficiency virus (both HIV1 and HIV2). He had also filed a patent through Astra that would allow him to develop a novel diagnostic kit for a brain infection called neurocysticercosis, a test that would help neurologists to distinguish between neuro-tuberculosis and tapeworm infection.

In applying to Small Industries Development Bank of India (SIDBI) for a loan to start his company, XCyton, Ravikumar needed a recommendation letter. He asked Bergström. At that time, the Nobel laureate wore three hats but chose to use the one that said chairman of the Nobel Committee in Stockholm, and for a good reason. The pithy letter said he knew more than 110 researchers in the field of immunology in India; they were all very good but 'if there is one of them who would develop a product, it is Ravikumar. If the Bank has difficulty in finding funds, I'll arrange it from [Astra's] national funds'.

'That letter worked like magic. The bank advanced its investment committee meeting and closed the deal,' says Ravikumar. Later, when he decided to commercialize his neurocysticercosis work done at Astra, he went back to Bergström and offered a proposal with 3 per cent royalty. Bergström looked at his offer and said, 'Thank you for your proposal but it is rejected. It's given free, as a gift.'

Like Padmanaban Babu, Ravikumar raised money from Astra colleagues and friends to develop a slew of diagnostic kits over the next few years. But he had merely seen the tip of the iceberg. The issue that disturbed him, and perhaps also Astra and others, on the idyllic scientific setting of Bengaluru, was that any product for public health had to go through the gruelling grind of Nirman Bhawan in Delhi, which housed the offices of the Ministry of Health and Family Welfare. Even after meeting all the stringent criteria for the kit validation, the government chose to import such kits, the expenses on which was supported by World Bank funds. The procurement specifications were such that no Indian manufacturer could even make a bid for the supply. 'It took three Union health ministers to finally amend the specifications to allow a portion of the business to go to Indian manufacturers, with Indian government money,' recalls G. Padmanaban.

From nearly nil expertise at the beginning of the 1980s, by the early 1990s, at least a dozen Indian labs had recombinant experience but not a single recombinant protein product was under development for commercial use. Once again, G. Padmanaban wrote about it furiously. 'In the twenty-first century, the West may dictate what hybrid seeds we should sow or what brand of recombinant insulin we should use or even what brand of detergent we should use to remove laundry stains,' he warned in a *Current Science* article.

Meanwhile, one frustrated entrepreneur in Hyderabad was getting restive.

First Recombinant Product

In 1992, K.I. Varaprasad Reddy had an existential crisis. As an electronics engineer, he had spent seven years in a defence research lab which he left because all that engineers did there was import substitution. That's when he met an academic entrepreneur who chose him to revive and run his specialized batteries business

SABNIFE Power Systems, which Reddy achieved effectively and ran for a few years, notching ₹50 crore in revenue. Still, he was 'unceremoniously' ousted.

As Reddy was considering going back to his native place to pursue farming, he accompanied his cousin, a scientist in Cincinnati, to a biomedical conference in Geneva. People discussed global health issues, hepatitis B in particular, with India and China having nearly ninety million infections. In the same conference, people also spoke about developing countries coming to an international forum with 'begging bowls'. There he came to understand that not only children, even adults needed the vaccine but it was expensive and not readily available.

When he returned to Hyderabad, he checked with a few pharmaceutical companies, but all of them discouraged him. Pushpa Mittra Bhargava was the only one to encourage him when he thought of starting a company to make the vaccine. From his cousins and Telugu friends in New Jersey, and by selling a part of his ancestral land, Reddy raised ₹1.91 crore and registered Shantha Biotechnics. When he was scouting for a scientific partner, microbiologist Gita Sharma at Osmania University heard about it and proposed a fair deal: Reddy would fund part of her conference travel to the United States since the government money was falling short and Sharma would identify a project to work on. Her own recommendation was interferon, an important cancer drug but exorbitantly priced in India. To that Reddy added hepatitis B and the two-product list was ready for an industry–university alliance.

Over the next several months, Sharma began working with help from molecular biologist Guntaka Reddy at the University of Missouri. They bought DNA of the hepatitis B virus from American Type Culture Centre (ATCC). At that time, at least two such vaccines were in the market and the patent on it would not expire until 2005. But if made with a different process, the product could be sold in India where product patent would apply only from 2005.

Meanwhile, Varaprasad Reddy was busy for the most part of early 1994 raising more money and doing market research for the two products he had identified. News of his courageous – although foolhardy in many eyes – venture had reached the foreign minister of Oman, Yusuf bin Alawi bin Abdullah, who could sense that Reddy was not the 'typical businessman, but a man in a hurry'. He agreed to provide ₹90 lakh after the royal doctor in Oman endorsed the project.

On the scientific front, Sharma and her mentor from Missouri hit a roadblock – it was as much due to opinion as hard science. They debated whether or not to use *E. coli*, a bacterial expression system, midway through the project, when they had started with the yeast expression of *Pichia pastoris*. Varaprasad Reddy shifted the research from Osmania University to the Centre for Cellular and Molecular Biology which had to choose the best clone from a bunch of clones that would act as the cell line for the vaccine. Director Gowri Shankar did not give the project 'more than a 5 per cent probability of survival'. He wondered at the electronics engineer, who had ventured into a highly specialized field which even big Indian pharmaceutical companies had stayed away from, and thought the project would need many things such as voltage stability and supplies of liquid nitrogen which were difficult even at his Centre. He found a principal researcher for the project but deep within, he knew the 'good intentions [of Reddy] were not enough, it could take two days, or it could take six months'.

Since hepatitis B vaccine would be the first recombinant technology product for human use in the country, Reddy had no small role in Delhi; some viewed it as a cameo, some as a tragicomic tale of a rebel. At the public sector vaccine unit in Kasauli, in Himachal Pradesh, the testing protocols and facilities to evaluate a recombinant vaccine did not exist. In the Ministry of Health, there was no pharmacopoeia – a rulebook and catalogue of medicines – and when Reddy made persistent visits, officials ridiculed him.

'When I would seek appointment with the health secretary Javed Chaudhary, he'd say, "You are an electronics fellow, what are you doing here? Don't waste my time,"' recalls Reddy. 'I would tell him that my company was working on this vaccine, and would request him to see that the pharmacopoeia is formed. I was talking about the expertise needed at Kasauli but he refused to even listen to me. His colleagues poked fun at me that I was trying to make such a vaccine in India.'

Under the 1989 rules notified by the Ministry of Environment, a Genetic Engineering Approval Committee existed but the Department of Biotechnology itself had not evaluated any application. Shantha's hepatitis B vaccine would become the first test case for its Review Committee on Genetic Manipulation. The first comprehensive guidelines for generating preclinical and clinical data for recombinant vaccines, diagnostics and other biologicals (biotech products) would come out only in 1999.

By the time Reddy built his factory in late 1995, funds also began flowing in easily, even from the government. Narayanan Vaghul's dream of technology development in India was coming true and ICICI sanctioned a loan of $1 million through a USAID (United States Aid for International Development) Programme for the Advancement of Commercial Technology. Reddy's Omani investor helped him secure a term loan at 4.75 per cent interest from Oman International Bank, a breather when the interest rate in India hovered around 19 per cent. Reddy's friends and family in the US pooled in some more money. If in the first round they were 'exonerating' themselves, giving Reddy money more for his passion than for the product, in the second round of equity investment, they could see the return in multiples.

The first batch of vaccines was produced in March 1996. The clinical trials were to be conducted at the Nizam's Institute of Medical Sciences (NIMS) in Hyderabad where doctors initially showed some hesitation and asked for some pilot test data. Reddy offered to be the first subject and a pilot test was conducted on eighteen company staffers before a larger trial took place. Results of the five-month study blew away everyone. Shantha's vaccine produced antibodies in more than 96 per cent of those vaccinated by the third dose, compared to 91.4 per cent for SmithKlineBeecham's. In KEM Hospital in Mumbai, 100 per cent cases had antibody production, a statistic which pleasantly surprised Philip Abraham in the gastroenterology department.

Creating a Market

After nearly a year of scaling up manufacturing and government approval, Shanvac was launched in August 1997. But the actual sales started a few months later.

When Reddy was knocking on the banks' doors, a general manager at Andhra Bank did some number crunching. India imported 1,80,000 doses of hepatitis vaccines which were sufficient to vaccinate 60,000 children, public health professionals or adults who could afford it. At 10 per cent of that market – which was the market size calculation norm for the bank – and ₹50 per dose – which Reddy wanted to price his vaccine at – Shantha's annual revenue would be ₹9,00,000. 'Against that I was seeking a loan of ₹10 crore. The manager looked at me in exasperation. He did not say, but his look clearly implied I was an idiot,' says Reddy.

Reddy certainly was not a savvy businessman to price it at ₹50 when the multinationals were selling at ₹840 per dose. His idealism cost him a marketing alliance with one of the biggest pharma companies in the city which was not ready to sell at ₹50; it wanted to price the vaccine at ₹499 after the competition dropped their price to ₹520. Reddy was left in a lurch. It took him four more months to recruit and build a marketing team.

Defying all estimates, Shantha sold half a million doses in the first six months and twenty-five million after three years. His original licence was for two million doses, so when Reddy went to the Department of Biotechnology to raise the limit on doses, the agency heckled, saying it wanted to study the environmental impact, and spun a long regulatory yarn. By then the quality of public sector units' vaccines based on cell culture was gaining a reputation of offering more 'psychological rather than immunological immunity'.

Soon after Shantha's vaccine, G. Padmanaban and his colleague P.N. Rangarajan at the Indian Institute of Science also cloned the hepatitis B gene which they licensed to two other vaccine companies in Hyderabad – Indian Immunologicals, and Biological Evans. By 1999, a host of manufacturers, Bharat Biotech, Wockhardt, Intas Pharma, Serum Institute and Panacea Biotec were making hepatitis B vaccines for the Indian market which made up the second largest pool of virus carriers, amounting to at least forty million.

All this was part of the second vaccine wave. In the 1890s, there were over a dozen vaccine research centres in India, a number which declined in the twentieth century to such an extent that when the British left, it took India three decades to come out with a new vaccine policy. The government production units supplied for a while, but by the 1980s, not only could they not catch up with new technologies and fail to produce routine DTP (diptheria, tetanus and pneumonia) vaccines, but India also had to heavily import oral polio vaccine in the beginning, and measles vaccine subsequently. In some cases, the government even discouraged local manufacturing centres – like the Pasteur Institute in Coonoor in Tamil Nadu – in favour of imports. It was Cyrus Poonawala, of the Serum Institute in Pune, who breathed new life into Indian vaccine manufacturing when he started supplying measles vaccine to the national programme.

By the mid-1990s, when a chafed Reddy took up the improbable challenge, the industrialized world had moved to recombinant technology, causing a shortage of vaccines produced by conventional cell culture methods. However, by the new millennium, the market had grown some immunity to global trends. Along with local technology transfers and development of molecular diagnostics, there was a surge in vaccine production in India, particularly from companies in Hyderabad, Pune and Mumbai whereas public sector vaccine units continued to wobble in government apathy.

At that time, one scientist who took a long-term bet in vaccines – it would turn out to be unusually long – was Krishna M. Ella. At Bharat Biotech, which he founded after returning from the University of Wisconsin in 1996, Ella had made a few generic vaccines but was getting edgy to try new molecules. At the All India Institute of Medical Sciences (AIIMS) in Delhi, paediatric scientist Maharaj Kishan Bhan had identified a novel strain of rotavirus and wanted to develop it as a vaccine candidate. As Ella got ready to pick up the project, the non-profit PATH showed interest, and so did the Bill & Melinda Gates Foundation the following year, in 2000, when it invited Ella for a public–private partnership. Former biotech secretary S. Ramachandran was an advisor to the Gates Foundation and he would facilitate a partnership that, over fifteen years, evolved into a prototype of clinical research and drug development that India had not seen – a multi-country, sixty-five-scientist vaccine study that spent $60 million in its clinical testing on 10,000 babies.

Ella had returned to India to make drugs for some unassailable neglected diseases; he was just getting started. A frozen Japanese encephalitis strain, isolated long ago by the National Institute of Virology in Pune, was waiting to be thawed.

Hit-and-Miss Biology

In the summer of 1985, Samir K. Brahmachari went for a short sabbatical to Charles Cantor's genetic and development laboratory at Columbia University. One day, Charles DeLisi, then director of the United States Department of Energy's health and environmental research programmes, called Cantor to conceive what would famously become the Human Genome Project. On his return from Washington, Cantor took Brahmachari and a few others from his lab for dinner and painted the big picture – how they would map and sequence the human genome, the three billion nucleotides that form a person's genetic make-up.

'At that time, scientists had the capability to sequence only 200 nucleotides per [electrophoresis] gel and they were talking about three billion,' recounted Brahmachari. Over the next one month, he had the privilege of listening to Cantor and watching him give a form and feel to what remains, till today, the world's largest collaborative biological project. 'My exposure to genomics was accidentally far ahead of what was going on in India. I saw how people dream and build projects.'

On his return to the Indian Institute of Science, Brahmachari tried to convince the faculty and held a workshop on genomics where he invited Cantor. Somewhat sceptical, Cantor came for the workshop but returned with cautionary advice: 'Indians are good at learning but they don't deliver.' Brahmachari took it as a personal challenge. In 1990, the Human Genome Project started and the following year, he became an elected member of the Human Genome Organization which fortuitously sustained his earlier accidental exposure to the genomics tsunami that would soon hit the life sciences.

A few years earlier, in 1988, about the time when America decided to invest in the Human Genome Project, Bhargava wrote a letter to Prime Minister Rajiv Gandhi suggesting that India should also invest in such a programme. In his meticulous calculation, the project cost for India would amount to not more than ₹300 crore, which meant an average cost of ₹20 crore every year for a fifteen-year project period. It was a pittance, less than the yearly grant of a good laboratory. Gandhi referred his letter to the Department of Biotechnology, which dumped it into bureaucratic cold storage, without any response to the scientist who had been a member of its high-power scientific advisory committee for many years.

What Bhargava was aspiring for India, Craig Venter's Celera Genomics in the United States achieved later – a parallel draft of the human genome at a fraction of the cost of the original international project. The Indian scientist knew that genome sequencing would throw up valuable short tandem repeats – specific stretches of sequences in DNA – which would prove invaluable in developing new diagnostics.

Indeed, by the early 1990s, one of the first repeats to be published was in mytotonic dystrophy which gave much insight into its onset and progression. Brahmachari had found CTG repeats in his informatics research at IISc. 'I knew my repeats would be functional, I could see where the world was going,' he recalls. In 1990, he had refused Cantor's offer to take up a teaching position at the University of California at Berkeley, swayed as he was by nationalism after he received the Shanti Swarup Bhatnagar award. The award would give him more bargaining power, he thought, as he hatched a big genomics initiative in his head. India, with thousands of ethnic and linguistic groups, is, as J.B.S. Haldane famously said, a 'living laboratory' for genetics research.

In 1995, Brahmachari once again organized a consensus-gathering meeting of the faculty at IISc. Fifty-four attended but other than one, no academic supported a large genomics programme; they said the field was for 'technicians'. Brahmachari wanted to sequence *Mycobacterium tuberculosis* genome by coordinating with all tuberculosis research institutions in India in the manner 100-odd laboratories in Europe, along with three other countries, had sequenced the yeast genome earlier. Sometime later, the IISc did submit such a proposal, but Brahmachari was not part of it. 'They said I was not a biologist, I did not know tuberculosis, so I couldn't do this,' said Brahmachari. The pathogen's genome was finally sequenced by a group of scientists led by the Pasteur Institute in France in 1998.

Angry and dejected, Brahmachari had an ally in Manju Sharma, secretary, Department of Biotechnology, even though, for nearly two years, he had assumed an activist's role campaigning against UNESCO's stance that genome was common human heritage. His activism, to some extent, damaged his publishing record. Journals would 'not touch his papers'. He even dabbled in the idea of setting up a research foundation since Sharma had promised that DBT would fund him wherever he worked. The Centre for Biochemical Technology in Delhi looked a reasonable place because AIIMS, located right in the neighbourhood, would allow him to get clinical collaborators. Under Brahmachari, the Centre experienced induced mutation of the subtlest kind.

While offering him the directorship in 1997, CSIR director general Mashelkar took an 'assurance letter' that Brahmachari would 'not disturb the system, use the existing talent well, and not ask for big money from him'. In honouring that, Brahmachari's inspiration was William Haseltine's Human Genome Sciences, the world's first genomics-based pharmaceutical company which patented human genomic sequences for medical use. He mapped the skill sets and lab expertise at the veteran's lab in the United States and with a generous ₹8.7 crore grant from the Department of Biotechnology, he refurbished the Centre for Biochemical Technology in Delhi. By 2002, some senior scientists said the name of the place should reflect its work. So the Centre was renamed as the Institute for Genomics and Integrative Biology.

The first breakthrough came when they hit upon a common founder mutation for dominant hereditary ataxia, a type of movement disorder seen in the Indian population in 2000. It was the first single-nucleotide polymorphism marker they patented, although defensively. In the last few years, a test for ataxia has been a routine procedure in neurology departments of advanced medical centres like AIIMS and the National Institute of Mental Health and Neurosciences (NIMHANS).

Mashelkar's initial stiffness slowly melted away when he saw

Brahmachari, in his own words, 'was willing to die for genomics'. In 2002, he sanctioned two big investments which stabilized genomics research in India and fortified Brahmachari's position as the champion – ₹25 crore for an Indian Genome Variation database and ₹47 crore for an 'in-silico' drug discovery programme.

'We could either put money on the table and join the global HapMap project where they wanted thirty samples of Indian nationals. Partha [Majumder, at National Institute of Biomedical Genomics in Kolkata] and others agreed that we needed a few thousand samples, not just thirty. Or we could create our own consortium and do it in India; and we chose the latter,' Brahmachari said. Following the HapMap method and working with twenty-four investigators, the consortium created an initial database of disease variation.

India makes up one-sixth of the world's population, yet it has been gravely under-represented in genome-wide studies of human genetic variation.

In Hyderabad, Lalji Singh had proposed setting up of four large sequencing centres in different parts of the country so that diagnostic applications could penetrate rural areas. Subsequent governments, bar none, turned a blind eye. Many years later, late in the first decade of the new century, Singh would again propose a comprehensive project for a genomics research centre with an associated hospital. By this time, he had some seminal work to his credit, including the complex genetic origin of Indians which made the cover of *Nature* – the only research from India to make the cover of an international journal – and the discovery of the genetic cause for inheritable cardiomyopathy, or sudden cardiac death, in Indians and the people of the subcontinent. Singh's proposal managed to pass all committees, get an approval and reach the Planning Commission which sanctioned ₹1,000 crore. In 2009, the project was mysteriously scuttled.

Sometimes, the politics of science is no less political than politics itself.

4

TRANSFORMATION: FROM ENZYMES TO DRUGS

THE CHANCE MEETING

In 1996, thought leader and author Stephen Covey was giving a talk at Oberoi Hotel in Bengaluru, where many business leaders had descended to listen to the celebrated speaker. During lunch, Kiran Mazumdar-Shaw met Dr Parvinder Singh, who had taken the reins at Ranbaxy from his father three years earlier. A chemistry doctorate from the University of Michigan, Singh was overhauling Ranbaxy radically; so naturally he seemed interested in the goings-on at Biocon. The two were meeting for the first time but 'they chatted most of the afternoon', and Singh, who had a late-evening flight, drove down to the city outskirts to visit the Biocon campus.

After that visit, he proposed to Kiran that they forge a research partnership. She suggested fungal pharmaceuticals; he recommended statins, a class of small molecules that lower the cholesterol level in blood by reducing cholesterol production in the liver. Lovastatin was a rage those days. Even though the drug was approved by the US Food and Drug Administration in 1987, a landmark study had been published in 1994. It dismissed the ambiguities surrounding lovastatin's beneficial effects in reducing LDL (low-density lipoprotein) cholesterol which significantly reduced recurrence of heart attacks. Pharmaceutical company Merck had commercialized the product, but its patent was expiring in 2001.

Biocon's willingness to develop lovastatin was instinctive. It was a fermentation product, one which was first discovered by enzyme researcher Akira Endo at Sankyo Corporation in Japan, a country where the earliest record of the Koji enzyme technology can be traced back to the third century AD. In the late 1970s, Endo had identified compounds, later named compactin or mevastatin, from the mould that infected the Japanese orange. But Sankyo dropped the project after some initial toxicity results. A few years later, Merck took it up and did larger studies to understand the mechanism of reported toxicity, and finally brought it to the clinics.

Kiran promised Singh that Biocon would develop high-yielding micro-organism strains, and the two companies' R&D teams got on to it with their respective strengths – Biocon using solid state fermentation, Ranbaxy using submerged fermentation. 'We saw it as an opportunity to get into manufacturing – we would have created two technologies; in any case, they were into marketing,' Kiran recalls.

By the mid-1990s, under its own strategic shift, Biocon sniffed the opportunities in pharmaceuticals and started research for lovastatin under the new company Helix, away from Unilever's scrutiny and interference.

'I had said if Ranbaxy gave us the strains, we could adapt and improve the strain for solid state fermentation,' Shri says. 'Sure enough, we did it. But it surprised the hell out of everybody when Ranbaxy, which was struggling to scale up its own laboratory work, changed its mind and decided to do it alone.'

Before the statin collaboration, Ranbaxy and Biocon had contemplated a business association when the former needed enzymes for its flagship product, penicillin, for which the starting raw material was a fermented product, 6-amino penicillin acid. Biocon was one of the leading enzyme producers those days, but, for a lack of capacity, most of which was already committed to the brewing industry, it could not produce enzymes for Ranbaxy.

On its part, Ranbaxy never intended to get directly into fermentation, primarily because it was a chemistry-driven company and wished to remain so. No less importantly, Singh was married into the Radhaswamy Satsang family whose guru was his father-in-law. 'So the question of Singh getting involved in manufacturing something that had anything to do with alcohol or intoxication was not possible,' said Bimal Raizada, a long-term Ranbaxy executive who handled different responsibilities at different times, at one point even running the non-pharmaceutical businesses of the family.

Singh was basically proposing that Biocon set up the production unit and Ranbaxy would consume the enzymes. The deal did not work out and Ranbaxy ended up making an investment in a small unit near Kangra in Himachal Pradesh. Gist-Brocadis helped transfer the technology to Max India to make the enzyme. The Singh family had a clear understanding that Ranbaxy and Max were separate companies and that the latter would do biotechnology. However, a director on Ranbaxy's board, D.D. Chopra, was a good friend of Kiran and he, to an extent, 'influenced Ranbaxy in building a bond with Biocon'.

By the early 1990s, it was clear to Singh, who had until then focused largely on anti-infectives, that major diseases in India would be related to hypertension and heart attack. 'We did take on a few blood-pressure-related products but we were unsuccessful. For cardiac cases, we had identified a range of statins and that's how Dr Singh wanted to collaborate with Kiran,' said Raizada, who passed away in March 2015.

To avoid getting into fermentation, which was becoming integral to many drugs it was producing, Ranbaxy signed a collaborative agreement with Hoechst – before it merged with the French company Rhône-Poulenc to become Aventis – to buy the state-owned Hindustan Antibiotics Limited (HAL) in Pune. There was going to be a three-member partnership which would form the biologics arm of Ranbaxy. But the government could not make up its mind on spinning off HAL, which had good manufacturing facilities for certain fermented products, including penicillin. A major producer of penicillin in Europe, Hoechst was meant to provide new strains to HAL.

While all this planning was going on in Singh's mind, in early 1999, he invited Kiran and Shaw to Delhi. At Ranbaxy House in Nehru Place, after a lavish lunch, Singh asked the others to leave and had a private conversation with Kiran and Shaw. 'Kiran, I want to make a proposal to you. I'm very keen to see if Biocon can become part of the Ranbaxy family. You are doing a tremendous job,' Kiran recalls him saying. He offered Ranbaxy shares, a board position in his company and the right to run Biocon.

'I told him,' says Kiran, 'it's a great honour to be asked by you but I am not ready to even consider such a proposal. He understood and said, "If you ever reconsider, let me know."'

Singh was thinking of biotechnology, but the rest of the company wasn't. 'If you ask me what the reaction was at that lunch meeting, people were saying: "You are doing well in biotech, I wish you luck; but I am good and doing well in chemistry",' said Raizada. That inherent aloofness, if not outright aversion, to biotech would come back to haunt Ranbaxy a few years later.

All plans fell apart later in 1999 – Hoechst merged with Rhône-Poulenc; the Indian government could not come to a decision on hiving off Hindustan Antibiotics; and Singh, fifty-six years old, tragically succumbed to cancer in July.

Statins and the Cash Flow

Since the two research teams – Biocon and Ranbaxy – were having differences, they decided to part ways, leaving some scope for joint commercialization once lovastatin was ready for the market. In Bengaluru, Shri and his colleagues had developed lovastatin strains and processes but had no downstream technology to count on. Manufacturing was certainly the draw for this collaboration but the timeline had got unduly compressed. Shri decided to use the existing solid state fermentation facility to make lovastatin – instead of using water, they used solvents, acetone or ethyl acetate to extract the statin. It was a non-messy process but the yield was less than satisfactory.

In December 1997, when Anand Khedkar reported for work at Biocon for the first time, leaving his all-in-one job at Khandelwal Laboratories in Mumbai, he was asked to join a meeting that afternoon which was nicknamed AAG – Aspertone Action Group (the acronym meaning 'fire' in Hindi) – which aspired to make lovastatin. From nearly 18 kg of biomass upstream, they were able to purify only 250 gm lovastatin. After that meeting, recalls Khedkar, whose training at UDCT was in process technology, it was clear that they would have to develop new processes to improve the yield.

Over the next several months, Khedkar and team improved lab productivity substantially, and they could purify about 17 kg of lovastatin. Scaling it to a production plant had its own set of challenges.

Ravindra K.C., an experienced hand, was hired from Cipla. In February 1999, when he joined Biocon, the latter was trading on a small scale in a few pharmaceutical products and lovastatin was in pilot production. The production team was struggling with just 500 gm to 1 kg of lovatstatin per batch. It was still a small fermenter – 1,000 litres – but it took a few months for Ravindra to get commercial production under way. The yield jumped to 27 kg. Now the business team was ready to go in for the kill.

Sometime earlier, Genpharm, Canada's largest generics manufacturer, had heard about Biocon making lovastatin using surface fermentation. Through their common partner, Eros Pharmaceutical, a small company in Bengaluru, Genpharm had visited Biocon and seen lovastatin in the lab. By 2000, when Biocon had a reasonably good quantity of lovastatin coming out of its fermenter, it began searching for generics makers. Since the liquid fermentation patent was expiring a year later, Biocon's lovastatin, made from a proprietary surface fermentation process, would help its early customers beat competitors to the regulated markets.

Bamzai and Sandeep Rao visited Genpharm in Toronto. Rao, a chemical engineer from IIT Powai, who had come back to Biocon after a two-year sabbatical at the Indian Institute of Management (IIM), in Lucknow, remembers sitting outside the Genpharm office in biting cold with Bamzai for hours to meet their purchase officer, Judy Dabey. After a long wait, Dabey heard them out but with an expression that said, 'Well, yet another Indian company.' 'I haven't heard of Biocon, why should we work with you?' was her curt response.

Rao speaks with clear, soft sincerity and that day in Toronto, he managed to impress Dabey. 'Why don't you give us our first chance?' he said.

Genpharm agreed; even held them by hand, so to say, through the FDA approval preparedness. Lovastatin was Biocon's first pharmaceutical product for the regulated markets; the Canadian company intended to sell it in the US market.

For most part of the year 2000, getting FDA approval was the prime preoccupation. Since no one had any experience, they would take guidance from wherever it came; even the regulatory guys of their distribution agents in the UK would come and audit the facility. On one such occasion, an auditor, seeing the same signature at an incessant ten-minute interval on all batch records, asked, 'This guy has not even gone to the washroom?'

'We were so ashamed,' says Jayaram. 'We immediately created shifts and made staff on duty write compulsorily.'

When the FDA inspection was imminent, Kiran and Tara Jayaram did their own inspections early in the morning. Teams were formed which did cross-inspections and plugged any loopholes. On the day of the inspection, as Jayaram accompanied the inspector, she offered to hold on to the diary which she found him carrying even to the bathroom. 'No, I can't give it to you,' he said. 'That's when I realized how serious it was. Second audit onwards, the inspector would carry a laptop which he'd keep in a locked case,' said Jayaram.

But it all worked out in the end. In 2001, Biocon became the first Indian company to be approved by the US FDA to sell lovastatin. It was also the first surface fermentation plant anywhere in the world with FDA approval.

The first order of a few hundred kilograms of lovastatin to Genpharm opened doors that would lead to many gilded doors in the future. Rao stayed in touch with Dabey. Many years later, when he asked what had made her give them the first break, she gave the most unexpected reason.

During the British rule in India, Dabey's father had left the country to work on a sugar plantation in Trinidad. She knew she was Indian in her roots – after all, they would eat 'dhal and roti' at home. She had those memories even as her family moved to Canada where she was born and raised. Somewhere, she had a soft spot for India and wanted to know which part of the country her second name, Dabey, came from.

Rao spun a tale, which, in hindsight, isn't so unbelievable. He told her, 'Dabey sounds like Dubey and it comes from the northern Indian state of Uttar Pradesh, so probably you came from there.'

*

Starting in 2001, in a matter of a few years, Biocon became known for statins. Since lovastatin was a precursor to simvastatin, customers started asking for it too. It was a two-stage product – the fermentation product had to be chemically synthesized. One of its earliest customers came from Schweizerhalle in Europe. Not a shutterbug at the workplace, Rao remembers getting a team photo clicked with the cheque, which in rupee terms amounted to ₹45 crore.

'We hadn't seen a purchase order so big,' he says. Bharadwaj, always the cautious salesman, told them, 'Let's make the supplies, have them accept and then celebrate.' People remember Kiran 'grinning from ear to ear.' The regulated markets had welcomed a new entrant and Biocon set up a small office in New Jersey in the US with Rao as its all-purpose manager.

A whole range of statins followed, each with its own process twist. In simvastatin, says Ravindra, people were scared to handle 1 or 2 kg of butyl lithium, a highly toxic substance used in the intermediate stage of production. 'Eventually, we ended up consuming 20 to 30 tonnes of butyl lithium every month, the highest in Asia then,' he notes with pride. Biocon was granted a patent on this method of production – it gave fewer side reactions and lowered the overall cost of manufacture.

Subsequently, pravastatin, atorvastatin, rosuvastatin and fluvastatin followed. In a matter of three to four years, Biocon gained nearly 20 per cent share in the regulated markets for statin, also becoming one of the largest suppliers to most Indian generics manufacturers.

One notable Indian customer was Ranbaxy. The pharma company was witnessing early successes in statin formulations and needed a strong technology-backed supplier behind it. 'Such collaboration was new in those days, though today, many companies do it. It was tough for me. I had to convince a few people at Biocon as some saw Ranbaxy as a competitor,' says

Rakesh Bamzai. At one stage, Ranbaxy was Biocon's biggest statin buyer in India with over ₹100 crore in business. The story had come full circle – the statin research collaboration had got axed but Ranbaxy still ended up buying statin-active pharmaceutical ingredients from Biocon.

From the late 1990s, when the company was barely beginning to produce a few pharmaceutical products to the middle of the next decade when the statin business was in full bloom, Biocon's growth was on steroids. Revenues grew nearly 100 per cent annually.

'Statins allowed us to transition from fungal R&D to proper R&D. We had the money and the demand, and we had learnt how to use it,' says Shri. He and Khedkar took their first mass spectrometry lessons at the Indian Institute of Science from P. Balaram in the molecular biology department, and soon, they were buying mass spectrometers quite generously. In the enzyme days, even access to high-pressure liquid chromatography was a luxury. Between 2000 and 2006, Biocon bought chromatography equipment by the dozens.

It was a narrow window of opportunity. The timing was right and the expiry of the lovastatin patent seemed to be perfectly made for Biocon. The business development team was regularly attending conferences and pharma exhibitions in Europe and the US, and Biocon's name as a statin maker was getting established. But predictably, the little biotech from Bengaluru was spoiling the party for some.

In 2003, after meeting the Biocon team at the annual pharma networking conference CPhI in Europe, two executives from the Israeli company, Teva Pharmaceutical Industries, arrived in Bengaluru. They met the senior team, spoke about building a strategic relationship and after a while, asked Bharadwaj and Bamzai to step out of the room. They wanted to make a proposition to Kiran and Shaw. 'Get out of the statin market and we'll compensate you for that,' they said.

'I said, "I'll never do it,"' remembers Kiran. They persisted, spouted some market wisdom, but she held her ground.

Over the years, Biocon has earned more than $1 billion in revenues from statins. It took statin manufacturing to a scale where others wouldn't think about entering the market. Today, Biocon supplies at least 35 per cent of the world's statin.

Real Pharma Flavour

In 1999, when Biocon was building its submerged fermentation plant, its agreement with Dyadic International to make textile enzymes fell apart, blowing up its carefully laid plans to fill capacity. They had identified just one fermentation product, serratio peptidase, and sourced the basic technology.

Adapting serratio culture to Indian production conditions proved to be a time-consuming process; even finding the right raw materials in India meant a cross-country search. They found a small vendor in Madhya Pradesh for the protein source of soya isolate.

That was the time when Biocon added technical and managerial muscle to its manufacturing. Pharmaceutical fermentation was going through a dip in India. China had entered the penicillin market, crashing prices. Max India, which had a partnership with Gist-Brocades, had to exit fermentation when the latter was acquired by the Dutch chemicals giant DSM, which wanted to close Gist's fermentation operations in India.

In this shake-out, B.S.V. Prasad had to exit Max and find refuge in Gujarat Themis Biosyn Limited, a company floated by some pharmaceutical entrepreneurs to make cephalosporins. A chemical engineer from IIT Delhi, Prasad was fascinated with fermentation but found it hard to acclimatize in his new company which was 'pretty different' from Max. He had heard about Biocon and decided to write a letter to Kiran. Never one to miss an opportunity to hire talent, she had him join Biocon almost instantly.

On arriving in Bengaluru, Prasad found his first challenge

awaiting him. He had been hired to run the submerged fermentation plant which was commissioned by doing 'water trials', but when the actual serratio process was run, the centrifuge did not work. There was no scale-up – the process was going from a few litres in the lab to 30,000 litres in the plant.

'I had to act fast. I needed expensive equipment, a new centrifuge from a vendor I knew in my previous company and who was not known to Biocon. In any other company, the situation would have slipped into analysis paralysis,' recalls Prasad. (Ten years later, he would again be surprised doing a major manufacturing acquisition in Hyderabad, thinking how in any other company, the decision would have slipped into a specialized merger/acquisition analysis.)

Serratio became a volume product for Biocon, getting it nearly 70 per cent of the Indian market and adding a steady revenue stream in the early years of the millennium at a time when it was building multiple product capabilities which were sucking up capital. One other such API was a rather boring-sounding supplement – iron polymaltose complex.

'It wasn't just another iron supplement,' says Bamzai, with a salesman's solemnity that considers all cash-generating products as equal. It was a novel compound, developed at National Chemical Laboratory in Pune, which had licensed it to city-based Emcure Pharmaceutical. When other iron supplements sold for less than twenty paise per tablet, the new compound, with the brand name Orofer, sold for three to four rupees. Emcure's Arun Khanna spun a marketing story around it, and Biocon rode the wave, producing 30 tonnes a month. It became the leading supplier for the country. The solitary product suitably fuelled the R&D engine for some time.

Around the same time, a new platform for immunosuppressant drugs sprang up around the Plafractor. Biocon was one of the first companies to make mycophenolate mofetil, which it later converted into a franchise success, with a full suite of generic immunosuppressants starting with tacrolimus. It was a class of drugs which was difficult to manufacture. Commercially, other generics manufacturers thought it would not work because cyclosporine generics had not succeeded. 'It was high-risk but offered high gains too,' says Bamzai. Most of the market lay outside India as organ transplantation wasn't big in India until recently.

Between 2000 and 2005, the research team kept pegging away at new processes, producing more than a dozen difficult-to-make active pharmaceutical ingredients. One of its customers was Kosan Biosciences, a company founded by chemical engineering professor Chaitan Khosla at Stanford University that was later acquired by Britsol-Myers Squibb. Kosan came to Biocon for process development and clinical supply of geldanamycin and later 15-F-erythronolide A. Geldanamycin is a naturally occurring antibiotic and difficult to produce in a lab. 'When we started, it cost ₹18 lakh to make a kilo. We changed the processes and brought it down to ₹60,000 a kilo,' says Khedkar.

In selecting differentiated products, something Kiran was fixated with, and which perhaps came from her own distinctive taste in everything she did at Biocon – from buying furniture to art – the company lost sight of taking those products to market under its own brand to garner higher margins. 'We were too busy building our platforms and making complex pharmaceutical ingredients' is the chorus of past and present business executives.

'As business guys, we could see the value in selling formulations. We would broach this with Kiran time and again but she thought drug formulation was a very crowded market,' says Bamzai. It still is. In 2014, out of some 20,000 registered pharmaceutical entities, more than 8,000 made formulations.

The spectacular growth of the pharmaceutical business changed the start-up atmospherics for the first time. Those working in enzymes felt 'they were not contributing enough'. Enzyme research saw an osmotic effect – people wanted to move to the pharma side. 'A competitive spirit began to surface and people began to have doubts whether to stay in enzymes or move to the pharmaceutical division, which was getting more revenue and recognition,' says Jyothi Kamath. She was asked to be involved in pharmaceutical research but she refused. It wasn't her interest, nor did she have expertise. A perfectionist at work, Kamath had fixed views on many things. In fact, Kiran wanted to merge the two research wings, but since Kamath felt so strongly about them being separate, it continued that way for a while, even after Kamath left in 2003.

When Kamath turned fifty, in 2001, she sent her resignation letter to Kiran, who promptly tore it up. Two years later, Kamath sent a resignation letter again, but this time to the human resource department. Her father wasn't keeping well and she told Kiran she was 'not open to any discussion'.

The Pivot

Just when statins showed promise, recombinant products offered an even bigger pie.

In the year 2000, Harish Iyer was 'living the American Dream' in San Diego. As a process science engineer with Biogen (now Biogen-IDEC) which had developed the celebrated biotech drug interferon, he had a cushy yet challenging job, a beach-facing office and a green card. Life gave no reason to carp and cavil, except that he had developed an obsessive distraction: to go back to India and make a difference. Iyer wanted to put his chemical engineering training from IIT Chennai and doctorate from Rensselaer Polytechnic Institute in New York to bigger use. As he was looking for work in India, he became open to even joining academics if industry did not have a suitable position.

Biocon offered him a job in 2001, at an annual compensation of ₹5 lakh. It was a tenth of what he was earning in the US. Reflecting back, Iyer is amused about it even today: 'Those days, I used to be more spiritual and would tell myself, "Come what may I'm going to have a positive attitude." When I landed here, I realized my wife's postdoctoral stipend in San Diego was much higher than my salary. But I had savings from my six years of work in America and I was going to do exciting work in Bengaluru.'

When he walked in the first day, Chandavarkar told him they wanted to make insulin; he said it with a casualness that made the recombinant drug sound like a painkiller. Iyer, who had earlier worked in Genentech, knew what a tough beast insulin was to crack even in the generics form. The product patent in India was not valid then, it would kick in only in 2005 even though the patent on recombinant human insulin, held by Eli Lilly and Novo Nordisk, was expiring in January 2003. Human insulin comprised just half of the Indian insulin market; the rest was porcine and bovine insulin.

At the time, Biocon and Shantha were negotiating a partnership to make recombinant human insulin. In Hyderabad, Shantha had developed the insulin gene clone in *Pichia pastoris* yeast after licensing the host cell from Research Corporation Technologies at Arizona University, one of the major producers of biological expression systems. Shantha's earlier product, hepatitis B vaccine, was also made in this yeast which, being a single-celled organism, is easy to grow and manipulate in the lab.

Researchers at Shantha had hit a wall after preclinical studies, one of the reasons being the smaller size of their fermenter. Since Biocon was already doing large-scale fermentation, Varaprasad Reddy came to Kiran with a proposal. *Pichia* as a production system was familiar to Biocon, which was using it to make recombinant phytase, an enzyme used in human health and animal nutrition. He said it was only rational that the two join forces, and they did.

In April 2002, they announced a 50:50 joint venture – Biocon-Shantha Biotech – to manufacture human insulin. But barely a year into the agreement, Kiran called Varaprasad Reddy to say the collaboration was not working and that they should part ways. Since the joint venture was yet to be formally registered, it was easy to dissolve it. When she broke the news to Reddy, he recalls, he was very disappointed but 'dropped the project philosophically'. 'I went to my board and said, "I am not here to fight." I did not want to break my friendship with Kiran,' says Reddy.

According to Harish Iyer, Shantha did not have the tools to pull it off. 'They did not have the analytical methods to examine the product or the right purification method to test the purity of the insulin they made,' he said. By Shantha's method, the purity of its insulin was 95 per cent; by standard pharmacopoeia, it amounted to just 50 per cent. In a quirky turn of events, Iyer, who led Biocon's recombinant human insulin programme and grew it into a significant portfolio, became Shantha's chief executive in late 2014.

'I have no reason to take sides,' he said.

Shantha had cloned the gene and had a 'rudimentary' idea of the process. Moreover, what was done wasn't done the industrial way. For instance, in a step called conjugation and de-blocking, they had used the wrong chemistry – tertiary butyl, instead of tertiary methyl. Even in tertiary butyl, Shantha used ether for precipitation. 'In an industrial setting, using 10,000 litres of ether would blow up in your face,' said Iyer.

At Biocon, a few months into the collaboration, the R&D team realized the joint venture had actually not yielded much, other than, of course, planting the idea of making insulin in their heads. They convinced Kiran to break off the partnership since it would 'dilute' the value of their work.

Pichia pastoris was a good choice though. It was a high-yielding biological factory which combined the advantages of a bacterial system and mammalian cell-culture system. It is no surprise that it became the dominant system of the Indian biotech industry, giving them the lowest-cost production technology. For Biocon, choosing the prevalent bacterial system, *E. coli*, could also mean hitting the process patent block at some point.

Still, that didn't mean anybody at Biocon knew exactly what it would take to make insulin. Iyer remembers taking a long, arduous six months to develop a purification process. Even a patient manager like Chandavarkar couldn't wait that long. He came to Iyer and said, 'You better tell me when you are going to do it.'

'I told him, "Go to hell." In all fairness, he didn't push me and understood,' recounts Iyer. 'We had to have multiple steps to get 99.9 per cent purity.' Iyer was back to bench science and programming machines after having managed a fairly large team at Biogen in the US. Here, all he had was one team member, a challenging project and meagre resources. Yet, he says it was a 'useful phase'.

Building the manufacturing facility was most interesting. They had large-scale fermenters but nobody knew how to process insulin. In their hunt for processing and characterization equipment, Iyer, Chandavarkar and Prasad went on a world tour, almost. All other drug companies were using *E. coli* to make insulin, so even vendor expertise on *Pichia* was missing. Finally, in France, they could identify the right equipment. But with no experience of using it, and no other way of trying it out without buying it, they bought two centrifuges for about a million euros. It was a gutsy move. 'In my sophisticated eyes, the way I would do it today is to get a consultant and ask someone for a recommendation,' says Iyer.

One thing becomes clear: experimentation was common. And exploration was not penalized. Even though the analytical expertise to characterize a large molecule like insulin – which has to be chopped into pieces for analysis – was missing, they chose to develop it in-house. Insulin is one of the few biopharmaceutical molecules that need to be manufactured at 1,00,000 litres; such is the demand. This volume game poses interesting challenges in downstream processing. Just when Biocon was working on insulin, Wockhardt had tied up with the German company Rhein Biotech for insulin and other biotech products, but they were never a competitor. It was the Danish insulin giant Novo Nordisk that Biocon wished to compete with on quality and market share.

ORAL INSULIN

Around the same time, in early 2004, when Shri was incubating new teams, he came to Khedkar one day and said, 'Anand, we don't know what to do with you. You are a manager now and you have to figure out your own programme.' Khedkar was closely studying the development in oral and inhaled insulin around the world. Since Biocon was already ready with its human insulin, he thought he could try new formulations which, if aided with new delivery technologies, could be delivered orally. It was wildly ambitious, because until then only a handful of formulations had been tested in animal studies in the rest of the world.

Historically, researchers have tried to develop oral insulin since the early 1920s but have failed consistently. Insulin is a large molecule and when taken orally, enzymes in the gut break it down into inactive amino acids. Taking insulin subcutaneously, through injections, is not the most desired route, either for patients or for doctors. Popping a pill, if possible, instead of pricking oneself a few times in the day is what most diabetics would choose. Medically speaking, if insulin survives the enzyme attack and is absorbed in the gut, it travels through the portal vein to reach the liver which is its original target. In the liver, this insulin controls the glucose to produce glucagon pretty much the same way pancreas-produced insulin controls glucose in healthy people.

Hence, oral, nasal or buccal (through the lining in the mouth) insulin continues to beckon businesses and academics.

Khedkar began by making micro-particles of insulin and showed that at acidic pH, these particles remained as they were;

there was no release of insulin at all. But the moment pH crossed 5.5, the micro-particles would begin dissolving and release insulin. His team captured the dissolution under a microscope. At the animal testing facility at Al Amin College nearby, they showed they could achieve a big drop in glucose in certain kind of rats. Shri was so excited he made Khedkar present it before the board of directors.

But their formulation technology was not efficient; it required high doses. They had been collaborating with an institute in Scotland which had an interesting technology to make micro-emulsion for insulin. It had a serious limitation though. The encapsulation was small, just about one unit per millilitre. They would joke in the lab that diabetics would have to carry a Pepsi-size 500 ml bottle of insulin to get their blood glucose under control.

Just when they were trying a number of delivery technologies, Nobex Corp, a small medicinal and polymer chemistry company at Research Park in North Carolina, came to Biocon for sourcing insulin, which it required in tonnes. Nobex had invented a new way to modify the insulin molecule by attaching polymers to points in the insulin that protected it from disintegrating in the gut. Earlier, in 2002, Nobex had signed a $283 million deal with GlaxoSmithKline to develop oral insulin and needed low-cost insulin for that programme.

Chris Price, founder and chief executive of Nobex, had met Kiran and Bharadwaj at conferences in the US and knew about Biocon, particularly its process innovation, which had convinced him it would consistently yield low-cost insulin. Price secured an insulin supply arrangement with Biocon, first for animal studies and then for human trials that GlaxoSmithKline would do in future.

Less than a year after the Glaxo deal, Price was walking down Fifth Avenue in New York one day, when he got a call from his business development chief. The pharmaceutical company had called off the agreement on oral insulin. As he walked past the tony stores around him, his mind was racing at the thought of fatal fallouts. He thought, 'Oh my God, we put all our marbles in this one deal and now they've backed out.'

Price immediately flew back to North Carolina to figure out what they could do. The deal was backloaded and GlaxoSmithKline, apart from $5 million of upfront payment, was to pay the rest of the deal amount on reaching milestones which were clinically driven. Looking back, says Price, he had made a mistake. 'Until then, GlaxoSmithKline had never worked with protein drugs and had neither the idea nor the tool kit. They lost faith in oral insulin very quickly because they already had two small molecules in diabetes which they were focused on.' As a small company, Price thinks, Nobex should have considered this in its scheme of things.

Biocon represented an avenue, rather the best bet, for Nobex. Price, along with a consultant who he thought would be helpful but eventually proved counterproductive, started making trips to Bengaluru. They were fairly impressed by the progress Biocon was making in building the 'right kind of research facility', but at the same time, they were concerned about the lack of clinical experience in the Biocon staff and their lack of depth in medicinal chemistry. After all, Nobex's HIM2 (hexyl-insulin monoconjugate 2) was a modified molecule, not pure insulin, and very few people had been successful in modifying insulin. They could get modified insulin through the gastrointestinal tract but their modification diminished the insulin's therapeutic activity. At that time, the team at Nobex was 'mystified' and had no real information on how the insulin molecule was getting across the gut.

Nobex knew there was a big challenge looming, especially since it was no expert in diabetes or insulin. Biocon, other than making insulin cost-effectively, did not have any of the other required capabilities either.

They were taking a significant risk, the board members at Nobex told Price, but they also understood that working with Eli Lilly or Novo Nordisk would present a lot of difficulties because 'neither of the two companies really believed in oral insulin at the time.'

In a way, recalls Price, Biocon and Nobex were two early-stage companies with a product idea, some data to support it and the manufacturing ability to make brute proteins for the drug industry. What Nobex did have was a group of knowledgeable people to consult and that included Alan Cherrington at Vanderbilt University, who had set up a nice dog model in his lab for testing insulin. 'I underestimated what it'd take to make the two companies work together. It was a very difficult time for us after GlaxoSmithKline, but Biocon was at the right place at the right time,' said Price.

Not he, though.

The way big pharma shifts its strategies, dumps deals and prioritizes portfolios, it often leaves its smaller partners reaching for their proton pump inhibitors. Some partners get cardiac arrest; some even experience sudden cardiac death. Nobex was a victim of the latter. The fallen GlaxoSmithKline deal brought the demise of the company. Price had to resign; he was 'taken out of the picture'. The consultant who accompanied him to Bengaluru had to salvage and seal the deal with Biocon but the fact that he and Kiran did not get along particularly well added further complexity. Biocon could not fill in the void left by GlaxoSmithKline; the Bengaluru biotech was taking time to evaluate what it wanted from Nobex and for how much.

A lot of the negotiations were done by the legal and business teams but Price remembers a few meetings when Kiran was in the room. 'She has a very strong sense of what she wants and she would greatly resent any attempt of manipulation or clever negotiation,' he recounts. Everything was pretty much black and white. 'She doesn't leave much on the table that is undecided. To an extent, she has that very aggressive business attitude which is often a trait of men in business, and, as we see, increasingly of women in business as well.'

Meanwhile, Nobex hurtled towards bankruptcy. In a smart move, Kiran chose to wait it out. She had sensed that Nobex would fall apart completely and then the acquisition of intellectual property would be easier. 'I'd have done the same in her shoes, although I don't wear women's shoes,' says Price with a soft laugh.

In late 2004, the two companies had made public their partnership to develop oral insulin and a heart failure drug – both in preclinical studies – and by March 2006, Biocon was bidding for the intellectual property assets of a beleaguered Nobex. On the day of the auction, board member Bala Manian and Kiran were up until the early morning hours in Bengaluru to assist M. Chinappa, vice-president of finance, in Delaware, place the bids and keep the paddle low. The prize came at $5 million. Biocon won the bid and full ownership of the two preclinical programmes besides some proprietary technologies around a few other therapeutic peptides, and a large patent basket.

INTO THE UNKNOWN

When Biocon initially paired up with Nobex for oral insulin, the molecule was in liquid formulation, not the kind that could be made into a regular tablet. To release the drug effectively, a tablet should disintegrate into smaller particles. What Nobex had would make an erodible tablet; it would have to erode, not dissolve like regular tablets, to release the drug. Nobex had hand-pressed it into pellets, a method that wasn't commercially scalable, nor could it withstand packaging and shipping stress.

Biocon worked on the insulin derivative of Nobex, oral HIM2, to improve its properties and developed a new molecule which it named IN-105. 'We had two objectives – to make IN-105 cheaper and convert it into a marketable product,' says Khedkar. It was a tough goal for the first-timers but Shri had taught them to not feel insecure about what they did not know.

At the time, Biocon was already making insulin, but going from the powder drug substance to a tablet took nearly three years. In standard pharmaceuticals, small molecules as they are called, making a tablet is easier. All the excipients – inert substances that are added to the active pharmaceutical ingredient to give it the consistency and form of a drug – are well defined. In the case of IN-105, new substances had to be tested. Nobex had discovered some of the excipients but it had not studied their impact in tablet formation.

Along the way, Nitesh Dave and Iyer devised a new strategy whereby they started making IN-105 directly, without going through the insulin route. Initially, the plan was that Nobex would make insulin and conjugate it, which would give 60–70 per cent conversion into IN-105. So the whole cost of insulin was built into it. But later, Biocon made a clone of IN-105 so that it could do away with some processes. The shorter production time gave them an impressive cost advantage. That was critical for its commercial success because every insulin tablet one takes, only a small part of it is absorbed in the body. Some of the earlier champions of oral insulin had dropped their programme because they did not know how to make insulin super cheap.

Every once in a while, the team would have open-ended, intellectually challenging debates. Even the list of unknowns was unknown. Nobody knew what would happen to insulin when compressed with high pressure on a turret. Should it be a dispersible tablet or a soluble tablet, with instant release or slow release? They would test their wits and ask each other what flavour or stamp it should have.

'How many people get a chance to name a molecule? Even today I get a high, just thinking about those days,' says Iyer, his booming voice softening with the memories.

Then it was time to test the molecule in clinics. The approach had stark contrasts: it moved between concerted efforts and plain old spitballing. Everybody carried the burden of over ninety years of injectable insulin knowledge, including Biocon, which had recently tested its generic human insulin. The understanding around insulin therapy is sound – doctors titrate insulin very finely, otherwise patients could have a high risk of hypoglycaemia, a condition with abnormally low blood sugar levels in the body. But the understanding around how insulin behaves when given orally was nil. Research publications on this have been sparse and sporadic. Companies like Novo Nordisk don't publish their work until they are past Phase II in clinical studies.

Not everybody was happy with Kiran's high-risk path, including some in the senior management, but she stuck to her belief. She went on to constitute an advisory board of distinguished professionals, including Alan Cherrington, past president of American Diabetes Association, and Harold Lebovitz, a noted endocrinologist at the State University of New York Health Science at Brooklyn. Lebovitz is part of the committee that made guidelines for comprehensive diabetes care in the United States.

Biocon had already established a relationship with physicians while testing its human insulin. Going back to some of them and asking them to be part of a clinical study of a brand new molecule was easy. Physicians loved it, it was high-grade stuff. The team had fun too, travelling to conferences overseas and presenting papers. As an Indian company, being featured in the new product category and given a chance to present data before 'thousands of endocrinologists' was a moment that Shri and Iyer cherish. Both had trained as chemical engineers but had flung themselves bravely and passionately into the medical brahminism that such conferences usually smack of.

Iyer distinctly remembers the European Association for the Study of Diabetes meeting in Rome in 2008 where he was a speaker. Soon after his talk, in which he presented the findings of the Phase II study, a big crowd of Pakistanis came up to him and said, 'Wow, we don't see anyone from our part of the world giving a talk. It's such a moment of pride for us.' It's true that physicians from the subcontinent do attend these meetings, but hardly anyone presents new findings.

'That was the highlight of my career,' says Iyer unselfconsciously.

CUBA: CIGAR, COFFEE, COMMUNISM AND SCIENCE

But insulin was not enough for Kiran.

The beginning of the new millennium saw the drug industry slot machine light up; many drug makers were winning jackpots. The discoveries of the previous three decades in monoclonal antibodies – from 1975 to be precise, when Argentinian scientist César Milstein first showed its clinical application – were turning into very effective drugs. Along with big pharma, traditional biotech companies like Genzyme, Genentech and Biogen had successfully launched such antibodies for a wide array of diseases, and many more promising drugs were waiting in the wings. Kiran was curious. Her characteristic hunt for the next big thing was on.

She was particularly interested in acquiring the know-how to manufacture monoclonal antibodies. By then she was a regular at global conferences, building her knowledge and professional network. At one such conference, the annual Novo Ventures meeting in Copenhagen, she met Lisa Drakeman who had founded the Danish biotech Genmab in 1998 to develop human antibody products. Drakeman had successfully led the start-up through many milestones, including a successful public offering and a celebrated $2.1 billion partnership with GlaxoSmithKline. On meeting Kiran, Drakeman had discouraged her and said nobody would give her that technology. 'We can develop the antibodies and give it to you for further work,' she had offered.

During one of the annual Biotechnology Innovation

Organization (BIO) conferences, Kiran went to Genentech but they 'made it look like such an out-of-the-world technology that it had to be closely guarded'. She was picking up similar vibes from most drug companies. Looking back, she says, 'It appeared that the manufacturing technology was nearly impossible to get. I think it was more hearsay than the real thing.'

In the business team, which independently selected the products to trade in and test waters, Bharadwaj was aware that some recombinant products, like granulocyte-colony-stimulating factor and streptokinase were being sold in the Indian market, particularly because India was not a signatory to the World Trade Organization and did not recognize product patents. Key Pharmaceutical in Delhi was one company that sourced these products from Cuba. When Bharadwaj and Bamzai met Key executives, they were blown away by how biotechnologically advanced Cuba was, their health sector in particular. Cubans had begun by copying biotech drugs developed elsewhere, like interferon-α 2b and had gradually started to innovate locally.

Key Pharma helped Biocon to hook up with Heber Biotec, the commercial arm of the Centre of Genetic Engineering and Biotechnology, a research institute in Havana. Initially, Kiran had doubts about doing business with the communist country but she overcame those when she read a feature on Cuban biotechnology in the journal *Genetic Engineering and Biotechnology*.

After some preliminary to-and-fro between the business teams, Kiran, Bamzai and Shaw headed for Havana in late 2000.

The land of cigars, beaches and coffee had morphed into a different place altogether after the literacy campaign that followed the Cuban revolution of 1959. Cuba went from 75 per cent literacy to total literacy in just one year. Fidel Castro's regime generously funded science to develop biotech products for improving public health. Research institutions were set up and by the late 1980s, many products were ready for the market, of which the meningitis vaccine caught the world's attention in 1985. However, by 1990, with the disintegration of the Soviet Union, the era of subsidy that came with Cuba's 'special relationship' with the communist Big Brother ended and so did its export market in eastern Europe. American trade sanctions became aggressive, asphyxiating the Cuban economy.

In that period of political and economic turmoil, Cuba intensified the process of exploiting the scientific capabilities it had already built. It actively sought new markets to sell into as well as partners to license its technologies to. By the mid-1990s, many of its institutions had a commercial arm and comprised the 'whole cycle', covering research, development, production, quality control and commercialization.

It was the first visit for Kiran and Bamzai but Shaw was familiar with Cuba. In his textile days, he had worked in Venezuela and could speak Spanish. Just like his intervention in the Unilever and ICI deals, he was the facilitator at meetings, though he admits that Cuba was more difficult than any previous negotiations, 'not least because getting to Cuba is tough and they take time to know and trust people'.

Heber Biotec had organized a meeting in Havana with Blanca Tormo, a researcher at CIMAB, the commercial arm of another institute, the Centre for Molecular Immunology. Once the meeting got over in the afternoon, and just a few hours before the three of them were to fly back to India, Kiran asked Blanca if they could visit CIMAB for a short while. That short visit lasted three hours. They met the wife–husband team of Patricia Sierra, president of CIMAB and Joaquin Villan, the technical director.

The Centre for Molecular Immunology had been developing monoclonal antibodies and vaccines since the early 1980s. By the mid-1990s, it was also manufacturing on a commercial scale but in Biocon they saw an 'established biopharma company which had bigger and more sophisticated plants'.

Sierra had been travelling to India every year since 1991, looking for partners to jointly develop products of CIMAB. She had heard about Biocon's enzyme story; when she met Kiran, she spotted her hunger and plans for expansion in other areas.

Kiran invited her to Biocon. Sierra had already licensed two monoclonal antibodies to Dabur, but the firm wasn't doing much with the anti-EGFR and anti-CD6 molecules. Dabur's licence would expire in three months; Sierra said that if the Indian company did not take the molecule further, she would give it to Biocon.

As Sierra had expected, Dabur refused to take those molecules into clinical trials. Kiran scooped them up with an eye on acquiring the mammalian cell culture technology which, in any case, was the natural progression for a biotech organization making products with microbial fermentation. Kiran offered to build a plant and bear all the expenses. The Cubans saw in Biocon a company that was good at making proteins and wanted to move to antibodies because it would be the same ultra-filtration, micro-filtration and chromatography steps that would apply to the manufacture of monoclonal antibodies. In addition, India had opened up economically, making it easier to import equipment while Cuba was reeling under American sanctions. An arrangement where Cuba would do research and development and Biocon would manufacture the products appeared attractive to both the parties.

In 2002, Biocon and CIMAB set up a 51:49 joint venture with an initial investment of about ₹90 crore towards setting up a mammalian cell culture plant. It would produce recombinant granulocyte-stimulating factor, erythropoeitin and a novel cancer monoclonal antibody – anti-epidermal growth factor receptor – which was in advanced stages of development and had shown promise in a variety of cancers.

For Shri, as R&D head, the deal in its early design looked drab; there was no role for his people. From his perch, he wanted to learn to ferment antibodies so that they could do their own programmes. He quietly began to build lab-scale facilities, even though he sensed that the Cubans were reluctant.

'I don't think Kiran appreciated how we had to go about doing it, as, on the face of it, we had to be seen as not competing with the Cubans. But I was determined,' Shri recalls. By then he had figured what made research and development tick – the urge to be able to generate knowledge first. They could follow the 'recipe' that the Cubans gave, but if a batch failed, it wouldn't be possible to fix it by dialling Havana. He began to build local research and development capabilities in the garb of supporting manufacturing. If insulin was a large, complex molecule compared to statins and other fermented products that Biocon produced earlier, monoclonal antibodies were a few orders of magnitude higher in complexity. Just one process, glycosylation, could impact the therapeutic properties of a molecule such as its efficacy, safety, half-life and manufacturability.

'I had to justify the purchase of those fermenters and other investments. Kiran understood,' Shri says.

Circumstances were conducive too. Because of sanctions, Cubans could not import some critical components like advanced cell culture media which only American companies made then. So the Cuban team could never improve their fermentation titre, i.e., concentration of antibodies. In Bengaluru, Shri had access to the new media but had no micro-organisms. The Cubans couldn't ignore his argument that in the time that the plant would be built, his team could use the new media and improve the titre. Those days, no one in India knew about mammalian cell culture other than those teaching it in classrooms.

Shri was invigorated. Once he had the high-efficiency strains, he could engineer them, ferment antibodies and build downstream processes. Process development chief Sohang Chatterjee at Millipore India spent several months in Cuba establishing some of the filtration and purification processes for products which were being transferred to Biocon; Cuba could not get it from Millipore US. Eventually, Biocon jumped right into the thick of mammalian cell culture technology.

The learning curve was steeper. During the early statin days, Chandavarkar took classes for the team in downstream processing. He thought some basic theoretical knowledge was essential for the people on the shop floor, particularly because most people were diploma holders, not masters or Ph.Ds. But with mammalian cells, derived from Chinese Hamster Ovary – or CHO cell lines – which are most often used as factories for production of monoclonal antibodies – because they allow post-translational modifications – everyone had to brush up their biotech skills. Mammalian cells need gentle, calibrated handling – they die if shaken violently or centrifuged at high speed.

The stakes for Kiran were pretty high; she was learning to do things by doing them. 'Betting on a new molecule is itself a big risk, then to get it from Cuba …' she says, surprised, even after a decade, at her own nerve. She would have weekly meetings and check on little details. For about a month, recalls Anuj Goel, she would call him every day to ask about the cell count as it inched up from two million to four million and upward. 'When we started working on the cells, we did not know how to grow them. So any growth was exciting. We also did not know when she'd call, and that kept us on our toes,' says Goel.

In cell culture fermentation, one ought to take care of cells like newborn babies – feed them just the right amount of nutrients to coax them to produce more and consistently spew out proteins. But making biosimilars – generics of biotech drugs – by this method gets trickier. Even if cells can produce more, one has to stress the cells to an extent that they produce what one wants them to produce in order to match the innovator company's product quality. Protein production in a cell is a cascade process – it's like an assembly line. As the protein goes on the endoplasmic reticulum, sugars are added, one by one. The rate of protein production will change the rate of addition of sugars. This has to be manipulated, through an understanding of each product, says Goel, an associate vice-president at Biocon, who arrived there after his doctorate at the National Chemical Laboratory, nearly two decades ago. Technology for these processes is closely guarded, what one gets in the public domain is theoretical knowledge.

Thirteen years later, all the monoclonal antibodies of Biocon – novel molecules and biosimilars – are emanating from the same mammalian cell infrastructure.

In the beginning, Biocon brought a handful of molecules from Cuba, even a few enzymes, but later, in 2004, it extended the basket with another novel monoclonal antibody, anti-CD6 and three cancer vaccine candidates. Eventually, it dropped most of the novel molecules and pursued two cancer molecules – nimotuzumab or anti-EGFR, and itolizumab or anti-CD6.

Sierra had licensed nimotuzumab to a few other partners with different territorial rights for marketing the drug. She found that among all her partners, Biocon moved the fastest in conducting clinical trials. She may not have been fluent in English, and still worries if her Spanish comes in the way of her English syntax and vocabulary, but dealing with Kiran was easy 'because even in the most complicated of situations, she was straightforward'. So when the next molecule from her lab, itolizumab, was ready to be licensed, it was not surprising that Sierra chose Biocon as the main partner granting it nearly worldwide marketing rights.

Biocon had upgraded its manufacturing – from fungal products to the most coveted and complex biologics.

5

DIVERSIFICATION: CLOSING THE LIFE SCIENCES LOOP

Sold on Services

The rise of recombinant technology in the 1980s had some unexpected outcomes. Researchers riffed molecular systems and began to identify new therapeutic targets in multitudes. But their traditional method of screening compounds against these targets for potential drug candidates did not keep pace. Drug companies too did not know how to accelerate the process for generating new compounds. So by the early 1990s, robotic systems that could test tens or hundreds of thousands of molecules on purified protein targets in one day were born. Start-ups were rapidly founded in the United States to build technology for high-throughput screening which produced 'hits', the starting matter for drug discovery programmes.

From among the early starters to mix and match compounds at high speed was Affymax, founded in 1988 by the consummate biotech entrepreneur Alejandro Zaffaroni and run by Gordon Ringold, a former faculty at Stanford. Ringold and former biotech secretary Janakiraman Ramachandran go back decades. Their initial student–teacher relationship has evolved into that of fellow scientists, innovators, and then stakeholders of the biotech boom times of California. Once the Astra Research Centre got off the ground, Ramachandran invited Ringold to Bengaluru. Getting to the city in 1992 was one of the 'worst trips' Ringold ever made. It took him three days to reach Bengaluru as planes were rerouted. Yet, Ringold came away impressed. He was keen on striking a working relationship between Affymax and Astra, though he understood the latter was a slow-moving but forward-looking company and it would take him 'forever' to negotiate with the Swedes.

By that time, Kiran was entrenched in Astra's nerve centre in Bengaluru and was more receptive to Ringold's idea. Ramachandran knew new compounds were needed by drug companies, especially peptides, and suggested that Kiran supply building blocks to the companies in the US – use low-cost base in India to make modified amino acids which could then be linked to make peptides.

Affymax had built a potent platform, so versatile that it spun off a handful of companies – the most notable being Affymetrix – and so irresistible to drug discovery that GlaxoSmithKline paid $500 million just for the technology when the company was barely five years old.

What Affymax needed then was some good organic chemists and molecular biologists in India so that it could outsource initial compound making. Ringold promised Kiran that if she set up a lab, he would 'guarantee a contract that'll pay her all the cost and a profit margin'.

In its enzymes business, by developing applications for customers, Biocon was used to the idea of doing research for others. At Astra Centre, Ramachandran had already helped Padmanabhan Babu start Bangalore Genei, which was researching and building molecular tool kits for others. Between Biocon and Astra, Babu had found committed customers. So the idea of doing high-quality science for others was not entirely new, although it was evident it wasn't going to be an easy sell to the rest of the world. Still, it offered a business opportunity where Kiran did not have to wrap her head around much uncertainty, at least in the early days. Moreover, information technology companies in her neighbourhood were showing how outsourced service could impact global businesses, their profits and proficiency included.

Sometime in the year 1992, over dinner and after a few glasses of Indian wine – which Charles Cooney believes has become drinkable since then – some seven-odd diners at the table wrote cheques. Together they amounted to ₹50 lakh, reasonable money to start Syngene. 'It was not like today, when you first ask for term sheets or decide who owns how much. We thought it was a cool idea. If it worked out, fine; if not, we'd at least have fun together,' recounts Cooney. For Astra, he would come to Bengaluru at least once a year. In her inimitable style, Kiran would often host dinners and the budding biotech community would gather to discuss what was hot and happening in science, life sciences in particular.

A year later, Kiran floated Helix (which was merged with Biocon later); Cooney wrote her a cheque again. Laughing, he remarks: 'How do you do foreign direct investment in 1992? You write a cheque.'

In 1993, Syngene, India's first contract research organization, was incorporated. More than half of the initial investors were from Ramachandran's centre or known to him; having their skin in the game gave Kiran confidence. Since generic pharma in India was already steeped in chemistry, Syngene founders had doubts about getting enough chemistry business from overseas and they chose to focus on molecular biology, which, as it turned out later, was an error of judgement. Molecular biologist Goutam Das had already worked with Biocon on a few projects and was the only researcher at Astra to have been offered shares in Syngene. He wasn't surprised when Ramachandran suggested to him, 'Why don't you join Syngene?'

Work-wise, Syngene would be a novelty but salary-wise, he would be downgrading himself, thought Das. So his first reaction was, 'I won't join but I will help them to build and grow'. Biocon then was making less than ₹25 crore in revenue. 'But when in a dilemma, you look internally and cling to your spouse's advice,' says Das. His wife, who was also a researcher at Astra, preferred to distribute the risk and advised him to join Syngene. Das left Astra to build Syngene but he would keep coming to the Astra Centre in the initial days for help and Astra produced large amounts of amino acids for him, which at one point got Ramachandran into trouble.

'Somebody got jealous and wrote a poison-penned letter to the president of Astra in Sweden. They sent one of their lawyers to investigate but I was acting under the mandate to help the scientific community, so it was settled,' says Ramachandran. He continued to help, even with the initial hiring. In mid-1994, when Ganesh Sambasivam, a fresh Ph.D from the National Chemical Laboratory applied for a position in Astra, Ramachandran called Kiran to say 'he had found the right guy' because projects from Affymax, a pioneer in combinatorial chemistry, had begun to pile up at Syngene.

What greeted Sambasivam at Syngene was a semblance of chemistry laboratory. 'I had no industry experience but Kiran gave me the feeling that it was my baby and I had to run it,' recalls Sambasivam. For nearly two years, his team cranked out molecules that were mostly non-proprietary in nature. Affymax was the sole customer, but making compounds for even one customer was fraught with challenges.

India was deep into generics and China was a big supplier of intermediates, the starting material for bulk drugs. Real R&D-based companies did not exist, so all chemicals for custom research at Syngene were bought from boutique companies which were based out of Europe or the US and took weeks to ship chemicals to India. Certain chemicals were classified as hazardous and had to be imported by sea, which took even longer. Infrastructure costs, from large air-handling units to high-pressure liquid chromatography – a technique to separate components in a mixture – kept the services' progress under check. Outsourcing role models in Bengaluru, which Syngene had looked up to, had none of these delays to deal with.

It was a slow start, with Quest International, the Unilever speciality and biotech division, coming in as the next customer. In 1996, Kiran and Das travelled to California to meet Ringold and to convey that she would not sell Syngene. In the throes of starting up, Ringold had made a gentlemanly verbal commitment to Kiran which implied that if she didn't want to keep Syngene, Affymax might want to buy it. 'Gordon found our decision extremely reassuring because he had already sold the company to GlaxoSmithKline and it would have been very difficult for him to sell the idea of Syngene to the big pharma,' recalls Das.

Even then, Kiran treaded cautiously for some time. 'In the early days, I'd ask her to buy a nuclear magnetic resonance machine, but she'd say it cost $300,000. I'd say borrow that money, you will recover it in no time, but she waited for the business to grow. She was tentative. But once John [Shaw] came, he gave her the confidence to be bold,' says Ramachandran.

Enter Big Pharma

In 1998, Das got a call from Balu N. Subramanian, the head of external R&D innovation at Bristol-Myers Squibb in New Jersey, who at that time was looking for new ways to improve the productivity of pharmaceutical research. While interviewing a candidate from Affymax for the medicinal chemistry position at Bristol-Myers, Subramanian learnt that Affymax did most of its synthesis work at Syngene. Those days, one of the proposals on Subramanian's table was on how to increase the number of full-time equivalents for chemical synthesis for the same cost without compromising on quality. The late 1990s were a tough period for big pharma as it struggled to put money into R&D, a situation the industry hasn't really been able to come out of since.

In his conversation with Das, Subramanian made it clear that he was engaging in a trial run – to outsource synthesis of compounds for drug discovery. In essence, Bristol-Myers was pioneering this concept because until then big pharma had outsourced process chemistry and manufacturing but not any work related to discovery. It was a risky proposition. Subramanian gave one full-time equivalent each to four companies – Syngene, and one company each in Europe, China and the US. Syngene and the Illinois company delivered the quality product but at different costs.

It was a small project, worth $35,000, which Syngene took but it proved consequential. 'Compare that with Y2K of the information technology industry. Today, nobody talks about what price Infosys worked at in Y2K projects,' says Das. After that first assignment, he says, Syngene never lost sight of building the business. One full-time equivalent grew to ten and more, but Bristol-Myers did not want to tie its scope to one company and distributed projects to Sunmar in Chennai, GVK in Hyderabad and ChemBiotek (now TCG Lifesciences) in Kolkata. It was avoiding errors of commission and omission.

Between 1998 and 2003, as Subramanian increased the outsourcing business to India, he had to educate people in India and convince colleagues in New Jersey. The issue with respect to most Indian scientists then, he says, was that they were not able to give a clear picture of the deliverables and were 'loose' about timelines. If they said they would deliver the compound by the week of 20 January, based on which the team in the US would plan experiments the following week, even by 28 January, there would be no trace of the compound. All Indian contract research companies suffered from this time lapse syndrome.

'It took us five to six years to shape raw talent into discovery science,' says Subramanian.

By 2000, leading drug companies were outsourcing nearly 25 per cent of all their work in these areas.

In the meantime, Syngene found other customers in the industry. It upgraded to making compounds for novel and experimental drugs. Its growth was cautious, not least because culturally too it was a different environment, particularly for those in white laboratory coats. Sambasivam recalls a researcher who had returned from a postdoctoral position in an American university and was working on a project for a big pharmaceutical client. The guy messed up the synthesis, and naturally, the client coordinator gave him a hard time. After being down for a week, when he got back to work, he was given a fresh set of synthesis requests. Since he was already struggling, he requested some preparatory protocol to start with. The coordinator in the US sent him the procedures, prefixing it with 'FYI'.

'Our guy was so nervous, he didn't sleep at night and came to me saying, "I've been trying to be good but this is not working. I know what he means by FYI – F*** You Indian,"' recalls Sambasivam with some amusement but without downplaying the fact that scientist-to-scientist interactions were often touchy and took a while to set right.

Through its first decade, Syngene was built on small-scale synthesis–making compounds from milligram to gram scale. It served two types of clients: research and development customers who wanted compounds only in milligram scale; drug companies having stumbled upon some interesting compounds in screens which they wanted to test further. The compound would then move to process research, which would make it in hundreds of kilograms. Often, what contract research companies do in small scale may not be ideal for large scale.

It was after 2003 that Syngene got into making pilot-scale

compounds – where you take a formula on paper to lab-scale production to pilot-scale manufacturing and then, finally, develop the process to be fit for a plant. For the next three years, it made more than a million compounds, only a fraction of which – as is the industry standard, about 40–50 – came back for scale-up. Eventually, many compounds came to Syngene which were for late stage clinical trials or on the verge of entering the market.

One of the earliest test cases of its molecular biology capability came when Biocon embarked on its insulin programme early in the twenty-first century, and Das, who had expertise in yeast molecular biology, cloned the insulin gene. Soon, Syngene was offering services in cloning and expressing protein targets. Yet, it was chemistry that catalysed Syngene's growth. By 2006, for each of the fifty biologists on its rolls, there were twelve chemists. The reason the biology business was muted was obvious. Most proprietary work rested in biology, and given India's reputation in infringing intellectual property in pharmaceuticals, global life sciences companies were iffy about putting their patented knowledge into the hands of Indian contractors.

The Clinical Touch

In March 2000, Arvind Atignal was visiting Bengaluru from Wales in the United Kingdom, where he worked as a medical director at the University Hospital of Wales in Cardiff in a rather unique role that allowed him to treat patients, do research and dabble in administration. One morning, he got a call from Kiran. She said there was an opportunity he might want to check out. Knowing her, he interpreted the call as: here is the opportunity, come and take it up.

It was about a start-up in Palo Alto, California, called Surromed, which was started by Ringold to look for diagnostic markers that would help stratify patients. Emboldened by the Affymax experience in India, Ringold wanted to set up registries in chronic diseases like diabetes, cancer, cardiovascular and others, where patients would be studied for a period of time to find biomarkers that could predict their complications. For instance, in diabetes, doctors often advise their patients to control their blood sugar, watch their weight and so on, but nobody can tell if a patient will develop any complication which to some, or to a large extent, may be related to one's control of diabetes. Surromed and Atignal wanted to set up a longitudinal study in association with several diabetologists in Bengaluru.

However, this idea, unlike the Affymax–Syngene collaboration, needed patient data whose generation, quality and integrity were paramount, but without a precedent in India. What was also less appreciated, perhaps, was that setting up a registry required more infrastructure than conducting clinical trials.

Atignal was holidaying in Bengaluru for two weeks but was adventurous enough to take the next available flight to Palo Alto to meet Ringold and his chief medical officer, Nancy Grove. After three days of discussions, Atignal laid out a plan before Ringold on an overhead projector and returned to Bengaluru to tell Kiran that 'it could be done'. Predictably, Kiran offered him the baby with the bathwater.

But the choice before Atignal was not that simple. He had a good job in Wales and when he went back to discuss with his boss the possibility of relocating to India, the Welsh chief executive Mike Jones told him he was being foolish. 'What will you do after two years when the registry is done?' he asked. Atignal had worked with Kiran earlier, when he was setting up a hospital in Bengaluru for the Mallya Group, owned by liquor baron Vijay Mallya. Kiran was a non-executive director in the hospital but 'she was never a non-involved non-executive director; she was always involved in decisions from the ceiling to the floor'. Atignal knew Biocon was planning to get into insulin and Kiran would not stop at just running the diabetes registry. He also sensed how vital the clinical work they were contemplating with Surromed would become for introducing insulin in the Indian market – position it aptly as a biotech drug.

Jones asked for one good reason why Atignal was leaving an enviable position in Wales. 'I told him getting a chance to be part of the science and technology scene of the emerging economy of my country was probably a lifetime opportunity,' says Atignal. Jones placed a condition that Atignal would have to spend a month in Wales for every three months he spent in India until they found a suitable substitute. He sweetened the term by saying that if Atignal wished, the arrangement could continue for two to three years. (It continued for ten years.) Jones was providing him a 'safety net' which he said he had not offered to anyone else.

Once Atignal made his decision, Clinigene was founded as a wholly owned subsidiary of Biocon which would work not just for Surromed but for Biocon and other pharmaceutical companies as well. It became India's first laboratory to get accreditation from the College of American Pathologists.

Apart from Surromed, Merck, known as MSD Pharmaceuticals in India, was one of its early customers. Kiran and Atignal were clear that they wanted to establish a research-focused diabetes group which would do clinical trials on oral drugs, injectables, intra-nasal insulin spray – any new or old diabetes therapy that anyone wanted to test. It was also a time when alternative routes of administering insulin were being vigorously researched worldwide. One of the keenly watched stories then was New Hampshire–based Bentley Pharmaceuticals' intra-nasal insulin for which Clinigene did some studies.

Companies were willing to outsource their clinical studies to Clinigene even though Biocon had its own generic insulin on the cards simply because it had built a 'robust firewall around data'.

'We were open about it. My first slide in every presentation said we are a subsidiary of Biocon which is working on insulin. Clients felt comfortable working with a contract research organization that was aware of the landscape in diabetes. Our negative became our positive,' says Atignal. Once that credibility was established, the company bagged clinical study contracts for new products from MSD – oral diabetes drugs Januvia and Januvet. It was not a coincidence that these two drugs, Januvia in particular, set a record for the speed with which Merck conducted parallel clinical trials and brought it to market.

Clinching a brand like Merck was important for Atignal, but he chose to be transparent about the limitations of Clinigene. When MSD managing director Naveen Rao wanted to audit Clinigene before outsourcing any study, Atignal told him that if he audited them, they wouldn't muster past the drill. To a guarded and somewhat confounded Rao, Atignal proposed a deal: 'You will have to trust that we will deliver the quality on time.' The two had a long discussion at a Windsor Manor restaurant, after which Rao agreed to take a chance, on the condition that he would closely monitor progress, almost on a daily basis. MSD went on to become an enduring customer.

Until Clinigene came about, Biocon's pharma plan had a cavernous chink. No biomedical idea escapes being shaped by clinical development. With a modest investment of ₹5 crore, Clinigene acquired the best training, setting up a twenty-six-bed human pharmacology unit at Sagar Apollo Hospital which allowed fast enrolment of patients and close supervision.

Serendipity

Ringold had started Surromed with Bala Manian, a successful optical engineer in the biomedical world who had built and sold a few companies in Silicon Valley but never looked back at India after leaving for the US in 1966 with twenty dollars in his pocket. When Ringold told him about Affymax's work with Syngene in Bengaluru, Manian brushed it aside with the cold shrug of a cynic, saying, 'You can't do anything in India.' By then, Syngene had proved itself, so Ringold, to impress Manian that even bankers in India were willing to back science-based ventures, described how at the inauguration of Syngene, ICICI Bank president Narayanan Vaghul spoke about the need for scientist entrepreneurs in India. He described how Vaghul had promised funding from his bank if scientists were willing to venture.

Now it was Ringold's turn to be impressed. 'Vaghul is my brother,' Manian said, quietly making up his mind to visit India and assess the situation first-hand. At the time of leaving India, Vaghul had seen him off at Mumbai airport but did not approve of his younger brother's decision to go to the US. They had not stayed in touch for over a decade.

By the time Ringold, Grove and Atignal got Clinigene going full steam in Bengaluru, the business environment had changed in California. Ringold and Manian struggled to keep Surromed alive as a service business. The diabetes registries had not been in place long enough to discover anything worthwhile. In 2003, they divested the biomarker business of Surromed to Pharmaceutical Product Development Inc., an existing investor and clinical services provider commonly known as PPD.

Objectively speaking, says Ringold, nothing medically valuable came out of the Surromed–Clinigene collaboration. In retrospect, he believes that if they had focused on one disease and turned it into a diagnostics company rather than a service provider across many diseases, they probably would have been more successful. 'I think it's very hard to make an impact in any area and at the same time become service providers to the industry. Those are not particularly overlapping areas,' he rues.

Indeed they are not, as Clinigene experienced later. Imagine: one big pharma firm comes with project A, another with project B, and neither is an entirely different project. The kinds of patients a service company may have to follow are different, the kinds of markers it needs may be different. But then to superimpose all these responsibilities to say that the service company would discover something for itself – though theoretically promising – was an almost impossible goal to achieve.

But PPD fell for it. As the largest shareholder when it acquired Surromed, it had a similar goal in mind: to discover biomarkers. But operationally, they ran into the same problem that Surromed and Clinigene faced. All the clinical experts serving the leading pharma companies could not get their heads around the notion of doing research for their own purposes. 'It was all cash-flow driven,' reflects Ringold.

So even PPD divested the biomarker division – which was largely a mass spectrometry, proteomics and metabolomics group – to a small precision medicine company in Canada named Caprion.

Surromed, on the whole, was a great idea, but it was fifteen years too soon. Even for America.

In January 2015, President Obama launched a new precision medicine initiative in the US 'to bring us closer to curing diseases like cancer and diabetes – and to give all of us access to the personalized information we need to keep ourselves and our families healthier.' Scientists and health administrators hope to assemble a longitudinal cohort of one million or more Americans who will volunteer to participate in research. This initiative intends to do all that Surromed (and a few others) wanted to do and some more. It is about time. Biology, in the past fifteen years, has followed the equivalent of Moore's law – the costs of reading and writing new genes and genomes are falling by a factor of two every eighteen to twenty-four months, and the productivity in reading and writing is independently doubling at a similar rate.

Surromed, and by extension Clinigene, met the fate which is endemic to being 'just service providers', and which, perhaps, has been the fate of many information technology companies in India – they excel at services but product innovation remains elusive.

Quality Stamp

After five years of off-shoring discovery services to India and other Asian countries, Bristol-Myers thought it was time to outsource strategically. Subramanian and his colleagues placed a proposal before the management to consolidate its outsourcing in one place in Asia. They consulted McKinsey and Boston Consulting Group and shortlisted three countries – China, India and Singapore.

By then, Kiran had got Subramanian, a champion of drug discovery science ever since he left India, involved in local scientific deliberations and policy making in Karnataka. The soft diplomacy of interpersonal relationships and confidence building was working in the background. In New Jersey, some of the senior managers were reluctant to move work outside the US. 'In China, I never had the comfort of knowing what I was buying,' says Tamar Howson, who, as a corporate vice-president, was one of the decision influencers.

When Howson visited Bengaluru in 2007, Subramanian and Das had been discussing a potential deal for sometime but were still nervous. In Bengaluru, not many – and this included Krishnan and Chandavarkar – believed Syngene could get into such a relationship with the pharma company, but Kiran saw the promise.

'She could see right through my first meeting,' says Das. Moreover, Wyeth, another pharma giant from New Jersey, had already struck a partnership with Syngene's rival, GVK Bio, in Hyderabad to set up a discovery research centre. There were sceptics on the other side too. Howson was quite fascinated by India – she had written a paper on Indira Gandhi in high school – but wasn't comfortable trusting Indian companies with quality research and timely delivery.

All this had prepped Kiran. 'I was told Tamar was a very tough lady to get to know and deal with. But when she came here, I found her very open and accessible and I said to myself, we can do business with her.'

The choice between China and India had a very small margin of error. But after meeting Kiran, Howson believed she was reducing the risk for Bristol-Myers and, compared to China, they had a much better chance of being successful. In Singapore, it was early days in the life sciences sector and the 'government involvement in everything you do' was a spoilsport. At the same time, Bristol-Myers had checked out a few other companies in India but it didn't quite like what it saw in the name of transparency. 'It was not that the contract research companies did not want to be transparent, they did not have books and procedures,' says Howson. In comparison, Kiran was 'extremely honest and it was clear that we wouldn't have surprises'.

Howson went back satisfied with what Biocon was promising to do. For the management in the US, the political climate in India 'was trending in the right direction'. Beginning 2005, India had amended its Patent Act, showing commitment to the Trade Related Intellectual Property rights (TRIPs) under the World Trade Organization.

Even though Syngene had nearly 200 people working on Bristol-Myers' projects, the latter was not too keen to invest much outside India. Instead, it asked Biocon to build a research centre to its taste and standard which it would compensate over time by way of full-time equivalents. A section of employees in the US thought this arrangement would take positions to India. 'We had to convince people that we were augmenting our capability in the US, and it turned out to be the case, actually. It took me about eight years and three presidents of R&D to get to starting the Biocon-BMS Research Centre,' says Subramanian.

As the discussions continued, Howson and Kiran came to know each other better. Howson even invited Kiran to the annual BioMed conference in Jerusalem, thinking the two countries could collaborate in some way. After the conference, he took her to the Dead Sea and then they drove down to the southern tip of Israel to the resort city of Eilat, crossing the border to see Jordan. Since Howson was there, he recalls, Kiran had to 'absolutely go to Petra', the Jordanian city which is one of the new Seven Wonders of the World, and ride a donkey. Much of the negotiation on the Biocon–Bristol-Myers deal happened during the drive from Jerusalem to Jordan.

It was a unique arrangement that Das and Subramanian finally came up with. Evenly spreading the risk and reward, it offered calibrated exits: the two partners could walk out after seven years, in which case Syngene would gain by having hundreds of scientists trained in drug discovery. If either party walked out prematurely, it would have to pay a penalty. Finally, after seven years, Bristol-Myers would have the option to buy the centre out and convert it into a captive outfit.

In 2007, the two companies formalized their arrangement and Bristol-Myers pulled out of all contractual agreements with other Indian companies. In some respects, it was starting afresh, particularly in managing security and training people to understand the nuances of intellectual property. Subramanian hired people to create training courses, down to instructions on how to send emails. No leak would be tolerated. In one instance of breach, a scientist wrote an email to her husband, who was doing his doctorate in a university, listing a few targets that the pharma company was working on. She was fired. No one was supposed to mention names of the programmes to anyone outside the centre.

As Syngene matured, it attracted other big pharmaceutical clients and grew in sophistication. Around 2010, a client raised some concern about two bioreactors which were used by turns for making compounds. The question was: how do you ensure that one client doesn't get a whiff of what is being made for another client? Scientists, after all, can sniff out a product just by looking at the chemical labels. That observation triggered a fresh layer of security measures with Syngene creating codes for each raw material of each product of each customer, so that even if the latter walked into a product area, they wouldn't know their own product unless the codes were revealed to them.

In 2012, Abbott Nutrition started a dedicated centre; Baxter followed in 2014.

When Syngene was conceived, in the post-dinner languor and pre-services hope of the early 1990s, it was meant to be a standalone business. It has remained so and Das takes much pride in stressing that 'not a single Biocon client has come to Syngene, rather it has been the other way round'. (Biocon later forged alliances with BMS and Pfizer.) Yet, it turned out to be, in splendidly serendipitous ways, a means to an end – to making Biocon an independent biotech company. Syngene allowed it to build capabilities in all spheres of drug discovery and biopharmaceutical manufacturing processes. If not for the funded contract activities of Syngene, Biocon would have had to invest several years and millions of dollars to build that capability organically. Whether it was borrowing Sambasivam's chemistry skills when Biocon was entering into pharmaceuticals or the yeast molecular biology expertise of Das during the cloning of the insulin gene for *Pichia pastoris*, the subsidiary proved to be a nimble enabler.

SYNGENE 2.0

By early 2008, in happy inadvertence – who could tell that it would turn into a nasty downturn – Kiran felt Syngene was ready for a public offering. Quite casually, she began discussing this at forums, hinting at the fiscal year-end for a stock market listing. She even issued a statement in January which said, 'We believe Syngene has attained critical mass that can be leveraged to deliver a strong growth trajectory.'

Quality veteran at Biocon, Tara Jayaram was moved to Syngene, as was the number two person in finance, Muckatira Bhemaiah

Chinappa. It required some mental shifts for Jayaram; she wasn't happy moving from a products company to a services company where technology, processes and approvals, all came from the customer. She remembers once going to Das and smugly narrating that she had said no to a customer when they asked for entry–exit procedures. 'Goutam told me, "If you say no, the client will say bye-bye". It did take some time to get used to the services culture,' she recalls. 'But I learnt more at Syngene in six years than I did at Biocon in twenty.'

But very soon, tendrils around the business began to tighten. The competition copied what Syngene had pioneered and it learnt to copy cheap. GVK Bio, in particular, began to take away its lunch. A seasoned generics business leader, D.S. Brar, who had just retired as chief executive at Ranbaxy Laboratories, joined GVK Bio as chairman, infusing fresh energy into the company. Apart from eroding business, inadequate – sometimes even adhoc – processes in operations came to haunt Syngene. One 'sizeable project' of a big pharma company failed, causing 'a significant loss of face, revenue and profitability'. The client eventually stayed on but with a 'lot of nurturing'.

Kiran read the warning signs and saw the event as a tell-tale signal of what could go wrong with the business. Her long-time financial associate Kunal Kashyap recommended Peter Bains, with whom he had worked as an Arthur Andersen consultant while the latter served as vice-president of international business at GlaxoSmithKline.

In the summer of 2009, when Kashyap was in London, he called Bains even though the two had not spoken for twelve years. They met up. Bains had left GlaxoSmithKline to explore new opportunities outside of the big pharma wagon, and was particularly interested in putting his emerging market expertise to use. India was a choice; he had declined China, despite having worked there while setting up SmithKlineBeecham's business. Kashyap advised him to meet Kiran.

Bains had served on the board of SmithKlineBeecham in India for six years and was reasonably familiar with the local pharmaceutical environment. During the peak HIV/AIDS crisis of the early 2000s, when the antiretroviral drug makers were locked in a patent battle with generic companies and healthcare advocacy groups, as business head of SmithKlineBeecham, which made those drugs, he had to go to South Africa to sign the 'compulsory licensing papers on television'. He also debated with Yusuf Hamied, chairman of Cipla, the company that electrified the world with its cut-price anti-HIV drugs, at the European Commission round table conference where Hamied first offered to supply low-cost cocktail therapy.

In brief, Bains understood the Indian market as well as the Indian mindset.

When he met Kiran, she initially wanted him to help her with some strategic thinking – what she should be doing with the Biocon Group. Perhaps she saw him as someone who understood the emerging markets better than the average biopharmaceutical executive. Strangely, Bains never headed any business in the US in the twenty-three years at GlaxoSmithKline (through all its previous corporate shake-ups) but had the title 'Head of Marketing'.

A few months after that meeting, when Kiran saw Bains was exploring other options and taking up board positions in companies, she pinned him down by offering him the position of a board director. He knew little about Syngene, so he said if he had to join the board, he would study it closely. He came up with a whitepaper to tell Kiran and the senior management how he saw the company. And he couldn't see very far. 'I told her Syngene was in a bit of a dilemma and it didn't have a clear vision. The market in which it was operating was moving very fast and changing shape; if Syngene didn't move very quickly, it could be compromised and end up with the commodity business,' recounts Bains.

He joined the board in early 2010 and by summer that year, Das wanted to resign from his post of chief operating officer. But Kiran did not accept it, at least not immediately. It was apparent Das and Bains had different styles of management; Kiran understood the company needed a change agent. By the end of that year, Bains and Das had a conversation in Kashyap's office and Das's earlier 'resignation' letter was converted into a 'retirement' note.

When I asked Das, why could he not sense Syngene's midlife crisis and bring about some change in a company he had built and run for seventeen years, he said: 'We could have done some things better but I don't know what!'

It took some patient persuasion for Kiran to get Bains to warm up to the idea of heading Syngene. The thought of running a company in India had never crossed his mind, especially with his family settled in the UK. Eventually, in January 2011, Bains took charge. He went about undertaking a 'change programme'. From his pharma days, he had watched how the industry had scattered its service relationships to such a degree that it spent more time managing processes and relationships than it did managing assets. Fortunately, he had also witnessed how GlaxoSmithKline consolidated its vendor, contract research and development activities. So at Syngene, his approach relied on integrated offerings on the discovery–development continuum.

For the first time, Syngene made a five-year plan. People were hired, empowered and made accountable. 'I had to undergo a shift in my mind as well,' says Manoj Nerurkar, who was pulled out of the formulations team to head the small molecules division and then groomed to be the chief operating officer, all within eighteen months. The largest team he had handled just three years earlier was under fifty, and now he was responsible for more than 2,000 people. Senior employees got a peek into the profit-and-loss account of their respective businesses, so they placed or cut their expectations accordingly.

Economics alone, Bains knew, did not keep R&D heads awake

at night. Innovation and productivity did. 'We decided not to be a cheap pair of hands; we chose to be an economical pair of hands attached to a brain,' he says in an amiably impersonal way. That translated into, say, moving away from making a library of compounds for a given scaffold to optimizing an antibody construct, which meant getting twenty scientists on board to make an antibody drug conjugate. There's a market price for the former but the latter is not an off-the-shelf solution.

Bains kept the focus on biotech and biopharma but expanded the service offering in many related fields – cosmetics, nutrition, agrochemicals, veterinary and electronics, where novel and extremely pure chemicals are mixed with polymers to make new materials. From the discarded cancer tissues at the Mazumdar-Shaw Cancer Hospital, 3 km away, Syngene has made and validated animal models. Pharma companies can use these to test their library of compounds and check which type of cancer they are effective on.

All along, Kiran continued to keep the initial public offer (IPO)buzz alive. In late 2012, GE Capital paid $23 million for nearly 8 per cent of the company. This was to set the base value for Syngene which, until then, had not raised private funds even if it meant compromising on expansion. One of the reasons its competition (the most inescapable comparison is with the Chinese company WuXi, which was started seven years after Syngene) has grown bigger is that they did commercial-scale manufacturing. Syngene shied away from this until 2015, when it acquired land in a Mangaluru special economic zone (SEZ) for contract manufacturing.

As with everything else in China, it's hard to appreciate, rather gauge, the extent of soft support that businesses get from the government. There's a broad state-controlled regulatory environment, adjacent to the commercial environment, which requires a pharma or a healthcare company accessing the Chinese market to do clinical work in China; all this inevitably benefits the contract research industry. India is a much more open and free market.

'I've worked in China. The country is uniquely capable of doing things because of the political system; it can play a long game in a way that no other major country can,' says Bains.

RIPE FOR PUBLIC LISTING

When GE Capital invested in Syngene, the broad understanding was that it would facilitate business with GE Healthcare, especially in life sciences manufacturing technologies. It did not work out because 'GE turned out to be like the Government of India, vendors had to go through a tender process' and Syngene participated in half a dozen tenders though it never was about the lowest price. By then, GE Capital had become a pariah in the GE universe and could not do much to fulfil the commitments it had made while investing. Kiran then considered buying back GE shares. India Value Fund, which had earlier invested in Biocon and got returns fifteen times their investment, came in. GE valued it at ₹1,600 crore, raising it to ₹2,800 crore when it exited eighteen months later. This was bumped up to ₹3,800 crore when India Value Fund bought 10 per cent shares in 2014.

As Kiran and Kashyap worked on moving the valuation needle, there was another clock that was ticking, its hands moving towards a set date: completion of the agreement between Syngene and Bristol-Myers Squibb in 2014. According to the exit clause, the pharma company could choose to buy out the partnership, in which case a good chunk of the Syngene business and a juicy bit of its corporate story would be knocked off; or, it could walk away, leaving 450 scientists on Syngene's rolls.

Either decision could nick the story that Kiran – after all, Biocon held 90 per cent of Syngene – was scripting for investors.

As it happened, Bristol-Myers chose to renew its partnership for five more years, clearing the way for the Syngene IPO.

Carl Decicco's argument in 2007 before the senior management of Bristol-Myers Squibb, that India would become a good player in the world of intellectual property, did not necessarily play out in the way he had 'pitched to the team'. But the other part – the scientific input and the level of productivity – turned out to be 'very strong'. Now its Bengaluru centre has all of the pieces that one ought to have to drive independent discovery and development programmes, says Decicco, head of discovery, research and development at Bristol-Myers Squibb. Ten per cent of its global research and development workforce is in Bengaluru.

'Syngene has delivered multiple drug candidates in collaboration with our people in the United States; it's pretty clear why we are still there,' Decicco noted. He refused to qualify 'multiple'. When pushed, he muttered, 'It's a very competitive environment. Everyone wants to have an edge over somebody else. Doesn't "multiple" sound like more than three?'

Continuing this relationship was critical for the company, and, by some stretch, for the industry too. The latter's credibility as a contract research destination was mired in steady reports of data being fudged or 'deleted' during contract research or drug testing. Once again, Kiran put her negotiating skills to work. 'She is very clear on what she'd like to do. At the same time, she is also a person who listens. She is someone you can talk to without a lot of emotion,' says Decicco, who, after forty trips to India, does not travel so often but relishes the 'unique cultural heritage' of the country.

Why did Bristol-Myers Squibb renew the contract? The reasons are both external as well as internal. Externally, the industry continues to reel under a decreasing productivity pandemic. The frenzied merger, acquisition and hostile biddings of 2015 hold up a mirror to that. Internally, however, Syngene showed 'progressive improvement'.

In the beginning, Bristol-Myers Squibb wouldn't give a

'programme' – camouflage for the specific science in this hyper-competitive industry – and ask researchers in Bengaluru to come with the final product. The contract research started with small molecules, but in the 'back-up strategy' of the company, one of Bristol-Myers' success formulae for speed-to-clinic. As the drug company moves its molecules to clinics, it develops backup compounds in case things go wrong with the first line of molecules. It got the Bengaluru centre to work on those backup molecules, for which a lot of biology was already worked out and the chemistry was already in place, providing a more advanced starting point. Over the years, says Decicco, it proved to be a very instructional way of building not just capacity but also confidence in the team.

In the early days, productivity was very low. 'It took us a lot of effort. Initially, people told us we'd never do world-class biology in Bengaluru, but today we are doing it and even the pharma development team here is a critical part of how we operate,' says Decicco. One of the things that Bristol-Myers is known for is the speed with which it gets a compound into humans – from the time of declaring a compound as drug candidate to testing it in humans. 'Syngene has helped us accelerate the process to the point that when we declare the candidate, we have the material and that helps us move fast into clinics.'

Gradually, Bengaluru got involved a lot earlier in programmes in oncology, neurology, immunology and hepatitis C. But there was one speciality area which Bristol-Myers seeded in Bengaluru. It was called pro-drugs, where teams took the compounds coming down the screens and improved the pharmacokinetics. 'We found that to be a useful strategy which has since delivered candidate pro-drugs,' says Decicco.

In the second innings, will the two players take singles and twos or will they swing for the fence? Decicco says that earlier they mostly did small molecules in India, but now biologics is a big portfolio in the US, so some bit of that work will move to Syngene.

CLINICAL RESEARCH BUBBLE

In 2009, one day, after returning from work, Atignal collapsed at the dining table. His kidneys had failed and he had to be on dialysis for about a year. Still, he continued to run Clinigene. Though Kiran was very 'compassionate', it was becoming apparent that he would need a transplant, after which he would not be able to pack much punch at work.

Clinigene hired a headhunter to look for a replacement and the search ended with Abhijit Barve. After twelve years at Astellas in Chicago, Barve and his family, like many first-generation Indian immigrants in the US, were contemplating relocation to India. He had already been interviewed at a large pharma company in Hyderabad but sometime during the selection process, the company's strategy changed and they offered him a position in the US; Barve then chose to stay back at Astellas. However, when the headhunter suggested he should meet Kiran in New York, he agreed.

At the hour-long breakfast meeting in the summer of 2009, Kiran spoke for most of the time. Before the meeting got over, she asked him, 'When are you joining?' That was her signature hiring technique. Not Barve's. After his Ph.D in biopharmaceutical sciences from the University of Illinois, he had worked in a big pharmaceutical company, during which time he took a sabbatical to attend Chicago Booth. The business school had taught him a few things. He told her they needed to go 'through a process, work on some numbers'. Fortunately, he recalls, because of the headhunter's involvement, there was a very detailed job description with role, expectations and critical success parameters duly defined.

'I've tried to do that for my hires, especially when people are making a big change,' says Barve, justifying his hard-nosed business approach.

When he joined Clinigene in April 2010 as its chief operating officer, he had moved to the other side of the fence – from a sponsor company to a service company. People in the US had warned him about moving to a contract research organization. 'I was told that in a services organization, nobody praises you for doing a good job but if things go wrong, you are at the receiving end. I was also warned about "losing self respect", in the sense that even if I saw something to be wrong from the customer's side, I could only counsel them, not take decisions on their behalf,' says Barve.

Those warnings did not come true, though. Most global pharma companies by that time had already moved to partnership-based services, though he did find Indian clients to be 'transactional'. Most of the Phase III clinical studies were for global clients, but in bio-availability and bio-equivalence studies – done to compare a generic drug with an innovator's drug – two-thirds of the clients were local. It was there that Barve had a challenge staring at him. The utilization in the human pharmacological unit was low. Clinigene was until then not audited by any of the top global regulatory agencies. It was something like the first job, where everyone wants to hire someone with experience. Because Clinigene had not done enough studies and submitted data, it was not audited. And because it was not approved by the regulatory agencies, it did not get enough studies. Eventually, it got audited in January 2011, for a study done in 2009. More audits followed and the bioavailability and bio-equivalence business got a lease of life.

But by then, the clinical research business was falling apart. It was a lull before the storm; rather, the lull itself was a post-hype reality check after a flurry of start-up ventures during the middle of the first decade of this century. In 2002, McKinsey made an audacious forecast which said the clinical research industry in India would be worth $1 billion by 2010, even though some of the foundational steps like a clinical trial registry, an accreditation body and a national position to drop the archaic stance on not allowing Phase I studies were nowhere in sight. The McKinsey report whipped up a frenzy; contract research start-ups began to pop up in the country. It wasn't just the entrepreneurs or expansion-hungry business groups which followed the pied piper, other advisory companies too – Ernst & Young, Frost & Sullivan and KPMG – brought out their respective reports on the contract research business as late as in 2008, even when India was far short of the earlier projected numbers.

The government in New Delhi wasn't deaf to this drum-beating. It took some policy measures, doled out a few tax concessions, but effectively left the pot only half-stirred. What also got lost in translation was the cold fact that a good portion of the estimate of over a billion dollars was to come from the knowledge process outsourcing business; the clinical research business was just a smaller pie, and a highly regulated one as well. Nobody parsed the forecast numbers, nor did the analysts, often quoted in the media, highlight the stark difference between business process outsourcing and clinical research outsourcing.

Consequently, the financial downturn of late 2008 dealt a heavy blow to standalone organizations. Nerurkar, before joining Syngene, was all set to start a contract research business for the Shapoorji Pallonji Group, a construction company which wanted to ride the clinical research wave but pulled out once the Lehman Brothers shook the global economy.

So when Barve came to Clinigene, the high tide was receding and many were seen swimming naked. Smaller companies had shut shop, bigger ones had bitten off more than they could chew in buying businesses overseas, and were busy cutting losses. Jubilant, SIRO Clinpharm, Manipal Acunova and others had acquired companies overseas, most of which did not pan out according to the buyers' plans.

At Clinigene too Barve and Kiran contemplated acquiring a business overseas. While limited to India, no contract research company could aspire to get global clients steadily. It was also one of the 'expectations' when he was hired – that he would expand

Clinigene to a few global sites. But Barve was not in favour of acquisitions. When he wore his earlier company Astellas's hat and asked himself if he would outsource to such outfits, he found the maths in cost structure to be incorrect. Clinigene chose to wait it out. It remained small, but it survived.

'I'd think, if I were a client sitting in the US and couldn't afford the big names like Quintiles, I'd give the contract to somebody who will stay in the business for three years; that is how long some clinical trials take. That's where we benefited from being a Biocon brand,' says Barve.

Soon after, all hell broke loose when the British newspaper, *The Independent*, reported in 2011 about irregularities and high death rates in three clinical trials conducted in Bhopal, many of the subjects being Union Carbide gas tragedy victims. Earlier, there were petitions filed in the Supreme Court of India which challenged the observational study being conducted in some states to evaluate the cost and feasibility of introducing the cervical cancer vaccine, caused by the human papilloma virus. The study was funded by Bill & Melinda Gates Foundation and carried out by the international non-profit health organization, PATH.

The petitions led to a court case. All clinical studies, even in teaching hospitals which were led by doctors and had nothing to do with drug companies, came to a near halt. The Supreme Court issued a series of orders, chastising the drug regulator, pruning its powers, and eventually banning the trials altogether. Years of administrative lethargy and political apathy reflected in the morality plays that got enacted, by turns, in the press, court, and inside Parliament until early 2015. However, it was the first amendment to the Drugs Act in 2013 which laid down compensation for injury and death during clinical trials that broke the industry's back.

It was a sweeping application of the amendment and would demand compensation for every death in clinical trials. No country has such a provision. With India accounting for less than 2 per cent of global clinical trials, drug companies shifted their attention elsewhere.

Like all contract research companies in India, Clinigene's clinical trials business dropped significantly. By late 2011, Barve had moved to Biocon as its R&D head. Two years later, Clinigene merged with Syngene to simplify and augment the latter's business. 'I wanted my customers to have all services in complete line of sight with no complications of having to cross another corporate line. Of course, there was reluctance to let go of a brand but it made sense. Syngene was reasonably recognized, but Clinigene was very small. Besides, building two brands is tough,' justifies Bains.

Building any Indian brand in pharmaceuticals has been challenging. One or the other company's regulatory faux pas have rocked the industry from time to time. The United States drug regulator's imposition of a $500 million penalty on Ranbaxy was, to a large extent, due to fudged data that Ranbaxy submitted for obtaining approval in the American market. In late 2014, the French regulatory agency inspected GVK Bio's facility and raised concern about data manipulation of the electrocardiogram in some studies, following which, the European Medicines Agency suspended a number of medicines in European countries. GVK Bio took a hit on business but the bigger hit was to the reputation of the industry. Some amount of GVK business landed in Syngene's pocket, but on the whole, it was another avoidable reputational hoop.

'New clients say data fudging has happened in GVK, how can you guarantee it'll not happen at Syngene? Why do I need to justify what GVK did or did not do? Look at us independently,' says Nerurkar.

To be fair, some amount of muckraking can be attributed to vested interests. The rise of Indian generics companies and their increasing global market share comes at the expense of other generics and innovator companies. For all the quality comparison narratives, several approvals that the overseas regulatory agencies grant in India never make the news headlines, in India or elsewhere. Crackpot correlations notwithstanding, the Indian life sciences industry has to bear the cross.

BIOCON PARK – THE BIGGER THE BETTER

At the start of the millennium, as Syngene and Clinigene found their foothold, Biocon could see rapid growth in pharmaceuticals, statins in particular. Between 2001 and 2004, revenue grew 300 per cent to ₹550 crore. The company acquired 90 acres in the neighbouring industrial park to build what would become India's largest integrated biotechnology park that did everything that an undergraduate learns in textbooks, just on a large scale. Built organically over the years, Biocon was getting ready to select portfolios that ranged from immunosuppressants to statins, recombinant proteins to antibodies.

Once again, the company stretched itself beyond limits. It built an expansion plan which ballooned from ₹250 crore to ₹450 crore. It would haemorrhage cash but Biocon was willing to bet its revenues, not just profits. In the past, it had done the same with the submerged fermentation plant, and a few years later, it would do it with a new insulin facility in Malaysia. Kiran had a habit of getting ahead of herself – when she was thinking insulin, her planned insulin capacity exceeded the total volumes sold in India.

It was gruelling for the managers. Chandavarkar must have lost most of his curly mop during those years. Biocon was building four fermenters of 1,25,000-litre capacity, scaling up from 30,000 litres; a chemical synthesis plant which would become the world's largest simvastatin plant outside the innovator company Merck; an antibody manufacturing plant with help from the Cubans; and its first sterile injectable facility. Always doing too many things at the same time, they were even building the country's first biotech SEZ. 'Every functional division – sales, legal, finance – was helping us.

There was no ready-made technology, we were learning through trial and error,' says Chandavarkar.

Halfway through this, they learnt it was amateurish to have become excited by the SEZ idea. It wasn't as rosy as it sounded in the beginning. The biggest draw, on paper, was its feature as a turnkey project – commission a plant and start making profits the same year. Hence, there was full exemption of income-tax for five years followed by 50 per cent exemption for the next five years. In reality, such plants never make a profit in the first few years, nor does the full capacity come into operation. After commissioning, there's a long period of validation and stability batches, filing for approval and getting the plant inspected by global regulatory bodies. All that takes two to three years; the five-year tax exemption window closes even before a penny in profit is counted.

When the fermentation block for antibodies was set up, the technology used was called perfusion, where the cells are retained within the bioreactor and the product is harvested. The industrial pioneer and user of this technology in those days was Centocor, which used it to make Remicade, a blockbuster rheumatoid arthritis drug, today sold by Johnson & Johnson after it acquired Centocor in 1999. So there was technological precedence globally, but in India, there were only novices. 'In biologics, we had the first-mover disadvantage, we could not poach from any company,' says Tambe.

Kiran also leveraged the ₹100-crore investment committed to the Cuban joint venture and built a common filling line for both insulin and antibodies. Until then, vials for insulin were outsourced.

The Biocon Park tested the project execution ability of many. Ravindra K.C. remembers being told 'just about the turnover Biocon would like to make from the plant', without any specifics on the products. 'How to achieve that was my role. I decided what I wanted. Kiran believed in her people and let them have a free hand.'

But she kept a tight control on the aesthetics, as she does today with an effortless recall of where each painting is placed. She went back to Yusuf Arakkal. She had first bought his painting, for ₹300, at an exhibition at Windsor Manor in 1989. For the second one, which she picked up from his studio when it was still wet, she paid three instalments of ₹1,000 each. As her business grew, she began commissioning his works. For the Park, she raised the bar and commissioned a large mural. 'Most business heads interfere with their commission, but not Kiran. After initial suggestions, she does not interfere. But she has her taste, you cannot sell a work of art to her unless she likes it. Harsh [Goenka of the RPG Group] is another corporate head whom you cannot force to buy,' says Arakkal.

Lavishing the buildings, walls and campuses with paintings – her collection numbers close to 1,800 – and sculpture pays off in most unexpected ways. In an inspection by the Japanese regulatory agency in 2014, the inspector was wowed by Arakkal's impressive mural. He told Sandeep Rao he had never seen a manufacturing facility which had granite flooring and murals. The visual elegance of the place stayed with him.

Kiran with her parents, Yamini and Rasendra Mazumdar, in 1955.

With her college mates at the University of Ballarat, Australia, in 1974.

Taking a break from work, with Pratima Rao and friends in 1979.

Kiran at the Biocon campus construction site in 1982.

Kiran (second from left) at the Biocon campus inauguration in 1983.

Having a good time with Biocon colleagues in 1983.

At work, cleaning fish maws at the plant in 1984.

Receiving the Padma Shri from the President of India, R. Venkataraman in 1989.

With Gordon Ringold at Syngene's inauguration in 1994.

Photo courtesy: S. Anand Kumar

Prime Minister Rajiv Gandhi inaugurating the Astra Research Centre in Bangalore in 1987, with (left to right) Sivaraj Ramaseshan, Janakiraman Ramachandran and S. Anand Kumar.

With Leslie Auchincloss in 1998.

When Nobel laureate James Watson visited Biocon in 1999.

With a copy of her colourfully illustrated book, *Ale & Arty*, on the history of beer, published in 2001.

With husband John Shaw at their home in Bengaluru in 1999.

At the groundbreaking ceremony of the insulin plant in 2001.

At an event to mark Biocon's listing on the stock exchange on 7 April 2004.

Receiving the Padma Bhushan from the President of India, Dr A.P.J. Abdul Kalam in 2005.

With the senior Shaws at Glenmore in Bengaluru in 2005.

With film stars Shah Rukh Khan and Waheeda Rehman at the launch of BIOMAb, a cancer drug, in Bengaluru in 2006.

With her two brothers and their families in 2008.

With US President Barack Obama, Indian Prime Minister Manmohan Singh and several Indian corporate leaders at the CEO Forum in New Delhi in 2010.

With John Shaw at the Malaysian insulin facility's traditional groundbreaking ceremony in 2011.

When Nobel laureate Kurt Wüthrich inaugurated the Biocon Research Centre in Bengaluru in 2012.

With former Irish president Mary Robinson after receiving the honorary doctorate at Trinity College, Dublin, in 2012.

An aerial view of Biocon Park located in the Bommasandra Industrial Area, Bengaluru.

With Devi Shetty (extreme right), Nobel laureate Harold Varmus and Paul Salins (extreme left) at the inauguration of the Mazumdar-Shaw Centre for Translational Research in Bengaluru in 2014.

At the christening of Mazumdar Drive at Ballarat in Australia in 2015.

6

START-UP BECOMES A CORPORATE

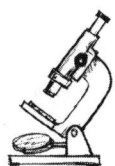

The Trigger

Once the Unilever hangover was behind her, Kiran's scramble for capital started again. Lovastatin was growing reasonably well in the labs and it needed a place of its own – in a large submerged fermenter. With no bank willing to lend, she called Kashyap for raising money. 'Can I see the business plan?' he asked. 'What business plan?' she snapped. 'I know there's a huge potential in statins; we have cracked it but I need money to build a plant.'

Kashyap went around selling the idea. A California fund, DLG, which showed interest with a cool shrug – 'Of course we understand biotech, we are from the Bay Area' – discussed the term sheet but did not honour the commitment. Mumbai's Infrastructure and Leasing Financial Services too shied away over some minor issue. The saviour was ICICI Ventures, which, in its earlier lending avatar of TDICI, had already invested in Biocon and this time it came around once again with $4 million for a share of 20 per cent. The understanding was that the private equity would get an exit in five to seven years, either through a public offering or some secondary route that would yield at least 25 per cent return.

In a storied corporate shuffle, most of the top management at ICICI Ventures left in 2001. Renuka Ramnath took the leadership position that Nitin Deshmukh had vacated but she seemed to carry the rumble to Biocon, and into its board meetings. Once seated at the table, she did not like how business was conducted, particularly how the chairman of the audit committee, Neville Bain, oversaw matters.

Soon after taking charge at ICICI Ventures, Ramnath also invested in a freshly minted biotech, Avesthagen, started by an agriculture scientist, Villoo Morawala-Patell, and would often compare the two Bengaluru women entrepreneurs at Biocon meetings. 'She thought I did not know how to run the company or report numbers. She would tell me, "I think you are not very intelligent, Villoo is much smarter. I am on the board of these two companies and I can see the difference. You watch it, Villoo will overtake you," recalls Kiran.

*

Investors can push a company on to the most adventurous paths. By 2002, Biocon began to understand that. Ramnath wanted an exit; Kiran, not having got along particularly well with her, was keen to oblige when one of the former's third-party buyers got Deutsche Bank to evaluate the deal but did not eventually buy. Once again, the onus fell on Kashyap, who was by then a partner at a boutique investment bank, Allegro Capital, to look for an investor. This time it wasn't hard for him. Biocon's growth story was emerging – insulin and novel molecule programmes had taken root and revenues were growing rapidly on the back of statins which were selling at ridiculously high margins – never known before and never to be heard of later.

Meanwhile, Kiran's vision had become grander with the Biocon

Park, but she did not want to run the private equity gauntlet again. Going to the stock market was the only option and the board began to discuss it in all earnestness. That made it easier for Kashyap as he went back to the American International Group (AIG) which had earlier refused investment because they did not understand biotech. 'I told them that this time they must invest. They agreed for two reasons: one, the company would go public; two, they said that since they did not understand the story, they would want a "downside protection", a "clause to protect their principal",' said Kashyap. Finding a middle ground, he said Biocon promoters would give downside protection but the American investor would have to give 'upside protection', which meant if the investor made any money, it would be shared with the promoters.

This says something about the cult of private equity and the legendary appetites of this risk-faring tribe. Here was a seller who knew the company was to go public, yet wanted to exit. And there was a buyer, who, knowing that a public offering was in the works, wanted its principal protected.

Both had their wishes fulfilled. Ramnath exited with 156 per cent return when American International Group scooped up 10 per cent of the company in 2003 along with Gary Wendt Capital, now called India Value Fund, which took a minority stake in one of its first India investments. (If Ramnath had stayed until the public offering, she would have made sixtyfold returns.)

Around the same time, Kiran went on a branding blitzkrieg. The tagline 'Working with Nature' was dumped. She wanted to move from something that made Biocon seem like an Ayurvedic company to something that was in vogue, even scientifically. For the rebranding, she wanted the chic branding and design consulting firm in the city, Ray+Keshavan (now part of Brand Union of WPP), but in an odd coincidence, its founder Sujata Keshavan had just taken on Avesthagen as a client and could not sign up Biocon due to conflict of interest. From among some experienced agencies,

Kiran finally chose tsk Design. A few years earlier, in 1999, she had given its founder Tania Khosla her first break when she was setting up a design studio; but all she had then by way of portfolio was some academic work from her master's programme at Yale University but no real work for clients.

In her second coming, though, Khosla had an interesting challenge. She had seen the enzyme business, she had watched the early pharmaceutical business take off, but the brief she got from Kiran – 'We want to be one of the top ten biotech companies of the world' – was way beyond anything her creative eye could foresee. 'It was a huge leap in every sense of the term. We had to come up with a future-proof brand; it had to look like a global biotech which could be from any geography. We had to capture the DNA of the company because, however sophisticated the technology might get, a biotech will always work with the genetic material,' said Khosla. After several months, she came up with the idea of 'Dynalix–Dynamic helix', because 'Biocon derives from Kiran's personality which is dynamic, bold and agile'. The double-stranded DNA structure became the corporate logo, with a strap – The Difference Lies in Our DNA.

Governance in Place

Among other things, Kiran needed a heavyweight board of directors for the IPO.

At a wedding reception at Taj Westend Hotel in Bengaluru in 2013, Kiran and Shaw met Suresh Talwar, held his hand, and they made him promise that he would come on board when the company went public. A seasoned corporate lawyer, Talwar had served on multiple boards, including a few pharmaceutical companies and the textile company Madura Coats where Shaw was the managing director. Importantly, he had seen the listing of pharmaceutical companies like Merck, Glaxo, Burroughs and Solvay on Indian bourses. Talwar had also guided Kiran when she was negotiating a buyout of Unilever-ICI shares and knew her well – well enough to notice that 'she did everything in style'. 'She is an unusual Gujarati in that sense,' he joked.

After securing Talwar, she turned to Charles Cooney, who, even as an academic at MIT had been swift in taking biotech discoveries into new manufacturing processes. As an industry-inclined professor, he was associated with Genentech for the first full decade of its existence and later, in 1982, he was involved in the founding of another biotech legend, Genzyme, where he continued as a director for the next thirty years.

'Since I was deeply involved in the American biotech industry, I could see some parallels. The way Biocon was evolving, it was similar to Genzyme, which was more of a manufacturing company making drug substances for rare diseases, and not an early-stage discovery company,' Cooney recounted. Coming from MIT – where students and professors off- or on-campus never tire of stressing that the 'T' in their institution's name stands for 'technology' – Cooney would prove to be an anchor resource. Biocon was building on technology-driven innovation, rather than the discovery-driven science of Western biotechs. During the Plafractor development days, he would grill Shri and Tambe, but also back them when the board would debate or be divided over sharing the always scarce funds for research.

In addition, Cooney had the experience of corporate governance, so he joined the Biocon board as a non-executive, independent director. In his decade-plus association with Biocon until then, he had found 'there was always the excitement of a new thing, new opportunities'. 'What was clever was to go to Cuba, which nobody else in the world could do. I had been in Cuba in the early 1990s and had seen what the country had done in spite of the American embargo. We were all cheering for her then,' recalls Cooney.

From the promoter's side, it was brother Ravi and sister-in-law

Catherine Rosenberg on two board seats. 'I don't think we are on the board because of our understanding of life sciences. We are very clear and Kiran is very clear about that too. We sit as observers and give our honest opinion,' says Rosenberg, who considers it is her 'role in life to tell Kiran the truth', which, after 2004, extended to the boardroom too.

A professor at the Waterloo University in Canada, Rosenberg works with telecom companies in France and the United States as a specialist in wireline and wireless networking and knows how boards, certainly the scientific ones, work. 'You have to know who was going beyond their call of duty and so you also have to know why you want them,' she says in her casual, no-nonsense way. Which is why even outside the board, she is the messenger. 'Anybody in the family wanting to tell Kiran something tough or unpleasant will ask me to break the news.'

Over time, theirs became a role of more than just loyal observers. Being top-notch academics – both are fellows of the Institute of Electrical and Electronics Engineers – and having lived in different countries, they nudged Kiran and the senior management to think about corporate issues in a societal context. When at times the company got too focused on its strategy in the United States, Ravi got it to rethink the 'fixation of being validated by America'. 'There are so many other markets where Biocon can make a difference,' he said. Recognizably French (his wife, Rosenberg, is French and so are his mathematician collaborators), Ravi's approach made business sense as regulated markets dragged their feet on biosimilars regulation.

Along with the board of directors, Kiran assembled some luminaries for a scientific advisory board. Some were figureheads, like the highly decorated Chintamani Nagesa Ramachandra Rao, who, though a fountain of chemistry know-how, hardly had any interest in pharmaceuticals. Others like Anthony Allison, inventor of the immunosuppressant micophenolate mofetil, added pomp to the product portfolio of Biocon, one of the few generics manufacturers to make the full range of anti-transplant rejection drugs. However, there was one scientific advisor who turned out to be unique: later in the year, Bala Manian was inducted as an additional director to the board.

In the mid-1990s, ICICI's Vaghul introduced his brother Manian to some eminent industrialists and executives like Ratan Tata, Azim Premji, Hindustan Unilever's Ashok Ganguly and others in the hope that Manian, a successful entrepreneur in California who had built and sold multiple companies, would find a reason compelling enough to develop some technology in India. Kiran was one of Vaghul's hopes, and as it turned out, the only one who struck up a formal and long-term relationship with Manian.

After selling his first company in 1984 to Matrix Corp, Manian thought he had so much money, he could retire. So, for the next three years, in return for co-investing opportunities, he did consulting for three venture capitalists in California and one of the investments he made was in Amgen, along with a few other companies in life sciences. Most of his biology learning was self-taught, though he had an advantage – he was married to a physician. 'I still have my chart of Amgen stock appreciation – sixtyfold between 1985 and 2005. That's what patience is,' he said. Other than the life sciences investing connection, it was his own inventive career and technology tinkering in Silicon Valley garages that Kiran found useful, even inspirational. Manian had worked with the first three employees of Pixar – the pioneering computer animation film studio that Steve Jobs acquired for $10 million and, years later, sold to Disney for $7.4 billion – where he invented special effects technology that got him an Oscar, a technical achievement award from the Academy of Motion Pictures Arts and Sciences.

Through the life cycle of Pixar, closely watching Jobs infuse life into the start-up, Manian learnt 'you have to give breathing space for innovation to happen'. At Biocon, he ensured he was Kiran's 'co-conspirator' in carving out that breathing space.

The IPO

Biocon's story certainly intrigued investors: a brewer, who had built a fermentation-based enzyme and a pharmaceutical business, possessed complex-sounding genetic engineering technologies which she was using to make insulin and antibodies, with no precedent in India. 'I never thought [I was the first woman entrepreneur taking her company public], I was too busy meeting investors and telling them we had a unique path forward,' recalls Kiran.

The insulin plant which was going to be Asia's largest – and capable of meeting five times the country's insulin demand – was nearly ready. A mammalian cell culture plant would follow since the agreement with the Cubans was in place and an antibody drug – anti-Epidermal Growth Factor Receptor – was under clinical development in Bengaluru. Fittingly, at the intellectual property cell, Anindya Sircar was furiously filing hundreds of patent applications. For investors, a recombinant DNA story was being scripted right here in India.

Syngene and Clinigene were strong subplots in the Biocon story. And if anyone doubted the integration of manufacturing, contract research and clinical services, Kiran had a slide in her PowerPoint presentation on the depth of the management team. It ended with: 'What keeps everything together: Biocon Culture. Our greatest competitive advantage is the culture developed over twenty-five years.'

There were no major fireworks in the road shows; if anything, brokers and investors were curious about India's first biotech, as the conventional biotech in the United States, always the biggest market, was hardly the hybrid model of managed risk that Biocon was describing itself as. Outside India, she met investors in Singapore, London, Zurich and three cities in the United States. Existing investor AIG had introduced her to their likely investors – Goldman Sachs being one who eventually bought AIG shares. At the end of it, she pulled off a breezy global whirligig.

Fifteen per cent of the company was kept aside for employees and in employee stock option trust, while Kiran and Shaw held on to 68 per cent. (Shaw sold some of his shares later when foreign institutional investors complained that there wasn't enough free float in the market.)

Before Biocon, a few technology companies – Infosys, Mindtree, Mphasis – had gone public, so Kiran found 'a lot of energy in Bengaluru'. 'I said to myself, "If these companies can do it, I can also do it." Going to the capital market was better than borrowing,' she says. Particularly notable then was Infosys Technologies which, after going public nearly a decade earlier, had turned out to be the sleekest wealth-creation machine in Indian corporate history. For her, N.R. Narayana Murthy and his co-founders were an inspiration on more counts than one. Infosys's initial public offering had devolved – it was the American investment banker Morgan Stanley which bailed the information technology services company out from being undersubscribed. So she sought Murthy's advice. He, at the time, wanted to induct her into the Infosys board, but she was too busy, and he waited, until 2011, when he ensured that she was in before he got out of Infosys. Murthy told her: 'Have eight very strong profitable quarters and when you know you can keep delivering on those quarters, only then go to the market.' That became her guiding principle.

When it came to employee rewards, the core team, particularly those who had stuck together for two decades, became reasonably rich, whereas among the rest, more than 50 per cent got shares. Biocon did not emulate Infosys in giving stock options like confetti, it was broad-based allotment, depending as much on the number of years people had served in the company as on the position they held.

Through his prism of Western experience, where employee stock options are not given across the board and are rather used as a retention tool for key management, Shaw found Infosys-style distribution of stock options as a fad of the time from a company which had a more socialist view. (When I asked Murthy in 2015, whether he regretted distributing so much equity at Infosys, he said, 'My regret is that many of them did not deserve it, but that does not mean that the principle itself is not right. I come from a socialist background and when I turned to capitalism, I became a compassionate capitalist. We gave, excluding the so-called co-founders, 35 per cent of equity which is worth $11-12 billion today. Never in the history of India has it happened and I don't think it will ever happen again.')

On his part, Shaw adopted a standard approach, designing a reward and retention scheme for people who were driving the business. 'Our definition of manager then was broad; with time we have narrowed it,' he says. All employees, right from the top management down to the supervisor level, received stock options. 'Many came and thanked me, saying they could repay their loan with this money. I had to clarify that the company had given them options, not me,' says Bharadwaj. 'Kiran asked us to recommend people, we did, and she allotted. It was very egalitarian.'

She made some 'allotment' herself too. 'During my visits to [the stock broking company] Karvy in Mumbai, I had it in mind that I have to play this joke on my friends. They said they had applied for Biocon's shares but all was left to chance. So I asked Karvy for a sample allotment letter, saying I wanted it as a souvenir. Susan and I worked on it, made sure it looked authentic and made a few fake allotment letters. I couriered them to my friends so that they would receive the letters on 1 April. They were all very happy but by evening, I told them, "I hope you've realized it's April Fools' Day,"' she laughs.

When the issue opened, investors bet the jockey *and* the horse. The country's first biotech offering got oversubscribed thirty-three times, within five minutes of the issue opening. On 7 April, the first day of trading, the scrip's price zipped past ₹500 to finally close at ₹435, an impressive 52 per cent premium on the offer price of ₹315. Biocon was valued at $1.1 billion. At the celebration party at Taj Mahal hotel in Mumbai, one guest was conspicuously gracious – Renuka Ramnath.

It was a billionaire moment: Kiran became India's first self-made billionaire, in rupee terms; the dollar billionaire tag came later. The title sat uneasy on her conscience – it still does – as she would repeat, 'Biocon is not about personal wealth creation but intellectual wealth creation', almost like a slogan, in several media interviews in the months to follow.

Yet, for all apparent modesty, new wealth liberated the company in many ways. For the first time in its history, in July 2004, Biocon paid dividends to its shareholders. Her long-time colleagues became rich too, each one by upwards of $10 million. Kiran gave up her white Daewoo Cielo for her first 'foreign' car, a silver-grey Mercedes S-Class. More than managing wealth, or the notion of being wealthy, what was hard was the frigid realization that now she would have to restrain her speech about company affairs. For someone as reflexively open as Kiran, it was a Herculean task. As the year ended, on a day of peculiar splendour, she called her friend Meeru Pai and said, 'See, I've learnt to keep my mouth shut [about Biocon affairs].'

The spectacular stock market debut placed Biocon alongside top-ranking pharmaceutical stocks. Market watchers clubbed it with Ranbaxy, Dr Reddy's, Cipla and Sun, even though, in the run-up to the public offering, Kiran and Bharadwaj had consciously avoided being called 'just another pharma company', deliberately clinging to the biotech tag. The ranking was more a media and analyst creation than the company's declaration, and it would come to bite them later, when the same analysts would compare its market capitalization with that of other pharma companies.

Battle for Insulin

Soon after going public, just when Biocon was getting ready to launch its insulin in India, the first branded formulation for the company, a Press Trust of India (PTI) report carried by many newspapers on 23 August 2004, shocked people. The report quoted the environment ministry's Genetic Engineering Approval Committee's response to a public interest litigation filed by a Mumbai NGO which said 'deaths occurred in clinical trials of genetically engineered drugs'. It implicated Biocon and Shantha Biotechnics for their recombinant human insulin and streptokinase, respectively.

It did not shock Kiran as much as it did others because the petition had been filed much earlier, just a week before the public issue opened on 9 March 2004 when she was in London. She had received a call from the Securities and Exchange Board of India (SEBI) which demanded clarification. In panic, she had called Raghunath Mashelkar for help. He was travelling from Delhi to Pune on that day but managed to fax a letter to the stock market regulator clarifying that all Central government clearances had been granted. Yet, to have a public response of that kind from the Genetic Engineering Approval Committee was strange. When the trade magazine *BioSpectrum* investigated the case later that year, it found a Mumbai organization – Adar Destitute and Old People Home – to be behind the PIL. It had an equally dubious existence with the official trustees turning out to be fictitious characters or proxies for some unknown corporate rival. But what was surprising, rather sinister, was that the 100-odd pages of the petition had well-researched references to the regulatory processes involving half a dozen government agencies, an understanding which could only be associated with people active in the life sciences industry.

Who could have benefited by blocking Biocon's public offering or delaying its insulin launch in India is an unsolved mystery, but its legal tentacles have not eased around on Biocon, even a decade later.

Emerging from a very public distraction, in November, Biocon launched its recombinant human insulin, branded as Insugen, a good ten months after Wockhardt had launched its product called Wosulin. Even though it was made by licensing the production technology from Germany's Rhein Biotech, which used a different yeast expression system – *Hansenula polymorpha* – Wockhardt managed to steal the show. 'This is a technology breakthrough not only for Wockhardt but also for India. Worldwide, there are only three manufacturers of recombinant human insulin. Wockhardt is proud to have put India on the global map,' Wockhardt chairman Habil Khorakiwala, had said at a press conference in 2003.

Still, when Biocon entered the market, it had girded up for competition with innovator companies – Novo Nordisk and Eli Lilly – and not a local manufacturer. Pre-emptively, before Wosulin's launch, the multinationals had slashed the human insulin price by nearly a third. So the real battle would wage between Novo Nordisk and Biocon in doctors' clinics. Since insulin was not covered by insurance – it still isn't – each prescription had to be earned.

Before insulin, Biocon had sold bulk pharmaceutical ingredients to pharma companies; Bharadwaj now had to create a new marketing infrastructure for a consumer business. He was caught between a rock and a hard place – Novo Nordisk had been selling insulin for decades and was entrenched in India; Wockhardt, on the other hand, was game for a price war. Bharadwaj wanted to be in between and was clear that Insugen would not be differentiated only on price, though it was 25 per cent cheaper than the innovators' product.

'Our story was good to some extent, we had the doctors' attention,' recalls Bharadwaj. 'I have to admit, it was a tough market. It is a prescription drug and doctors who have to prescribe it have a long-standing relationship with companies like Novo and Lilly, who would have trained them, taken them to international conferences and medical education programmes. So there's intense loyalty to these big companies who have a complete lock on these drugs.'

Biocon managed to break that lock to some extent. Initially, it only had basic insulin whereas innovators had begun pushing formulations and long-lasting insulin. Its first full year of sales in 2006 amounted to ₹15.5 crore, which was more than anything the company had sold in its first year after statins. Competition was giving insulin pens free, even Wockhardt launched its own pen, but Biocon had no pens; it chose to pace itself. Then in 2006, Wockhardt received a body blow. On consumer complaints, the drug regulator in Maharashtra asked it to withdraw Wosulin from the state. Biocon's market share grew as Wosulin – mischievously referred to by some within Biocon as Woesulin – got mired in quality checks. It aggressively adopted a patient-centric approach, even launching new dosage forms, of 3 ml and 5 ml, which were not sold by anyone anywhere. More than a decade later, in 2015, Bamzai, who keeps packs of Insugen and related products at his workplace, gets excited by how engaging with patients earned Biocon goodwill.

In the US market, Abhijit Zutshi, who was selling diversified pharmaceutical ingredients, broke into a small but niche insulin market which was until then dominated by Novo Nordisk – insulin for cell culture, where it is used as growth hormone. It signed a pact with Invitrogen Corp., to market insulin to the global cell culture market. As insulin in the developed markets moved to veterinary use, so did Biocon's supply to brand manufacturers. It kept finding new avenues.

Even then, by 2009, Insugen had peaked and stagnated in the Indian market. The diabetes market was undergoing a shift. New oral products were arriving and older ones, like pioglitazone, suffered a severe price drop. When new oral drugs arrive, insulin gets pushed for later because general physicians, who treat a large number of patients in India apart from specialists, want to keep the hassle of insulin management at bay. It's the specialists who understand, better than physicians, that initiating insulin treatment early in the diagnosis can result in better outcomes. Understandably, the human insulin business took a hit; Insugen needed a shot in its arm.

The Flashpoint

Biocon's corporate team needed one too.

'Kiran is accommodative. You will have to look hard to find a harsh decision she's taken,' claimed Raizada, who, as Ranbaxy henchman, knew her well and served with her on government committees. But it isn't hard to find; she took one in 2006.

As revenues, pressure and the product mix grew, Bharadwaj's big-picture yang and Bamzai's nuts-and-bolts yin – which brought terrific growth from 2001 to 2005 – started losing their magic. In the role of marketing head, Bharadwaj complemented Bamzai, a salesman to boot, who lived out of a suitcase for days together. This would often get his father nervous and make him walk up to Krishnan who lived in the same complex, and ask: 'Where is my son?' Bamzai, who would rustle up sales numbers before quarterly closing, had restless energy running through his veins. Bharadwaj, meanwhile, used to play golf and had a relaxed air about him.

But those complementary skills soon became alter egos – same company, same responsibilities and competing ambitions. If Bharadwaj owed his cool competitive spirit to his parents' migration from Pakistan, Bamzai credited his army-school training in Kashmir for his fierce focus. He was, in his own words, 'heavy-lifting the business'. He would often bypass Bharadwaj and discuss matters directly with Kiran, who, if she did not encourage it, did not discourage him from undermining his boss either.

Those days, corporate culture was not well ingrained, protocols were just taking root. One day, Kiran was meeting a candidate for a senior marketing role and had asked Arvind Atignal to pick up the potential hire on his way to work. During the drive, the candidate asked Atignal, 'Whom do you report to?' As they neared the Biocon campus, Atignal responded with his typical dry humour: 'Well, first I report to the security; then I report to the receptionist (a person with weak eyesight to whom everyone made their presence felt by saying their names aloud); and then I report to Kiran.' The visitor was psyched; he never took the job offer.

More seriously, Kiran was in a fix. Apart from the quarterly pressure, the company was facing the Chinese wall. Manufacturers from China had flooded the market with cheap statins and prices crashed in no time. Lovastatin, which was selling for $2,000 a kilo, dropped to $400; Simvastatin dropped from $10,000 to $2,000. Biocon had to fortify its capacity and significantly reduce cost of operations to stay afloat.

In the midst of all this, Suresh Talwar, who was on the board of Merck, told her that Merck Serono's senior management officials were visiting India and wanted to meet her and invest in Biocon. Thinking that a large family-owned company's investment in Biocon could prove strategic as the Biocon Park loomed ahead, Kiran agreed to begin discussions. After the first meeting at the expensive Laguna Beach Hotel in California in 2006, Kiran, Shaw and Bharadwaj visited Merck's headquarters in Germany. 'We had multiple discussions. They wanted to take 10 per cent of the company and then gradually increase it to 51 per cent. They offered me a board position in Merck Serono and said they would make sure I ran Biocon comfortably,' Kiran says. The maximum she was willing to sell was 15 per cent, which, for a listed company, was the standard limit. She was not interested in selling her stake. Between husband and wife she wanted to keep 51 per cent of Biocon, but the German company said its board would not allow the investment unless they had the controlling stake. The talks ended there.

Meanwhile, the bickerings between Ajay Bharadwaj and Rakesh Bamzai spilled over into mundane affairs. On Biocon Day, (29 November), when the annual performance awards were given, the two would ask human resources head Nirupa Bareja for multiple score revisions so that the winner came from their team. As the squabbles became more public, Kiran saw it was poisoning the atmosphere, forcing junior-level employees to take sides. Eventually, when Bamzai marched up to Kiran a few times, offering to resign, she had a discussion with each of them separately where Bharadwaj made it clear she would have to choose one over the other. She tried to resolve it by offering him the top position at Syngene but he refused, saying he did not understand the contract research business. Instead, Bharadwaj proposed a management buyout of the enzyme business where he would 'backend the payment'. By then, enzymes were a slowing business for Biocon and the company was already talking to potential buyers for divestment. To agree to Bharadwaj's proposal would mean eroding significant shareholder value. 'I could not play to his emotional expectations, he was not being practical,' she said.

Two days after that discussion, everyone in Biocon received an email informing them that the business division was being divided into two – Bharadwaj would be responsible for enzymes and formulations, Bamzai would lead the pharmaceutical division.

'This decision is not acceptable. After so many years, if I have to learn this from an email, rather than from you, it means indirectly you are telling me I am not required,' Bharadwaj told her and walked out of Biocon.

'It all came to a point when I had to choose between the two and I chose Rakesh. Ajay holds that against me. He considered himself an integral part of Biocon and he's right. But enzymes was a sunset business for us,' says Kiran.

Analysing it later, Bharadwaj felt that Kiran must have held one of his earlier career moves against him. In the late 1990s, when

Reliance Industries was starting its life sciences business, it tried to lure him with a fourfold jump in his salary. Bharadwaj broke the news to Kiran saying, 'It's too good an offer to refuse'. 'She asked, "How could you even think of any other place, you are a founding member of this company," but he insisted that Mukesh Ambani had asked him to join Reliance Life Sciences. I told him how shattered I was,' Kiran recounts.

The senior management had an all-hands-but-one meeting at her residence where Bamzai assured everyone that Bharadwaj would stay on; it was just a passing phase. Bharadwaj did stay on, until that day in April 2006 when Kiran chose to secure her company's position. 'It was a mistake on my part. Either I should have left or kept quiet,' he says, referring to the Reliance offer.

Bharadwaj's exit came as a rude shock to many. He was a popular manager and some felt a combination of him, a suave extroverted marketer, and Chandavarkar, an efficient introverted problem solver, would have given Biocon the right successor to Kiran. Except, that even for a biotech company, making such a recombinant manager was not possible.

After the showdown, as Bharadwaj was leaving, Ganesh Sambasivam walked into his room. 'What will you do now?' he asked. 'I don't know, maybe improve my golf,' Bharadwaj replied. Sambasivam proposed to start a contract research business which he understood well as the chief scientific officer at Syngene where, he thought, he was increasingly becoming the 'chief apology officer'. 'There was a lot of pressure to compress timelines. In 1994, when we started, people were patient when we showed our delay with supplies; by 2000, nobody had the patience. Syngene did not have a purchase department and going through Biocon's purchase department was constraining,' he explains. Both the companies had grown to such a size that turning around processes was glacial. A separate purchase department with enough buying power had to be created; it was, but after Sambasivam's departure. By then he was kicked about the idea of entrepreneurship and he called Ravindra in the production division, who agreed to join them in a jiffy.

'In services, clients look for differentiated offerings. If you keep offering the same thing year after year, you get marginalized. I wanted to be more creative,' said Sambasivam. 'To be able to do something new at Syngene was becoming difficult, considering how the sales target was going up every year. We were basically fighting fire. The leadership, in principle, understood that more resources needed to be infused and somebody had to implement it.'

A soft-spoken scientist, Sambasivam never found himself at the receiving end of Kiran's occasional outbursts. 'She believed in everyone she selected. Many companies develop a parallel system to drive home the point that either you deliver or the other person takes the lead. That never happened here,' he reasons. Entrepreneurship seemed desirable; he was ready to feel his oats.

That marked the first high-level group – if the threesome can be called one – exodus from Biocon. The small organization that thrived on interpersonal vitality was now bigger, processes were in place which slowed things down, and systemic checks and balances left little room for decisions to be made on 'gut feeling', no matter who that gut belonged to. Ironically, Bharadwaj, who had refused the Syngene leadership position, set out to found a contract research services company, Anthem Biosciences. He also lured away a 'few tens' of people from Biocon and Syngene, including some well-established professionals.

A few months later, it was Shri's turn. As someone who liked exploring new ideas and believed R&D was the 'toughest sales job', he sold his exit plan rather directly and swiftly. 'I've always had a blast in Biocon, but now I am not enjoying what I am doing,' he told Kiran. It was the time when lovastatin was fading and programmes like the Biocon Park and clinical trials were guzzling most resources. The enzyme company that Shri had joined had become a biopharmaceutical company. 'Research and development not only faced a space crunch – their separate building was inaugurated in 2012, which ideally should have happened three to four years earlier – they also had less money to push the frontier. We had to squeeze ourselves and that was a realm less exciting for someone like me,' Shri said. He left in 2007 but stayed in an advisory role for two more years. He took on a government assignment in Delhi for some time before reverting to his first love, enzymes, by founding Sea6 Energy to make biofuel from seaweeds.

This period when two key members of the first management team left in quick succession was a trying time for Kiran. Once again, Manian was by her side and he interacted with both. 'People cannot differentiate between a project failure and personal failure. Shri was not happy when he left but he differentiated it as a personal failure. The job had outgrown him. But Ajay could not differentiate between the project and personal failure. Organizationally, things needed to change at Biocon,' Manian said.

A month before Shri left, Biocon sold its enzyme business to Novozymes for $115 million. The Danish enzyme leader was paying for the market share in India, the only place where it operated as number two. Because by then, Biocon, apart from its own prized pectinases and other enzymes, was sourcing raw material from major companies like Genencor, DSM, and Finsugar to control the Indian market. It was an I-know-it-when-I-see-it moment for Kiran. All the years of investment in intellectual property was paying off. With this deal, Novozymes eliminated competition, even though it had to shed an overlapping distribution network which was later acquired by Anthem. The sale gave Biocon enough cash to fund its joint venture with Cuba's Centre of Genetic Engineering and Biotechnology to build the mammalian cell manufacturing facility – Biocon Biopharmaceuticals Private Limited.

CELEBRITY STARDUST ON A BIOLOGIC

The first product of that manufacturing facility was rather special, especially its launch.

On 17 September 2006, Bollywood superstar Shah Rukh Khan was at his emotional best. As he spoke about his father's death from cancer in the 1990s when drugs weren't very effective, some doctors in the audience cried, a few others had resentment writ large on their faces. A heavy smoker was launching a drug for head and neck cancer at the Leela Palace in Bengaluru. But it was a conscious star cast by Biocon: the contrast couldn't be starker, nor the brand recalls any better. For the actor, it was about lending his star appeal to innovation and not about an endorsement fee, which he did not take. The drug was Biocon's first monoclonal antibody BIOMAb for treating solid tumours of epithelial origin. It could be used in a number of indications but Biocon chose head and neck cancer which has been a dominant cancer in the Indian subcontinent, owing its morbidity to tobacco-chewing habits.

Subir Basak, who was driving the launch, had been part of a global drug launch team at Amgen in the US when Kiran spotted him. At a Confederation of Indian Industry (CII) symposium in New Delhi in 2003, both were speakers. In his session, Basak spoke about the launch of Amgen's Neulasta, a long-acting pegylated filgrastim used to boost white blood cells in cancer patients. The drug had grossed one billion dollars in just twelve to fourteen months. For an Indian audience, such a conversation on the launch of a drug was impressive, even rare. Basak answered a lot of questions that day, particularly from students in the room. 'It was so warm and nice, I got swept away,' he recalls.

Kiran stayed connected with Basak, pursuing him for nearly two years before he agreed to come back to India. In the beginning, she didn't know where to place him, so he did investor relations for a few months, jazzing up her presentations and sharpening the

Biocon story before she asked him to create a new business unit for monoclonal antibodies. He took the most clinically advanced molecule, BIOMAb, which had been licensed from Cuba a while ago but was lying dormant for want of commercial attention, and started Phase II studies in India. The idea was to pitch it directly against the competitor's product in the market, Merck's Erbitux, and show non-inferiority – in the same manner that Biocon's insulin was directly compared with Novo's insulin, showing that structurally and functionally, Insugen was similar.

Atignal at Clinigene helped design a clinical trial that was suited for Indian conditions. The standard care in head and neck cancer is radiotherapy and chemotherapy, to which doctors add antibody therapy if and when the patient can afford it. The nutritional condition in Indian patients is such that they cannot stand chemotherapy alone. The rival Erbitux was not expected to be combined with the standard of care; it was approved only along with radiation. A cancer registry, on the lines of the earlier diabetes registry, was set up. 'Indian doctors hardly get to see, let alone generate, Indian data. So when we gave them a chance, some of them were very interested,' said Basak. Tactically, the clinical team designed four arms of the trial: radiotherapy; radiotherapy plus chemotherapy; radiotherapy plus chemotherapy plus antibody; radiotherapy plus antibody.

To do a head-to-head comparison in a relatively small sample of patients was a risky approach. Basak looked for examples abroad and made the regulators of different countries talk to each other to harmonize the rules. There was a 'night-and-day' difference between what he did at Amgen and what he was doing in Biocon. Those were crazy times with crazier commitments. He recruited a bunch of people from Dabur (then a company with deep oncology talent), Sun Pharma, Dr Reddy's and a few multinational companies, and built a team.

In its first year, BIOMAb netted more than anybody within the company had imagined. With it, Basak built the oncology franchise by licensing another drug, Abraxane, from the American company Abraxis. He would not talk much about his strategy, which he likes comparing to 'grandma's recipes, a bunch of things which nobody can copy', but he brought the zest and understanding of scientific marketing to Biocon.

The competition would tell patients that getting skin rashes was a sign that the drug was working and since Biocon's drug did not give rashes, it meant the drug was a dud. But the fact was that BIOMAb *was* a better molecule, a humanized antibody, so it had fewer side effects like rashes than Erbitux, which was a chimeric antibody with genetic material sourced partly from humans, partly from mice.

'We gave the explanation at a molecular level about how humanization impacted the binding of the molecule to the skin receptor, which decided whether the patient would get a rash or not. We explained the engineering at length,' says Praveen Bose, who worked with Basak.

But the early win couldn't be sustained. For the sales division, Basak's first full-year sales of ₹14.5 crore was probably not even a topping on the ₹1,000-crore revenue pie. 'Nobody was interested in BIOMAb. We were a minority in that group,' recalled Basak in early 2015, when he was with Jubilant Life Sciences. Sales was quintessential; strategy just a passing reference in the business division in those days. It was the phase when Biocon was transforming from an active pharmaceutical business – which is all about disposing what you have – to the branded formulations business – which is all about marketing and generating a need. Bamzai and Basak had different business development styles and the latter, even though he admitted he had learnt the 'basics of sales from Bamzai', felt 'he would be screwed if he stayed on'. He left in 2007 for Dr Reddy's Laboratories.

Being Tactical Was Hurting

Not only could BIOMAb not build on its impressive debut, but even for Insugen growth was stagnating five years after its launch. 'It's all right to be opportunistic when you are building your business but when you reach a level of critical mass, you have to be strategic. I think Insugen's strategic thinking was not optimal,' Kiran admits.

To introduce Insugen, Bamzai had brought two senior executives from Novo Nordisk, one of them its sales head. Coming from a giant like Novo, whose brands had a monopoly and the products sold almost on autopilot, the salesmen missed out on the strategic marketing of Insugen. Instead of garnering fresh prescriptions, they wasted a few years 'chasing Novo's doctors'.

It was damaging for Biocon because diabetes was at the top of its therapeutics heap. In 2009, it had signed an agreement with Amylin to jointly develop and market a new peptide drug for diabetes. Kiran had met Dan Bradbury at a US BIO conference. Bradbury was then chief operating officer of Amylin and was looking for a manufacturing partner to help them scale their technology in a cost-effective manner. Amylin had a technology that stitched two peptide hormones together to make fibrids, combination pills with dual activity. Conventionally, most molecules either deal with weight loss or reducing the glycaemic index of diabetics.

'The chemistry we were using was great in small scale but making these molecules on a large scale would be very expensive. We found Biocon, which did an extraordinary job of lowering the cost for us,' said Bradbury. Not to miss any manufacturing opportunity, Kiran struck an agreement that would make Biocon more involved in developing new products and at the same time, have commercialization rights in some emerging markets, including India.

Getting a good handle on the diabetes market was therefore critical. Merck's two new oral drugs, Januvia and Janumet, although expensive, were already causing doctors to push patients away from insulin to oral drugs. Biocon needed to add discernible value to its product. It relaunched its 'Winning with Diabetes' campaign, hired scientific officers in the field, increased the field force and took the feedback from doctors as a 'south-centric company' seriously. 'When I went to north India, I was told you are a south Indian, your company is south-focused. You are a Page-3 company. On top of that, we still don't spend money on doctors,' says Sudhir Nayak, who had joined from Zydus Cadila and now heads the metabolic business unit.

Biocon did expand to north India and also launched the generic version of the global best-seller, long-acting insulin glargine. For some reason, Sanofi – innovator of glargine – had not been aggressively selling it in India even though it was a rage globally. It sold it as a premium product but when it pushed it in 2010, Sanofi took Novo by surprise. Glargine was a golden chance to ink a fresh social contract with physicians, not just specialists, because it is peak-less insulin, does not cause hypoglycaemia and is good even for type 2 diabetics who make up more than 90 per cent of cases.

Nayak's dilemmas were not yet over though. Doctors were graduating patients to devices and analogues, neither of which were present with Biocon. Everyone else was selling glargine in cartridges and pens, but Biocon came out with smaller vials, which were cheaper to get the patient initiated but couldn't compete with pens. Nayak would budget for insulin pens every year but they would never come. Kiran was adamant she would only import best quality pens, which she did in 2011 from the German device-maker Haselmeier. These were manufactured in three bright colours, in contrast to the standard steel-gray insulin pens sold or given free by the competition. Nayak's team also started pharmaco-vigilance as other multinational companies were 'putting seeds of doubt in doctors' minds'. 'We followed up on any complaint within twenty-four to thirty-six hours. Doctors appreciated our sincerity and over time, the competitor's ploy became publicity for us,' Nayak narrates.

As the diabetes market was being fortified with a successful glargine launch, Kiran came to Iyer one day and said, 'Harish, you must form a clinical advisory board. It is critical for you. This would give us credibility and peer review in our programme.'

That was something, Iyer said, he had not thought about at all even though he was heading R&D after Shri had left. 'My mindset is not to spend money; I'm very Indian in that sense,' he said merrily. But having the clinical advisory board transformed the team. 'We knew what to have before going for due diligence; earlier, we were naive. Usually Kiran is hands-off and seldom gives advice, but in this case, she insisted.'

Perhaps Kiran was grooming Iyer for additional roles. She sent him to Harvard Business School for an executive programme, the first person from Biocon to get such an opportunity. By Biocon's measure, Iyer was more strategic. 'Maybe I am less strategic at Sanofi. In Indian companies, most people are very operational,' he said. At an off-site in Goa, she asked Iyer to talk about strategy – why the company was in-licensing certain molecules or technologies, why they needed a certain kind of pipeline, why the Abbreviated New Drug Application approach was not enough, what their net present value was, and the full nine yards. 'We had to explain what the net present value meant. Not everybody understood; the team was not aligned,' recalls Iyer. Interested in events beyond research, Iyer had been reading up on strategy and product positioning in trying to build a framework around what Kiran was doing. He would accompany Kiran and Chandavarkar to the annual JP Morgan healthcare conference in the US where they would discuss and rehearse the Biocon story to present.

In his earlier days in the US, Iyer had observed how biotech companies built their narrative, even mythologized their founders or the discoveries they made. Personally, he liked stories. (When he was interviewed at Sanofi, he told them Biocon stories, about the early days of platform development, which impressed the

French company. When they raised the point of poor quality that many Indian pharma companies are accused of, he doled out more stories. He would tell them how Western companies got beaten up for rules and regulations and learnt it all in a different era, not in the Internet age when publicity – good or bad – is instantaneous. Indian companies will also learn it with time, he would tell them.)

Power-packed Partnerships

Once insulin business gaps were identified and plans to address them afoot, Kiran turned to securing global partners for biosimilars. At least $25 billion worth of biotech drugs were going to lose patent protection in the next four to five years, opening up a massive market for biosimilars. Until then, Biocon had not sold its pharmaceutical formulations in the developed markets – regions which brought Indian pharma companies their value and profitability – and it was apparent that despite having the ability to develop and manufacture biosimilars, it would need a partner with a global marketing footprint and experience with regulatory affairs. Mylan was already buying its active pharma ingredients in India from Biocon but had an imperative to add biosimilars to its generics basket. It was talking to many other companies for possible alliances but when its chairman Robert Coury met Kiran, the former felt that he was most certain the two would partner.

Those who know Coury – he has a reputation for being tough – and Kiran were not surprised that the two sewed up a tenacious partnership that could run to several years before all the products reached the market. Kiran and Coury are similar in some respects; giving primacy to relationships is one of them. 'My style is somewhat unconventional. I like to know what it's like to be in the trenches with somebody. Is that person sincere, genuine? That's what I saw in her. Leaders are how they treat their own people, how they deal with other partners. Everything else is mathematical and maths can be replaced,' Coury says.

The two partners did their maths fair and square: they would share development, capital and certain other costs in getting the five biosimilars – trastuzumab, pegfilgrastim, bevacizumab, adalimumab and etanercept – to the market. Mylan would have exclusive commercialization rights to most developed markets and would share profits with Biocon. In all other markets, they would co-exclusively commercialize the drugs.

In Coury's words, it was 'a surgical' deal. 'We were behind the curve and I knew it. With this [partnership] we've moved from the back of the bus to the front. We brought the core competencies together and set up a strong structure. Anybody can walk into the shoes because people grow old or move on, the structure will last.' (I spoke with Coury in mid-2015 when an industrial drama of bidding and acquisition was being enacted where Mylan was pursuing a hostile takeover of Irish drugmaker Perrigo for $35 billion even as it was trying to fight off Israel-based Teva's $40 billion offer.)

To see its Mylan partnership go through, Biocon had to end another partnership. In April 2010, it bought back the Cuban share in the joint venture Biocon Biopharmaceuticals. In the complex and high-stakes partnership, Mylan would not have welcomed a third partner.

Biocon was climbing up the ladder fast. In October 2010, Kiran made public another partnership, this time stunning the world with the size and scope of the transaction. Smack in the middle of her globalization plan, she had scooped a worldwide commercialization agreement with the world's largest pharmaceutical company, Pfizer. For an upfront payment of $200 million, and an additional $150 million in milestone payments, Pfizer would have exclusive rights to commercialize four insulin and insulin-analogue products worldwide, with co-exclusive rights for all the products with Biocon in India, Germany and Malaysia.

Pfizer chief executive Jeff Kindler was a professional

acquaintance. When Kiran approached him with her insulins portfolio, Kindler said later, he found the drugs 'a really good addition to Pfizer's' and was convinced about biosimilars in general and insulins in particular. After all, he had overseen the development of Pfizer's inhaled insulin Exubera which turned out to be a disappointment, only to be dropped by the company in 2007. Kindler was also convinced that biosimilars, where Pfizer did not have a strong programme then, would one day clear regulatory hurdles and be a mainstay in global healthcare. However, barely two months after this agreement was signed, Kindler stepped down unexpectedly and David Simmons, who led the established business products, was given charge of the insulins. 'Initially, he was reluctant, but later he bought into it. Yet, I noticed a sense of reservation among a section there,' Kiran says. The collaboration was then entrusted to Diem Nguyen, a general manager of biosimilars, who was also supervising an in-house programme of biosimilars of monoclonal antibodies which included the popular breast cancer drug, trastuzumab (Roche's brand name: Herceptin). After the Biocon partnership, Nguyen had two competing streams – insulins and the internal monoclonals programme.

'Our insulin programme was moving very slowly,' Kiran recalls. 'We signed the agreement in October but had the first meeting only in December; it took that long to form the joint steering committee. A group of twenty-five people came to Bengaluru and everyone wanted to influence the programme. Finally, after six months, they said let's focus on one product – glargine.' By then, Eli Lilly had made public its alliance with Boehringer-Ingelheim to develop glargine. With this news, Pfizer altered the spreadsheet; suddenly a competitor had entered the market. Internally, Pfizer executives decided the competition should be factored in the contract. 'They wanted us to reduce our expectation on royalty stream and transfer price for the product. Diem said to me, "Kiran, we need to revisit the financial model,"' Kiran recalls.

Kiran's logic was that Eli Lilly was a good competitor to have because it won't slash prices. But Pfizer did not want to play second fiddle, which meant it would have to speed up the clinical trials, and that would cost them more. And since it was going to cost them more, they wanted to renegotiate the entire deal.

'Why should I? I dug in my heels,' Kiran argued. That sent Nguyen back to her drawing board. In the presence of notable competition like Eli Lilly, she found the value from insulins to be not as attractive as the in-house antibody biosimilars. By then, Ian Read had taken over as the new chief executive, and Pfizer had a significant organizational restructuring in which David Simmons left to join PPD Inc., a contract research company.

'I knew Ian, he is a finance person. I told him, let's be fair. I am a small company and I have to monetize my assets. You are Pfizer, your brand value and marketing powers will get you much more value, which is I why I'm partnering with you. If Eli Lilly has come, why should I pay the price? He understood,' Kiran explains. She was not willing to renegotiate the financial terms.

After a while, Kiran took her assets back but hung on to the upfront payment of $200 million. 'I was able to retain the money because they were withdrawing midstream, I did not commit any breach. I had already lost so much time. Who would bear that opportunity cost? Moreover, I was banking on this money to fund the Malaysia facility, which I could not renege on.'

When Coury heard about it, he called Kiran and 'just asked if everything was okay'. 'We've all been there. I think Kiran has fared pretty well economically. She may have, on the surface, appeared to face public rejection but I don't think she got the short side of the stick,' Coury says.

On 13 March 2012, when the two companies announced they were calling off their partnership, Biocon shares fell 6.3 per cent on the stock exchange but in the following weeks and months, the slide continued. Even as the market grasped the full implication of the break-up, stories floated that Pfizer had dropped the programme because there were 'quality issues with insulin'.

'That's a stupid hypothesis,' Kiran shot back. 'If there was a quality issue, they wouldn't have left money on the table.'

However, that money created a flutter when a research firm, Espirito Santo Investment, wrote in its report that Biocon had done 'aggressive accounting' with the Pfizer payment and questioned its validity. Fact is, Pfizer's money was only for the insulins programme development under their contract and Biocon would not account it as 'one-off earnings' to its revenues.

In the sad silence of a broken partnership, a state that could have driven many an entrepreneur to the brink, Kiran resumed her search for a new partner. Within a year, Biocon and Mylan announced they had extended their biosimilars alliance to include three insulin analogues – glargine (generic version of Sanofi's Lantus), aspart (generic version of Eli Lilly's Humalog) and lispro (generic version of Novo Nordisk's Novolog).

With the Pfizer breakup flotsam still in public memory, how did Mylan ensure the stories were mere rumours?

'It's not fair to ask me because I know Pfizer very well; I've ongoing partnerships with Pfizer,' Coury says. 'From the outside, people look at it as a multi-billion-dollar behemoth, and at Biocon as an Indian company which started from enzymes. The biggest falsity in the world today, not just in the US, is the general impression that bigger means better, in every form and fashion. Which is why I personally do due diligence, I go to lengths where most executives do not go because either they don't know how to go there and get their hands dirty or they do not want to step on the wrong shoes.'

In those two-odd years, working and breaking off with Pfizer, Biocon learnt a life lesson. For generic products, it was better off with partners who would look at the products through the generics lens, strategize and plan how to substitute and what to substitute in the regulated markets. Generics makers cannot possibly do full-blown clinical trials to substitute a product. Biocon finally understood it did not have to think like Eli Lilly or Novo Nordisk.

By the middle of the year, it seemed, Biocon had more partnership accounts to sort through. Its three-year-old partner, New Jersey–based Optimer Pharmaceuticals, was acquired by Cubist Pharmaceuticals for $535 million for the same prized drug for which Biocon had a supplier's agreement. The product was Dificid (generic name fidaxomicin), the first antibacterial drug approved in more than twenty-five years in 2011, whose roots lay in fermentation and the raw material back story in Bengaluru.

Way back in 2005, Shankar Hariharan, chief scientific officer of Par Pharmaceuticals, and Paul Campanelli, their head of marketing, were on a plant tour in Bengaluru with Zutshi. They realized it was no ordinary manufacturing facility, and soon confessed that it was indeed the best they had seen so far. 'The meeting agenda was modified from discussion on generic ingredient supplies to contract manufacturing a complex novel API that involved fermentation and chromatographic purification, a difficult and unique combination capability at a large scale,' recalls Zutshi.

At that time, Par was a licensee to the American commercialization rights to fidaxomicin from Optimer. Both Par and Optimer were searching for a reliable fermentation company to manufacture this product for them. They could not find one that could scale up their process and manufacture Phase III clinical requirement in a record six months. The product was then manufactured on a pilot scale by an Asian company. Since Optimer had received a fast-track review status from the American regulator, it meant an early market entry upon successful completion of their development.

Zutshi remembers getting the bacterial strain in a Petri dish in his hand baggage. The challenge in Bengaluru was to scale the process without any change in the product specification as that could risk Optimer's regulatory approval. 'And we did it,' beamed Zutshi. 'Even though this opportunity seemed relatively small compared to our existing business, the challenge was enticing.

Not to forget that we were going to be enablers for a first-in-class global therapeutic molecule.'

Biocon bagged exclusive manufacturing rights for this product for the US market and became the only supplier for all other markets. It netted some revenue until December 2014, when in another big pharma shake-out, Merck acquired Cubist for $8.4 billion, chiefly for its flagship drug Cubicin, another antibiotic. That left Biocon at Merck's mercy, and is yet to decide where fidaxomicin, a speciality antibiotic ideal for a boutique firm to market, fits in its large scheme of antibiotics.

Was it déjà vu for Kiran? A few years earlier, a company called GlycoFi which had developed technology to engineer *Pichia* yeast strains to produce glycosylated antibodies – attaching sugar structures to proteins for better therapeutic effect – had approched her. Biocon being the world's largest producer of *Pichia*-based recombinant products, GlycoFi wanted a partnership to manufacture its products. Before the contract could be concluded, GlycoFi was acquired by Merck in 2006 for $400 million. Afterwards, Merck did meet Biocon but decided to build internal capabilities.

Kiran has learnt to vaccinate herself against big pharma's acquisition moves and strategic shifts – off again, on again, gone once again.

'You cannot constantly be in fear of that,' she says. 'You have to move on, I am very resilient. We didn't care when Pfizer came and went, each partner has their idiosyncrasies, but you have to deal with these companies from a position of strength. For example, Pfizer did not have any clue about biosimilars when we walked in, so we realized this was our strength.'

Somehow, in this partnership walkathon, she managed to winch herself up. She had used her Pfizer agreement to convince the board to agree to a manufacturing facility in Malaysia. 'Pfizer's name gave them a comfort feeling,' Manian said. By the time the deal broke, she had worked out a fantastic arrangement with the

Malaysian government because the Pfizer money would be spent on insulin development, not on infrastructure.

In the latter half of the first decade of the millennium, Kiran was advising the Malaysian government on biotech policy as it tried to compete with Singapore, which had a strong biotech programme going with Biopolis. She told them that since Singapore was focusing on research and innovation, Malaysia should focus on bio-manufacturing. 'I told them the problems of bio-manufacturing, its dependence on high-cost utilities, capital intensiveness and gestational timelines, and suggested their policy should address that. A few years later, they came and said, "We've done all that you suggested, so now come and set up a plant in Malaysia,"' she says. The Malaysian government wanted to use Biocon as a bait for other companies.

BETS THAT DID NOT FLY

At the BIO conference in San Diego in 2004, Kiran and Bala met Vaccinex, a clinical-stage biotech company founded in 1997 by Maurice Zauderer and Deepak Sahasrabudhe. By then, Biocon had started its antibody programme and needed to build a pipeline. Its Vaccinia technology to make biobetters looked promising, and Biocon made a small investment in the company, licensing two molecules, BVX-10 and BVX-20, but soon abandoned the former since 'it was not up to the mark'. It took BVX-20 to clinics to evaluate whether, as a biobetter of the old drug Rituxan, it had any future.

In the early years of the new millennium, nobody knew if biobetters or biosimilars would rule the roost. Antibodies in those days were considered black-box molecules which regulators believed were so large that they could not be characterized. Hence, there was no way to prove their safety other than by doing clinical trials. Moreover, there were no non-human models for the antibodies. 'So you had to try it on humans – analytical data and science wasn't so mature that you could do everything around that antibody,' said Shri. That meant if one made copies of the existing antibody drugs, one had to go through all phases of clinical trials and if the drug had more efficacy than the innovator drug, the regulator would approve it. Some safety concerns would remain but in the end, the copies could be 'better'. That was how the biobetter story came about.

As time passed, characterization science progressed rapidly. People could copy the innovator molecule because they precisely knew the underlying science. The American regulators' guidance document of 2010 brought out the idea of substitutability which was never there before. Until then, the biggest bottleneck was that unlike small molecules where generics could substitute, biogenerics could not. But the moment substitutability came on the horizon, the risk of doing biobetter versus biosimilar was large and it made sense for companies to go for just substitutability.

(It's ironic though, that a generics company cannot bring out a better copy of the drug because of substitutability. The advantage innovator companies have is that whatever they first submit to the FDA becomes the standard, even if it's not the best way to do it. So companies copying them have to know so much about the process that even if it's not the best way to make it, they have to consistently make it inefficient so that it looks like the innovator's molecule.)

Gradually, everybody understood that even innovator products vary. So companies now have to take batches of the innovator product, characterize them and find the range of variation, and then make their process such that the specs fall in that range.

As attention and regulation shifted to biosimilars, BVX-20 was put in the slow lane. Its target, CD20 antigen, is a crowded space, so the regulatory path is getting tougher. 'Unless you show it is vastly superior, your approval and market access will not be so easy. Clinical trial is also difficult because ultimately you have to do it in refractive patients – those who are not responding to Rituxan. Your drug becomes the third or fourth line of therapy,' says Kiran.

At the San Diego BIO conference, Bala and Kiran had another

partnership meeting, with Nobex of North Carolina. While the latter's oral insulin delivery technology has been used and significantly improved upon, the rest of the patent basket that Biocon bought after Nobex's bankruptcy has remained largely unused. 'We were only knowledgeable about oral insulin; we inherited a portfolio we didn't know much about,' Kiran admits.

This may have to do with the philosophy of patents at Biocon. When Anindya Sircar moved from microbiology to set up the intellectual property cell in the late 1990s, he was the only scientist who was interested in patents and the company developed a thinking that was defensive to begin with. It made sure Biocon did not infringe on others' patents. Over time, the company filed patents aggressively, but, Sircar said, 'The portfolio, including Nobex, was good enough to do business in different parts of the world, never big and varied enough for value creation by licensing.'

Creating patents that would make Biocon commercially very strong is an area that needs work, acknowledges Kiran. India as a country has a weak understanding of patents. However, Bala Manian, who strongly favoured buying the Nobex patents, thinks otherwise. 'People who were selling intellectual property [at Biocon] did not believe in any such property, not just Nobex. You need to sell the potential, you need to be a visionary. You have to walk the talk before you talk the talk. Talking the talk is what needs to be done in selling intellectual property,' he said. 'If a used-car salesman does not believe in the car he is selling, he cannot sell the car.'

When Sircar, not happy at the way he was 'rising in the company', resigned in 2010 to work at Infosys, Kiran did not try to stop him.

Yet she continued her pursuit of valuable intellectual property. At Johns Hopkins University School of Medicine, Atul Bedi had a few brilliant ideas and some research in progress that would one day allow development of a wide spectrum of immunoconjugates – monoclonal antibodies that are coupled with other molecules to make them more targeted – which could engage with the immune system to kill tumours or pathogens. In 2008, Biocon made an equity investment in IATRICa, a company founded by Bedi and his colleague, Rajani Ravi. Bedi had a few ideas but he had not figured out which molecule to pursue. 'One of the most brilliant people I've ever met, Bedi is very passionate about curing cancer and wants to go for the big one,' Iyer recalls about his interactions.

Strangely, in 2013, Biocon announced it was stalling work on the monoclonal antibody fusion proteins that it was developing with IATRICa. What could have happened? It was a perfect partnership – an outstanding scientist, a savvy business leader and a company with low-cost biologics manufacturing prowess in India. Perhaps, in holding dual positions, Bedi could not secure clear intellectual property for IATRICa, forcing Biocon to stop development. 'We made a mistake. After doing some joint work, Bedi started filing patents on his own,' is all that Kiran would say. (Bedi did not respond to emails and phone calls. With his colleague Rajani, he was granted two patents in 2015 for discovering immunomodulatory antibodies and fusion proteins that reverse the immune tolerance of cancer cells.)

All these years, as she made eclectic scientific bets, Kiran rarely paid attention to buying businesses, either within the country or outside. However, in 2008, soon after divesting the enzyme business, she made an exception and bought majority shares in a German pharmaceutical marketing and distribution company, AxiCorp, for €30 million. She felt it would pay to have a strong marketing footprint in Germany and Europe as Insugen and other analogues would receive regulatory approval. Disappointingly, soon after the acquisition, the German government wanted to rein in healthcare costs and began pressuring the local industry to lower costs. By then, AxiCorp had begun eating into Biocon's profits. So when Pfizer came on board in 2010, having AxiCorp made little sense. Biocon sold its equity in 2011 for €40 million. Sometime later, when the Portuguese investment bank, Espirito

Santo, questioned the accounting in the AxiCorp transaction, saying the company had 'had a cash loss of €10 million and a notional loss of €21 million in buying back the intellectual property rights', Biocon clarified that the transaction had a mix of intellectual property and cash infusion and its 'impact on the profit-and-loss account was neutral'.

THE SHIFT

For a few years after 2009, Biocon was drinking out of a fire hose. It had loaded partnerships with serious financial and human resource commitments for clinical developments which had to be executed in a regulatory environment that was anything but clear and final. It was not the cookie-cutter ANDA (Abbreviated New Drug Application) path that generics companies follow. One little notification from the FDA meant a few more years of work. And it was happening to Biocon. It was a constant struggle to plan and foresee how, or if, American and European regulations would harmonize or be different. The pressure ran high. In the midst of that, Iyer dropped a bombshell.

Kiran was 'nervous' when he sought time to speak with her; he had already met Chandavarkar. She had not imagined Iyer would leave. 'She asked me, what I wanted; I said, "Nothing, nothing would stop me,"' Iyer recalls. Sanofi, the French owner of Shantha Biotechnics, had pitched the job in a way that Iyer could not refuse.

'You will succeed Varaprasad Reddy, they told me. How can one say no to that?' Iyer says. 'I had grown tremendously in Biocon, but working in a leadership role in a global company and reporting to the Sanofi-Pasteur chief executive was a big opportunity. On top of that, they said, "We will make sure you succeed."'

Apart from handling multiple programmes and travelling all the time, which was strenuous for sure, there was another reason Iyer chose to make the switch. He had come to India wanting to make an impact in the developing world, but realized 'Biocon's products were high-end ones, not going into public health'. With

Shantha's vaccines, he thought, he could fulfil his dream. 'The role at Shantha was good. I don't think I'd have got that role easily at Biocon.'

Kiran sent him off with a grand farewell which more than fifty people attended at Glenmore, the warm hearth where she often gives her business relationships a personal touch. (A business strategy she adopted right from the beginning when busloads of Irish colleagues would descend in Bengaluru and parties would be hosted at her residence. 'It was cheaper and also cosily comfortable for a woman business executive to mix business and socializing,' recalls long-time friend Meeru Pai.)

After a few months, Clinigene's Abhijit Barve stepped in as the new R&D president. As someone with a clinical background, he came at the right time, when most of Biocon's programmes were entering clinics and needed someone to make sense of the regulatory maze in different continents. But Iyer's departure made Kiran think hard about the organizational structure because even Chandavarkar 'needed more ammunition to fire on more cylinders'. In early 2013, she brought McKinsey to restructure Biocon into strategic business units. It took a while for it to work though; dual reporting lines did not sit easy on some senior managers. Two business units reported to Chandavarkar and two to Bamzai.

However, Bamzai, one of the most fervent proponents of restructuring, quit a few months later, in December. Internally, it was known that Chandavarkar would head for the corner office, even though Biocon had not made anything public. Bamzai left for a plum position – as chief executive and managing director of Mylan India which, after the Agila acquisition in 2013, is the second largest employer in the Indian pharmaceutical industry. A year later, he poached Sandeep Rao, head of the insulins business unit, who was driving the Mylan insulins partnership. Suddenly, the advantage that Biocon enjoyed for long in not having big pharma companies in the city to poach executives was eroding. Bamzai would not comment on the exits; he had serious corporate resistance to any business question – he described nineteen years of work at Biocon in ninety words. All he muttered was: 'I gave nineteen years of my life to Biocon, I have a much bigger role here.'

A month later, in January 2014, Biocon named Chandavarkar as its chief executive and Ravi Limaye as the new president of marketing. When Limaye met Kiran for his interview, first she asked why he wanted to leave a big company like Novartis to join Biocon; then she said she had only two expectations from him. She wanted somebody 'who understood science because Biocon was not a me-too company', and she did not want 'someone tactical'. Limaye said he did not quite get what she meant by tactical then because he had worked at Novartis and GalxoSmithKline and knew being tactical could take a speciality company – which Biocon was aspiring to be – only so far. Kiran was aware of this hole in Biocon's business fabric and had been taking small steps to patch it.

In early 2013, she had hired Mahesh Gowrishankara. When he was with Bristol-Myers Squibb in the US, at one of the quarterly town-hall meetings, he had seen Kiran address the research and development staff, something that had not happened before and has not happened since. As someone who worked with Elliott Sigal, head of research and development, and Francis Cuss, head of discovery, and supported the strategy group to make informed decisions, Gowrishankara was impressed with her town-hall talk. A few years later, when he thought of relocating to India, Biocon was the only option, as his knowledge of regular Indian pharmaceuticals came from his father who had spent a lifetime in Cipla.

The interview lasted twenty minutes and she offered him the title and the reporting line. Since then, Gowrishankara's primary role has been to help 'establish the future path of itolizumab' and find the right partners who would work on the science and have the ability to commercialize it. His pedigree and passion flank his position. 'Bristol-Myers patented receptor CTLA-4 in 1987 which led to one of the first immunotherapy drugs, ipilimumab, in 2011.

They worked on it for nearly twenty years. In fact, in 2008, it was the only company working on this target. That's the journey you have to take,' he says solemnly.

Since his arrival, three new board directors with distinctive drug development and pharmaceutical business experience have joined Biocon. If the earlier directors like Cooney, Talwar and Manian – all retired in 2015 – honed a start-up, the new additions have the task of shaping a mid-size Indian company into a global entity.

After the fibrids agreement with Amylin, Kiran kept her communication link with Dan Bradbury alive. Bradbury found this unique. 'When you do such deals, you never hear back from the chief executives again. But we used to have phone conversations once every month or so,' he says. Being British, he follows cricket even though he lives in California, and it turned out to be a common interest. Other than cricket, they would discuss their respective philosophies of what they were trying to do with their companies. When Bradbury read C.K. Prahalad's book *The New Age of Innovation* and brought it up, 'Kiran was like "I know CK". It was more a meeting of the minds.'

Together they would envision that like the iPhone – designed by Apple in California and manufactured in China – their products would say, designed by Amylin in California and manufactured by Biocon in India. It was another matter that Amylin's future lay somewhere else when Bristol-Myers bought it in mid-2012. Bradbury then left to pursue other roles in life sciences; Biocon board director was one such role.

Still, she needed someone who had run global business to guide her. She had known Jeremy Levin, 'a fund of knowledge', for ten years and when he stepped down as chief executive at Teva in October 2013, she checked with him if he would join a big pharma company full-time. When he said no, she proposed a board position. When Levin moved from Novartis to Bristol-Myers as its head of alliances, he had 'inherited' the Syngene–Bristol-Myers relationship and thought Kiran 'was unique in having established the beginnings of biotech in Bengaluru'.

But what made her different from other dealmakers?

'Kiran takes chances. Most people in larger companies don't like making deals because, if they go wrong, they lose their career; if they go right, their superior takes the credit. You have to live in an environment where, to make a deal successful, you have to make everyone successful or everyone own the failure; you have to know what the risks are and what the [chances of] success will be. In Kiran's case, she likes to make everyone around her feel successful; it's very different and very interesting,' said Levin.

Levin has always been interested in emerging markets. Reading the local newspaper the *Deccan Herald* in Bengaluru, 'he doesn't feel like a stranger'. Unlike many global executives, he says he 'understands the governments. I've negotiated with them; I really understand the intellectual property issues – the conflict between United States–European Union and India. I've participated in it and I'd like to have a small role there.' Biocon could perhaps give him that role.

There was yet another role that Biocon needed to fill – a scientific advisor, especially to help with itolizumab. The research team's search concluded in Cambridge, Massachusetts. At Harvard Medical School, Vijay Kuchroo suddenly received a lot of emails from people he knew in the university town saying Kiran would like to meet him; one of them was Tyler Jacks, director of the Koch Institute for Integrative Cancer Research at MIT. When the two met for lunch in Boston, Kuchroo 'liked her a lot, there was no formality, only straightforward talk'. 'She said, "We have this great molecule" and I told her I knew about it. Then she said, "You discovered Th-17 pathway, and our molecule inhibits that pathway. Would you help us out?"' Kuchroo remembers.

A neurologist much sought after, Kuchroo has founded four biotech companies – two of which were bought by GlaxoSmithKline and Novartis – in the field of immunology, which, after twenty years of basic research, are now yielding a whole array of new drugs in cancer and autoimmune diseases. Even for Kuchroo, itolizumab presents many scientific possibilities. 'We know it blocks Th-17 cells and that is like dowsing the fire in any inflammation, but it doesn't explain the durable response this drug provides. I think its [mechanism of action] brings back tolerance, which gives it a long-lasting protection and that is unique to this molecule, distinguishing it from all other compounds,' he said.

A native of Kashmir, Kuchroo left India in 1980 to pursue his Ph.D in Australia and has been in the US since 1985. Through his interactions with clinicians in tertiary health centres in India, he is aware that doctors in general are not trained or interested in building 'bio-banks of patient-derived material', something that is critical for building value for itolizumab. 'If we have the responder and non-responder material, we can do the whole genome analysis and can tell you what kind of patients will respond to the drug and what kind will not, so that you don't give it to everybody. You do a blood test beforehand and improve the outcome. That's how Genentech does it.' Biocon would like to do it too.

Kiran is therefore steering Biocon towards a new orientation. Limaye is shifting to more scientific business development, shedding smaller brands, bulking up bigger brands with deeper penetration. 'Most multinationals were like this seventy years ago,' he says. For the first time, in 2014, the company filed four ANDAs in the US for some of its difficult-to-manufacture active pharmaceutical ingredients.

For now, Limaye wants to be selective, and secretive, but it's anybody's guess that the ANDAs would be in immunosuppressants, a niche segment where the company makes all the APIs and where payers in the regulated markets would be willing to offer a premium for quality. In the immediate future, he plans to make products like trastuzumab and glargine the global brands they ought to be. By which time he would also have Kiran's audacious wagers, her wide-angle view on novel molecules, manifesting with their prospects or pitfalls.

7

BIG, HAIRY BETS

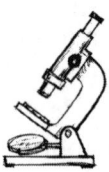

The Pin-up Molecule

'We need six runs off the last ball in the over,' Kiran said.

The research team was back from the heady conference of European Association for the Study of Diabetes in late 2008 and planning for a larger, late-stage study of oral insulin. In the earlier four studies, they had tested safety and dosage; they now wanted a shorter trial to test the clinical efficacy. But confidence in the results thus far got the better of Kiran. They would go straight for a six-month study.

Biocon had a stellar group of endocrinologists advising it on the clinical trial. The previous study had shown a near-perfect dose linearity – drug response was in proportion to the dose – and a significant blood sugar drop after meals. The key test ahead, the gold standard of diabetes treatment, was HbA1c, which is a measure of blood sugar control over three months.

'This will tell us the real positioning of IN-105 as an early insulin intervention for patients with early onset of diabetes,' Kiran had told me in an interview then. 'Obviously this will mean a new therapeutic paradigm for diabetes that has enormous business prospects for Biocon.' She had hinted the drug could be launched in 2010.

Alas, the molecule was going to be anti-diabetes, not an antidote to uncertainty. In January 2011, Biocon announced that the Phase III study in India had failed to meet primary end points.

Moreover, the drug did not meet the target of lowering the level of glycated haemoglobin by 0.7 per cent compared with a placebo. It was the first multiple-dose study of the molecule that Biocon had done and it experienced more than normal placebo response even though this patient group was not exactly on a placebo, but on the standard drug, metformin. In the group, though, there was more than expected benefit in the post-meal glucose reduction.

The news headlines were loud. Along with Khedkar and team, Bala Manian had diced the data to pin the failure on the placebo group's behaviour. Kiran was taking all the slamming on her chin. 'Clinical trials are not a slam dunk. You are lucky if you get outstanding data at the first shot. We had a higher-than-expected placebo effect that masked the primary end point. It is well known that early diabetics, especially type 2 diabetics, have a tendency to modify lifestyles. And if you suddenly exercise or cut down on your carbohydrates, it will impact on certain parameters,' she told the *Times of India*, a week later.

The results had sent shockwaves down everybody's spine, including the clinical advisory board of Cherrington, Lebovitz and Gilbert Alexander Fleming, endocrinologist and a former FDA regulator.

'One of the challenges we had faced was that there was no literature to guide us on what happens to patients on multiple doses of oral insulin,' said Khedkar. In designing the trial, the team was caught between an oral medication and insulin. While the former is always a double-blinded study (in which subjects and doctors do not know who is receiving what treatment), the latter is never a blinded study for fear of hypoglycaemia or insulin shock to the participants.

After much debate, it was decided to give the trial participants glucometers and let them measure their glucose levels once a week. Human psychology sometimes works in the weirdest ways. In the four-week stabilization period, even before the dosing began, patients showed an improvement in glucose levels as they had started changing their lifestyle, knowing they would be closely monitored. In the placebo group, the study got inadvertently unblinded because the subjects, perhaps new diabetics, on not seeing any blood sugar reduction, began to make lifestyle modifications which their doctors had advised in any case.

Lebovitz says he's been involved in studies in populations where the level of diabetes care is low and 'good placebo effect' is recorded if glucometers are given to participants. However, the only people who show this effect are those whose diabetes is not very severe at the time. In other words, if you are on two or three medications and you have had diabetes for a long time, even though you know what your glucose level is, you are not going to benefit much from a lifestyle change. In a recent diabetes study of a big pharmaceutical company of which one half was done in eastern Europe and the other half in western Europe, 'We saw no placebo effect in western Europe but a dramatic effect in eastern Europe,' says Lebovitz.

As an academic who had an abiding association with India since the mid-1980s, consulting for pharmaceutical companies as well as running educational programmes for diabetes specialists, Lebovitz was aware of the diabetes burden of India. So when Biocon approached him to be on its clinical advisory board, he readily agreed. He found IN-105 to be a 'unique' molecule, one that is rapidly absorbed and releases insulin for the body just like the pancreas releases insulin when a normal, healthy person eats meals.

'Some of the other insulin molecules being tested are not easily absorbed in the body; they are released when they get to the lower part of the intestine, which is not a valuable way to deliver insulin,' he says. The ultimate goal of diabetes treatment is to lower the glucose in a manner that is safe and has relatively little side effect. On that count, IN-105 scores high; it causes very little or no severe hypoglycaemia at all.

The trial results rattled not just the markets but some board members as well. The senior management also showed signs of edginess and a lack of faith. Manian and Khedkar had studied the data from which it emerged that this oral insulin would be a godsend for those diabetics or pre-diabetics who essentially had trouble controlling their diet. It wasn't a sixer, but taking singles wasn't too difficult. For Kiran, it was the solidity of the parsed data and an understanding of the science that there is no real substitute for insulin for diabetes treatment that let her don the solitary fanatic hat. She had two options: either to do a study overseas – which would be expensive but get her international validation – or take the risk of doing it again in India but factor in the high placebo effect into the trial design.

Since the team's confidence had taken a beating, Kiran chose to bide her time. Meanwhile, Khedkar and Iyer met several big pharmaceutical companies – AstraZeneca, Britsol-Myers Squibb, Johnson & Johnson and Eli Lilly. 'Our challenge was how much we could share with these companies, they could just beat us hands down. After all, they did not get this idea to make insulin into a tablet form that is so cheap,' says Iyer. All the companies seemed interested, in varying degrees and for various reasons, but few were willing to make long-term commitments. Scientists at Bristol-Myers were convinced by the full analysis and saw merit in it. In one of the consultation conversations, Simeon Taylor, former research and development head of Bristol-Myers, who is now at the University of Maryland, got excited at the prospect of 'lowered blood sugar without sustained hypoglycaemia'.

In late 2012, Biocon made it public that it had entered into an 'option agreement' with Bristol-Myers to further study the molecule up to Phase II. If successfully completed, Bristol-Myers would have the right to exercise an option to obtain an exclusive worldwide licence to the programme. Biocon would get a licence fee in addition to some milestone payments and royalties on commercial sales of IN-105 outside India while retaining exclusive rights to the drug in India.

The tug Bristol-Myers felt towards oral insulin was also because of a $7-billion acquisition it had made a few months earlier, of Amylin Pharmaceuticals, a diabetes-focused California company with a rich portfolio of molecules. As it happens in the small world of big pharma, Biocon, by then a roving partnership striker, had an existing relationship with Amylin to develop a hybrid peptide molecule for diabetes. Familiarity bred confidence. Bristol-Myers, which also had an ongoing seven-year contract with Syngene, became IN-105's champion, even if conditionally.

A few months later, in November 2013, Bristol-Myers had an internal research restructuring where it decided to stop broad-based basic research in diabetes and sold its diabetes business to AstraZeneca, with which it had an ongoing alliance. However, it chose to keep a 'number' of research and manufacturing employees related to diabetes. Presumably, IN-105 fell in that 'number'. For Bristol-Myers, it made sense to remain invested in a promising new molecule without having the pressure to perform.

By mid-2015, four Phase I studies of IN-105 were nearing completion in the US. The studies were complex and designed to seek answers to multiple questions about drug and food interaction as well as its performance in relation to some existing short-acting insulins.

ONE IN THE CROWD?

The diabetes world is in the grip of two trending crazes – rising obesity leading to swelling population of diabetics, particularly in middle-income countries, and a pack of new molecules from the veterans of the industry like Novo Nordisk, Sanofi, Eli Lilly and others like AstraZeneca, that target type 2 diabetics. Some of the new molecules could turn out to be revolutionary, like Novo's semaglutide, which is in an advanced stage of testing as a once-a-week injection as well as an oral drug which in mid-stage studies has shown glucose reduction as well as weight loss.

In early 2015, Sanofi's inhaled insulin Alfrezza entered the market. The metabolic memory may not be the same that a diabetic suffers from, but the market does have an overhang of Pfizer's 2007 failed stab at inhaled insulin, the expensive Exubera. Alfrezza has got off to a slow start and its labelling, which requires it to be kept away from a patient with any lung disease or asthma, adds one more layer to patient stratification.

Among the oral insulin contenders, Israeli company Oramed's insulin capsule is undergoing clinical studies in the United States for safety and efficacy under an Investigational New Drug application. For the sake of comparison, by early 2015, Oramed had given 1,600 doses of its long-acting oral insulin to patients whereas Biocon had administered at least 1,50,000 doses of its short-acting IN-105. In terms of being out there, IN-105 has gone the furthest.

In mid-2015, Novo Nordisk said its oral insulin, under a seven-year technology partnership with Merrion Pharmaceuticals, had completed a single-dose Phase I trial and would move further into a proof-of-principle study.

Most of the new oral diabetes drugs are insulin sensitizers, coaxing the bodies of type 2 diabetics to produce more insulin. Theoretically, it's the insulin – in whichever form the drug makers make it accessible and affordable – that can treat a patient whose body makes less or no insulin at all. Delivering it through an injection leads to weight gain because it gets deposited under the skin and keeps circulating in the body for a longer duration, causing hypoglycaemia, which people often treat by taking more food.

Oral delivery of insulin, therefore, has remained the most important goal of endocrinologists over the past eighty years. And they cannot rule out surprises, not yet.

'Surprises are always there. The reason we do research is because we are looking for answers, we never expected to see the placebo effect in Indian studies,' says Lebovitz. Surprises, particularly in metabolic diseases, continue to spring even after the drug has been launched. 'There's a lingering question whether glucagon-like peptide-1 receptor agonists [GLP-1, a class of insulin sensitizers] cause pancreatitis,' he says. Additionally, in mid-2015, the American regulator issued a warning that a new class of drugs, sodium-glucose cotransporter-2 (SGLT-2) may cause ketoacidosis, a condition where the body produces too many acids called ketones.

As similar as the drug insulin may be to the hormone insulin secreted by the body, the fact that its oral delivery has not been studied over a long term, Lebovitz and his peers are prepared for the unknown. 'The key is to have a company which is doing scientific work and is following up with careful clinical studies,' Lebovitz says.

On that count, Biocon often exceeds its own brief.

ITOLIZUMAB – THE NEW KID ON THE BLOCK

In January 2006, when Enrique Montero arrived from Cuba, he hoped to seamlessly transport his lab work from the Centre for Molecular Immunology in Havana to Biocon in Bengaluru. Kiran had licensed a brand new molecule, itolizumab, from the centre which he had co-founded, and Montero, as one of the inventors of the molecule, had come to get the Bengaluru team up to speed in developing it further. The physician scientist had earlier worked in labs in Switzerland and Israel in his postdoctoral career, and what he found in the name of a molecular biology lab – which did not even have a fluorescence-activated cell-sorting machine – at Biocon was disappointing.

Later that night, when Montero met Kiran, Shri, Iyer and Shaw for dinner, he did little to hide his feelings. Without an animal house and a better-equipped lab, he would find it hard to carry forward the science done in Havana, he told them. Next morning, at 8.30 a.m., Kiran, Shri and Montero were walking around the campus to figure out where they could set up an animal house. 'I was amazed at the speed with which they moved,' recalls Montero.

Kiran was trying to cleave to a vision. In choosing itolizumab from nearly twenty molecules that Montero's centre was ready to license at the time, she had shown rare insight and courage. 'The probability of success in drug discovery is less than 10 per cent, and to bet on a single molecule of this nature was very brave,' says Montero.

There were many firsts to itolizumab. It was a novel molecule that was addressing a new target; its origin was in mice and was later 'humanized' to work better in humans; and it was made in a cell line, Non-Secreting Null or NS0, which was not the most preferred biological expression system. Most researchers and companies had moved to CHO cell lines.

On top of that, immunotherapy was no longer the red-hot area of research bristling with many potential blockbusters as it has been in recent times. Only one such drug, adalimumab (brand name Humira of Abbott Laboratories) had been approved in 2002 for rheumatoid arthritis; by 2015, it was the world's largest-selling drug.

What Kiran pinned her sight on belongs to a new class of drugs called immunomodulators that tweak the immune system – inhabiting some pathways and activating others – to treat autoimmune diseases. The Cubans had done an exploratory study on eighteen patients to show that the molecule was somewhat effective in rheumatoid arthritis; yet the results were not resoundingly in favour of any particular indication among the autoimmune diseases. The topical application of this drug in psoriasis looked promising but the clinical trial had failed to meet its end point.

Over the next few years in Bengaluru, Ramakrishnan Melarkode and his team worked on the molecule. They changed the cell line to make it safer and commercially viable since most large-scale manufacturing happens in CHO cells. As the team began to understand the biology of this molecule, it finally struck gold. In Cuba, Montero's team had pursued a certain pathway, T helper 1, or Th-1 cells, in studying how it facilitates the body's immune cells to kill an infection. In Bengaluru, during the early and middle stages of clinical studies in rheumatoid arthritis and psoriasis, Melarkode found that along with other pathways, T helper 17, or Th-17, was extremely active in mediating a drug response.

More by chance than design, this was also the time when the scientific world was awash with new data on how Th-17 cells were involved in some of the most common autoimmune diseases like psoriasis, rheumatoid arthritis, inflammatory bowel disease, multiple sclerosis and others. These are a new group of cells that play an important role in mopping up fungal and bacterial infections, and, importantly, they do this by working the body's autoimmunity. For a long time, it was not clear how these cells worked, until 2006, when Vijay Kuchroo and his colleagues published their seminal work in *Nature*, characterizing these cells for the first time. The authors described a method to generate these cells and showed a relationship between regulatory and effector T cells. In short, Kuchroo and his colleagues synthesized a whole new understanding around T cells, a type of protective cells in the body.

Melarkode and his group now needed to test their hypothesis and the abounding theoretical knowledge in clinics. In 2010, Biocon convinced its Cuban partners to take a decision to test itolizumab in psoriasis to understand the mechanism of action. That was also the year Montero, who had been spending several months in Bengaluru, moved to India with his family. It was not the usual movement of an offshore collaborator. Kiran had to seek ministerial approvals in Delhi to employ a Cuban national but that hardly weighed on her mind. She may not have paid for a pie-in-the-sky investigation, but rooting for itolizumab was still a gamble and now she was sensing a pay-off.

All this while, Manian stood beside her, scouring scientific literature and connecting the dots. He was the one to have found a journal paper that pointed to the Th-17 pathway. It was a struggle for the board every time she needed to put more into research. Kiran was dogmatic about her belief in the molecule; Manian was dogmatic about her belief. There's always some give-and-take in their relationship. 'I derive energy in her enthusiasm, just to be able to see that out-of-the-box thinking. I vicariously live my Indian dream through her,' says Manian.

The Aha! Moment

If there were a pecking order of autoimmune diseases, psoriasis would rank pretty high in the eyes of drug researchers. They inevitably start with this disease when they have a new molecule to test. It's simply the ease of seeing the effect, visually. Psoriasis is a skin disorder where the immune system sends out flawed signals which speed up the production of new skin cells, causing them to merge and form itchy plaques. Till date, there's no cure for it. Some of the new drugs send the disease into remission, but only for a few weeks.

With much anticipation and some trepidation, Melarkode and his colleagues began their Phase III clinical trial on 225 patients. As weeks went by, from twelve to twenty-eight, the number of patients with at least 75 per cent improvement – Psoriasis Area and Severity Index score as it is called – increased steadily. What was revealing, though, was that the patients who responded well at week twelve and stopped taking medicine did not have to go back to taking it. Simply put, itolizumab was working upstream –

through pathway Th-17 – to block the disease for a longer time, much longer than some of the existing biotech drugs in the market were known to do.

'It was then we thought we may have a blockbuster on hand,' says Kiran. By then, the team in Bengaluru had acquired a fresh patent which extended protection on the molecule until 2028.

The drug was launched for psoriasis in India in August 2013, at half the price of similar drugs in the market. Incidentally, no head-to-head comparison between drugs exists in the field of immunomodulatory molecules. All successful drugs, beginning with the blockbusters Humira, Enbrel and Remicade, each blocking a similar path – tumour necrosis factor or TNF – were approved for psoriasis first and gradually moved to other indications, but no one set of data can be compared with another. Each trial is different, each patient population is different, so you can't take data from one and compare it with another, says Kuchroo.

Nonetheless, claims Ramakrishnan Melarkode, 'Our efficacy data is very similar to Enbrel, we are equal to Enbrel, if not superior.'

More than two years into the market, itolizumab is showing efficacy and doing well. But the question is: In the larger drug development market, where there are as many compounds in the turnpike as there are approved ones for psoriasis, where does itolizumab stand in comparison?

In early 2015, Novartis launched a drug, secukinumab, which is the first biologic to be approved as the first line of treatment for psoriasis as it nearly clears the skin for most patients. All other biologics, including itolizumab, are approved as a second line of treatment.

'Is there a disease against which itolizumab can achieve such a spectacular response? I suspect this drug will have its own indication. But the question is: Is it multiple sclerosis, is it Sjogren's syndrome, is it inflammatory bowel disease or something else?' asks Kuchroo. The way science evolves is through step-by-step clinical trials, and that's what Biocon is doing.

It's an expensive affair but Biocon is in a unique position – a mid-sized company doing novel biologics while earning the margins of speciality generics and harbouring the ambitions of an innovator company – which is usually a big pharma earning huge margins. Being public, it is accountable every quarter for the revenue numbers it shares, unlike a small biotech which is venture-funded and not tied to revenue generation.

The anecdotal evidence from itolizumab clinical trials and post-marketing studies shows that the drug has a durable response, not often seen with many biologics. Kuchroo thinks that lurking in this drug is potentially a completely new, lasting mechanism of action. What most existing drugs, anti-TNF, do is 'turn off the blaze, not turn off the flame'. They don't build the tolerance mechanism against inflammation in the body, so one needs to keep consuming the drug to keep the blaze under control. 'Itolizumab has the potential to do both – turn off the blaze and then turn off the flame. Not many drugs in autoimmune diseases do both, they do either one or the other, and one without the other doesn't quite work,' Kuchroo says.

As an academic who has started four biotech companies in Cambridge, Kuchroo is excited about discovering the biology of CD6 that Biocon's pursuit offers, but as someone who grew up in India, he is worried that the lack of research training among clinicians in India will impact further development of this drug.

'Clinicians in India always want to treat patients but not understand why. They do not know how valuable the patient material they have is for understanding the basic mechanisms of a drug. You have to have [Antonio] Salieri to understand what Mozart was playing. For everybody else Mozart was playing music, but for Salieri it was a gospel from God,' he says.

When Kuchroo became a board director in 2015, the task before him was to advise Biocon on developing itolizumab for further indications, but the catch that he finds the company in is that unless it has uncovered some more biology for big pharmaceutical companies – which are certainly intrigued by the molecule – it will find it hard to license it. The molecule works in the clinic, but at a molecular and academic level; people don't know about its functioning.

Around the time Biocon was welcoming the immunologist, Merck said Mumbai's Sun Pharma had paid it upwards of $80 million to license exclusive worldwide rights for a psoriasis drug, a monoclonal antibody called tildrakizumab. Under the arrangement, Merck would continue all clinical development and regulatory activities to be funded by Sun. After the approval, Sun would take all ownership.

At best, it was a commercial transaction for Sun, at worst, it was dumping of a molecule by a big pharma. It was the third molecule in its class to reach Phase III. Two years after Johnson & Johnson launched ustekinumab (brand name Stelara) in 2009, Abbott decided not to commercialize its drug in the same class even though it had completed all studies and acquired regulatory approvals. The field was getting crowded, and Merck, after a commercial restructuring, also chose not to commercialize it. But for a generic company like Sun, even if it rakes in a few hundred million dollars, it would be a reasonable commercial success.

Where does that leave Biocon's itolizumab, especially in the Indian market where it is already selling?

Gowrishankara, intense to the point where even food seems a distraction, has a habit of quoting from the technology industry and believes even the commercial prospects of the two drugs are not comparable. He says, 'You could go back and look at Steve Jobs and Bill Gates. Gates's vision was to come up with an operating system on every desk; Jobs's vision was something different – not to have his product on every desk, but to build something distinctive. You can't compare the two.

'We are moving to a point where we want people with a chronic disease to do daily chores. Therefore, to strike a balance between efficiency and safety is important and that is what itolizumab addresses. In four to five years, the biology of CD6 – an antigen which has been preserved in the biology of humans for over two million years – will get described more and we will take front position.'

THE CROSS BEARER

The position that Biocon started from is unenviable. I met Kiran the day Sun Pharma broke the news of licensing Merck's psoriasis drug. At the time, she was reading Peter Gotzsche's book, *Deadly Medicines and Organized Crime*. 'This book tells you how big pharma creates hype around its drug by marketing. For me,' she said, 'the biggest challenge is credibility. India has a terrible record in terms of new molecules. Two molecules from Dr Reddy's Laboratories' – Balaglitazone and Ragaglitazone – were returned. In reality, all glitazones had a problem. Now look at the dichotomy: for the same reason that big pharma returned Dr Reddy's molecules, i.e., for bladder cancer, Avandia (Rosiglitazone) was a big success until it was pulled out of the market. So if you think about it, this data of tumour was there in those drugs too, but they still went to the market. Yet, Dr Reddy's molecule was returned.

'Once [late] Dr Anji Reddy [founder of Dr Reddy's] told me, "I really feel bad that my drugs did not make it to the market and these drugs – Rosiglitazone and Bioglitazone – made it to the market. My drugs were just as good, if not better,"' says Kiran.

(Later, Dr Reddy's Laboratories said Balaglitazone was ready with Phase III data but a similar drug was banned in Europe, so it could not find a partner. It proved to be the straw that broke the camel's back. Even a diehard discovery champion like Dr Reddy, who kept throwing money at discovery research despite several consecutive quarters of declining profits in 2004, gave up on it and became party to the decision to slash the company's research budget. It was restored to previous levels only after ten years, but more for innovation than discovery.)

Now, with even fewer Indian companies developing new molecules, Biocon has a hard time making a case that its science is solid and its data genuine. 'Look at itolizumab. How am I going to prove its credibility when no one is working on anti-CD6? Bristol-Myers Squibb once worked on this antibody and later pulled the plug. Now when I have the molecule, people say if Bristol-Myers could not make it work, how will Biocon do it? I have valuable data to show that we have targeted a different domain from Bristol-Myers and the drug works,' Kiran says.

India as a country and generics companies as an industry have not done cutting-edge science around molecules; it's mostly incremental innovation around existing ones. No first-in-class molecule has come out of India. 'I am doing it and so I have to bear the cross,' Kiran said, a trace of contempt in her voice. 'If you ask my clinical advisory board, they are so excited. They are talking to our licensees, but the latter ask why BMS dumped such a molecule. But clinical advisors always say good things. I have to do a lot of hard talk and some clinical work outside India.'

It doesn't end with the West looking askance at Indian drug data cap, local clinicians sit on the fence too. 'They often ask, "Where is the data?" and I say, "Why don't you create the data?"' she adds.

One widely followed strategy for new molecules is to test them in rare diseases, also termed 'orphan indications', where standard care is inadequate or does not exist at all. The regulatory pathway is simpler and faster. So one day, when Kiran learnt that NIMHANS in Bengaluru had a team of neurologists which works in neuromyelitis optica – one of the orphan indications and a subset of multiple sclerosis, a disease of the central nervous system where itolizumab is in global clinical trials – she rushed to them.

The Bengaluru institute indeed gets neuromyelitis optica

patients every month, but for reasons never articulated, the neurologists neither said yes nor said no, keeping the trial decision in limbo for a year. The see-saw was surprising because the molecule was already approved for psoriasis in India. Then, in early 2015, a doctor at Amrita University in Kerala, who had returned from Cleveland Clinic in the US, offered to run the trial. The NIMHANS team then came forward to be part of the trial as well. In this academic flip-flop, one year was lost.

This was a crucial year because there's a pattern in drug discovery: companies select an area where they know the mechanism of action and build an understanding of the disease around it. Unless a company knows that mechanism, it will only be able to make general medicines. For instance, prior to 2000, doctors liberally prescribed a drug called taxol, a general killer of cells which when administered, killed many healthy cells too. By 2002, different approaches arrived in the field of medicine. Researchers found the mechanism of action in this drug in the orphan indication of cancer – chronic myeloid leukaemia.

At that time, there were just about 50,000 patients suffering from this cancer, perhaps because most of them had died. In any case, all of them died in five years, so the population was never bigger. Jeremy Levin was at the marketing table in Novartis when the senior management was discussing whether to proceed with the drug or not, once the mechanism of action was understood. The marketers around the table were not interested in investing in the disease because the patient pool was so small. The genius of Daniel Vasella and his colleagues was to ask – does this drug stop the disease? When the answer was 'yes', he said, five years from now, there won't be just 50,000 patients. Novartis proceeded with the drug development. The drug was imanitib, which was launched with the brand name Gleevec and is today on the World Health Organization's list of essential medicines.

'They took an orphan disease and impacted it with orphan

disease pricing. It went from 50,000 to 1,00,000 and eventually, more than 2,50,000 patients. They created a nearly $8 billion per year marketplace from an orphan disease,' says Levin.

Back in India, Stempeutics Research in Bengaluru received orphan designation in the European Union in 2015 for its stem cells product for Buerger's disease, a rare condition in which there is reduced blood flow to the limbs. A pioneer in India in stem cells research, the company has been stuck in India's muddled regulatory environment for some time but will now get multiple benefits from this orphan designation, including ten years of market exclusivity from the day of the product launch in the European Union.

Forced by the demands of unsettled science, complex regulation and brute economics, drug companies are learning what genetics always knew – rare diseases are not that rare.

There's yet another road less travelled that Biocon is treading once again using rare diseases as a gateway.

Upping the Ante: Antibodies to Nucleic Acid

At the annual biotech conference in Bengaluru in 2013, when the opening panel discussion ended, Daniel Zurr walked up to Kiran and introduced himself. The Israeli entrepreneur had heard her enzyme-to-antibody story and was impressed by the massive biologics manufacturing capabilities that Biocon housed. The products his company was developing in Israel and California were a natural progression from antibodies, and he thought he could find a production partner in Biocon.

The two met and one conversation led to another; their chemistry was organic. After having worked in the pharmaceutical industry for nearly two decades, Zurr started Quark Pharmaceuticals in 1994 to build technologies to identify genes that shed light on disease processes. In a few years, he realized he also needed to develop therapeutics to treat those faulty processes, and chose a newly discovered technology of gene silencing. It was RNA interference, a discovery that later won the Nobel Prize in 2006. It's a method for turning genes off selectively by using short double-stranded RNA molecules that the DNA makes to produce proteins. It shuts off production of any protein that is associated with a disease, a target which was earlier not 'druggable', i.e., reachable by ordinary drugs.

Unlike Kiran, Zurr came to entrepreneurship 'rather late'. 'I thought it would be some bit of adventure, we all die in the end anyway,' he says wryly. The adventure has lasted twenty years. Zurr built a team of over 300 scientists in Israel and 600 in California, 80 per cent of whom have stayed with the company.

When he met Kiran, Quark Pharmaceuticals had three products for five indications in mid-stage development; two of them were licensed to Novartis and Pfizer. For the third molecule, which was tested on a small sample in a mid-stage study and had impressed the American regulator with its findings, he was looking for a late-stage clinical trial as well as a manufacturing partner.

In less than a year from that meeting, by late 2013, Zurr and Kiran worked out a three-pronged partnership. Syngene would manufacture the experimental drug which has an orphan drug designation for an eye condition called non-arteritic anterior ischemic optic neuropathy, a hotchpotch of medical jargon that goes by the acronym NAION. Simplistically, it is accelerated glaucoma, a disease of the optic nerve which leads to loss of vision. Clinigene, now part of Syngene, would conduct the Indian arm of the global trial; and large-scale manufacturing, if and when the drug was approved, would come Biocon's way.

It was a comprehensive, relatively risk-free arrangement for Biocon, but Kiran had learnt from the Cuban partnership that unless local scientific research capabilities are in place, alliances remain flaky. She wanted a partnership in Quark's preclinical molecules, one of which targeted acute lung injury and was in the preclinical stage. She told Zurr, in order to close the manufacturing and clinical studies deal, they would have to come to an agreement on preclinical as well. She was clear that her researchers needed to understand the 'science better and learn how to select the best molecule at the end'.

That was asking a lot. Zurr, who likes to use the parent–child analogy, thought she was asking to be the mother of the baby when the baby was already born. He was hesitant, so she came up with an idea. 'Through the Investigational New Drug application approval and Phase I study, the baby belongs more to you, but I will put in more money, and by the time we end Phase I, the ownership will be fifty-fifty,' she told him.

'But I started to haggle. She cut me short – two-thirds investment hers and one-third mine,' Zurr recalls. It was difficult for him but he liked the concept where 'she adopts the baby and gives more care'. They signed the deal in New York.

A year later, in Bengaluru, Zurr was happy at the speed with which Biocon was moving. 'A deal with big pharma is like human pregnancy, it takes at least nine months to move a step; with Biocon it was less than two months,' he says. The tough negotiation was behind him. 'There are people who are tough negotiators, who enjoy the power of negotiation so much that they don't care if at the end of the day the deal has failed. Kiran knows how to close a deal.'

Common Aspirations

Before founding Quark, Zurr was the president and chief executive of Plantex-Ikapharm, which was acquired by Israel's largest pharmaceutical company, Teva. He left it to start a biotech company, one of the earliest human genomics companies in the world, in the mid-1990s, but the pharmaceutical flavour stayed with him. Now that Quark has developed some clinical-stage drugs, Zurr wants it to grow into a pharmaceutical company.

'When small companies license their drug to big pharma, they invariably have to give away the worldwide commercial rights.

'And if drugs are successful, all that small companies do is go to the bank to collect royalties. They never learn how to sell,' says Zurr. With the Biocon partnership, he retains the marketing rights to some markets, which he believes will help Quark sell a product and become a pharmaceutical company. (That also partly explains why he changed the name of his company from Quark Biotech to Quark Pharmaceuticals in 2007.)

Zurr was born in Israel to a Polish father and a Ukrainian mother who had fled Europe during the holocaust. His father founded and built one of the largest agrochemicals companies in the world, Makhteshim. Still, after completing his doctorate from the Imperial College in London, the idea of starting up never occurred to Zurr since most companies in Israel those days were state-owned in any case. His chemistry training under Nobel laureate Sir Derek Barton helped him launch into an international pharmaceutical executive's career but the past grew a kind of guilt in him. In his growing-up years, he was 'brainwashed by his father to dedicate his life to the welfare of Israel'. Attempting to fulfil it, he returned from the United States to build Quark in Israel, a company he had incorporated in California in 1994.

Four years later, he ran into Mugasimangalam Raja in the US, when the latter was working on the mutating specificity of restriction enzymes at Sidney Kimmel Cancer Center in San Diego. Prior to that, Raja had worked at Weizmann Institute in Israel, developing some techniques for DNA sequencing. He often confided in his colleagues that he missed Israel and that given an opportunity, he would like to return. When Zurr asked him what plans he had for his career, Raja, who had worked in the Human Genome Project at the Argonne National Laboratory in Illinois, made no bones about his desire to go back to India and start a company in genomics.

'That is a very honourable thing to do,' Zurr said, and made him an offer. If Raja went to Israel and helped Zurr's team solve a tricky problem in microarray technologies, which Quark was using to serve many Japanese pharmaceutical companies, he would give Raja a big enough project that would help him start his dream company in India. Zurr did not specify the problem Quark was facing but somehow felt Raja could do 'some Indian black magic' with his sequencing skills. Raja accepted his offer and spent two years at Quark in Israel, developing two new methods for constructing complementary DNA – which is used to clone some genes – microarrays.

Zurr kept his gentlemanly promise and gave Raja enough business to start Genotypic Technology in Bengaluru. Late though he was to entrepreneurship, Zurr knew that securing business was more important than signing up investors.

The two remained friends. Sometime before 2009, Zurr began travelling to India. His molecules were advancing and he needed a large, diverse population for the study of rare diseases. In Cipla's Yusuf Hamied he had a potential partner. The two have a common friend in the famous conductor Zubin Mehta, apart from Hamied's old connection to Israel because of his mother, who was of Jewish origin. Zurr also made a few trips to Bengaluru. He had heard about Biocon, which by then had become Genotypic's customer, a steady source of revenue in the city after AstraZeneca, but he could never meet Kiran despite having a few meetings at Biocon.

Sometimes visionaries cannot build, but in Kiran, he said, he found someone 'who had managed to combine vision with perseverance'. He felt he had some things to learn from her. So at the Bengaluru biotech conference, he just walked up to her and introduced himself.

In the first few years of starting up, Zurr had raised venture capital from a handful of Japanese investors but the company's rites of passage through the classic 'death valley' was arduous. Zurr ended up 'diluting' himself early on. He blames his minority position in Quark to his 'weakness' of not being interested in money. 'I was lucky to be born in a wealthy family, so I never had the need or urge to earn big money,' he says, poker-faced. 'I can drive a Volkswagen, I don't have to drive a Mercedes.'

At sixty-seven years of age, what drives Zurr is the obsession to bring a new drug from an Israeli company to the global market, an obsession he shares with Kiran. The preclinical deal which he haggled over in New York showed that Biocon's appetite for risk was increasing. Since RNAi (RNA interference) is a new category of therapeutics, which if successful, could launch a totally new commercial path for Biocon, Kiran needed an anchor researcher for this initiative, someone who would take ownership.

A few months after the agreement was signed, Manian, who chairs the board that decides the Bill & Melinda Gates Foundation's India-specific grand challenge applications, was one day advising a scientist who wanted to take up intellectual property management as a career. (Manian holds at least fifty patents.) When the meeting was over, the lady said that her husband, also a scientist, was in the car and wanted to say hello to him. Manian agreed. The man turned out to be Vasan Sambandanamurthy, who was looking for a job after AstraZeneca had shuttered its Bengaluru research centre in early 2014 and was actively considering a position at Shantha Biotechnics in Hyderabad, even though he knew it was a manufacturing company. Manian told him, 'We can't let you go out of Bengaluru,' and called Kiran and said he had found someone to run the Quark programme.

When Zurr visited Bengaluru a week later, Sambandanamurthy met him, Kiran and the senior management of Biocon; within fifteen minutes he was 'on board'. After his Ph.D from the Tuberculosis Institute in Chennai, Sambandanamurthy had worked at Howard Hughes Medical Institute in New York, Novartis Institute for Tropical Medicine in Singapore and AstraZeneca in Bengaluru in a career spanning over twelve years. Manian found his discovery research and big pharma experience valuable at a time when Biocon had to establish the regulatory and clinical pathway for RNAi while also building a knowledge platform in Bengaluru based on technology transfer from Quark that would allow it to discover new siRNA (short-interfering RNA) molecules.

In some respects, siRNAs are similar to small molecules; chemical in nature, they are screened to find lead molecules which are then 'optimized', i.e., designed to work best with the target. The similarities end there. These molecules are high in negative charge and to get across any cellular membrane in the body, they need to be made amply stable, a process that involves plenty of chemistry. One of the reasons Zurr kept coming back to India was its chemistry talent. In the West, it is a dying profession, according to him.

If chemical synthesis of a small molecule typically involves three to five reactions to get to the end product, in RNAi synthesis, as many as sixty reactions are required to get to the final product. To get into such uncharted territory, Sambandanamurthy needs to build a basic research culture, different from the industrial or applied research that Biocon traditionally does. So he has been placed in the Mazumdar-Shaw Centre for Translational Research in Narayana Health City. The new location also insulates his tiny team from the quarterly pressure that researchers face at the Biocon Research Centre.

For the clinical programme which began with a global Phase III study in NAION in September 2015, Zurr, through Raja, found Atignal as his focal person in India. After exiting Clinigene due to a sudden illness, Atignal lay low for some time, but is now back with a vengeance as a consultant. He is spreading himself thick, advising Tata Industries (which is entering the healthcare market), Acunova, a contract research organization, and is growing his wife's Milan Fertility Centre into India's largest in vitro fertility service provider by getting some strategic investments.

'Working with Kiran and married to Kamini [Rao] – two high-strung women who probably have one new idea every day – has honed my entrepreneurial skills. They are passionate about what they do and are not afraid to fail,' says Atignal as he mounts fresh clinical efforts to run India's first RNAi clinical trial.

Vulnerabilities

Racing past small molecules, which launched and sustained the pharmaceutical industry for several decades, biologics have now come to rule sales charts – seven of the top eight best-selling drugs in the world were biologics in 2014. It is believed they will continue to dominate until the early 2020s when new categories of therapeutics – RNAi being one of them, especially for chronic and rare diseases – will begin to influence prescriptions.

Since RNA interference is a naturally occurring cellular process which was first observed in plants and later in worms, its use to silence defective genes for curing diseases is only commonsensical. This also explains why its discovery won the Nobel Prize just eight years after the first paper was published, perhaps one of the few scientific discoveries to move from published paper to the coveted prize so swiftly.

In the initial days, the technology worked as a research tool in labs, both in universities and industry, for studying gene function, analysing pathways and validating drug targets. Eventually, scientists made siRNA, which could slip inside mammalian cells without causing any immune reaction.

All factors considered, it's the delivery of this technology which has stumped scientists because the body sees the siRNAs as foreign substances and attacks them. About half a dozen RNAi companies leading the charge – Quark being one of them – are developing delivery technologies to skirt this issue. Nanoparticles are being commonly used to deliver RNAi to the cells, some so potent they're able to target ten proteins at a time. For the Phase III trial of NAION, Quark will direct intravitreal injections into the eye.

Zurr's two-decade journey is heading towards fruition. The molecules licensed to Novartis, after some tweaking of the end point in Phase II, have entered Phase III, as has Zurr's older agreement with Pfizer. With the latter, Quark has entered a late-stage study in another eye disorder called diabetic macular edema. It's been pocketing millions of dollars in milestone payments, but it's also 'burning cash'.

By bearing a 'fraction' of the cost of the trial – Phase III is the most expensive of all stages – Biocon gets to be part of one of the earliest studies in RNAi molecules in the world. If the trial is successful and the drug is approved for NAION, which affects only 15,000 per year in the US and a slightly higher number elsewhere, it could unravel the underlying science of this drug. The two partners would then test it in glaucoma since the molecule, QPI-1007, in early studies has shown promise of curing glaucoma.

If that happens, Quark and Biocon could be looking at a potential billion-dollar market as there is no cure for glaucoma – all that patients receive today is drugs to reduce intraocular pressure.

Another possible commercial opportunity could come from agriculture, perhaps more in manufacturing than in developing new products. RNAi is being used to improve pest resistance, nutrition and yield of crop plants. Such crops are already approved for cultivation by regulatory agencies in Brazil and most of the developed countries.

What may look like a small financial risk for Kiran today could pay off disproportionately, if not immediately, maybe in a decade.

'She takes a gamble, but a very, very calculated gamble. Maybe it's also intuitive,' Zurr says brightly, warming to the theme of what drives entrepreneurs. 'She has reached a point where she can enjoy the process of doing new things.'

That may be, but for the industry, doing new things is still like a tent poorly staked, often dealing with seasonal storms.

8

THE START-UP INDUSTRY

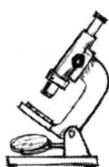

RISK OF THE RHYME

'When are we going to see an Infosys or a Wipro in Indian biotech?' asked a journalist at the first BioInvest conference in Mumbai in 2005.

'Never,' retorted Kiran. 'Biotech is not about body shopping. Today you have a hundred people, within a month you can scale up to two hundred and by year end, to a thousand. That is not possible in biotech, so it'll never be where they are. Is that clear?' she asked rhetorically.

The journalist was only partly to blame. The turn of the millennium saw a Western frenzy in life sciences that did not need a visa to reach Indian shores. If the millennial fright of Y2K could bring fortunes to IT companies, many assumed the same would repeat in life sciences. The Human Genome Project draft was getting ready to be made public and it was widely believed that the decoded DNA would offer a goldmine of data-driven opportunities. 'IT is India today, BT is Bharat tomorrow,' proclaimed Prime Minister Atal Bihari Vajpayee. But other than the common suffix, there was no commonality.

As a metaphor though, Vajpayee's slogan was right. Biotech is an industry of tomorrow. And with the explosion in genomics and other related sciences, DNA has become a programming language.

Way back in the mid-1960s, when America under Lyndon Johnson was critically evaluating the fruits of biosciences and asking for tangible practical results, politicians noticed that voters shared a belief that the 'biological sciences could mend many of the wicked evils of modern life'. The scope of life sciences ranged from virus to society. And, it hasn't diminished over the decades.

In Bengaluru, the seedbed of the IT business, entrepreneurs and policymakers were extrapolating that scope in search of the next wave to ride. If biotech 'biomania' as it was termed, in the 1980s had the rhetoric of perpetual growth associated with it, in India, people linked it with instant growth. In the relay race, they saw biotech taking the baton of high economic activity from information technology.

It was also the time when President George Bush imposed restrictions on the embryonic stem cell lines which could be used by American research labs to qualify for federal funding. Of the sixty-four approved cell lines, ten belonged to Reliance Life Sciences in Mumbai and the National Centre for Biological Sciences in Bengaluru. In a chest-thumping article, newsweekly *India Today* said the Bush announcement had 'opened a new pot of gold' for Indian science and business. India, however, had no policies covering stem cell research.

The giddy times made Karnakata move swiftly, though. It was the first state to formulate an IT policy and Vivek Kulkarni, the bureaucrat cheerleading that department, wanted to nearly clone it for biotechnology. 'We were hearing a lot about bioinformatics, so we thought we should not miss the opportunity,' recalls Kulkarni. The one-upmanship between Bengaluru and Hyderabad to be the preferred technology destination was suitably fired up by Andhra Pradesh chief minister Chandrababu Naidu's sloganeering –

'Bye-bye Bengaluru, hello Hyderabad'. It was a race for a race. A fresh returnee from the US, Bharat Biotech's Ella, presented the concept of a biotech park to Naidu. At ICICI, Vaghul wanted to do something substantive for early-stage technology development and came up with the idea of a knowledge park. In any case, his bank had considerable exposure to pharmaceuticals; he knew the new patent policy would require companies to be innovative. Naidu had visited Singapore and understood the urgency. The chief executive at ICICI, K.V. Kamath, gave nine months to complete the park. By late 1999, a bio-cluster called Genome Valley with ICICI Knowledge Park was ready, in part, in Hyderabad, to provide customized research and development facilities to start-ups. Deepanwita Chattopadhyay was pulled out of the telecom advisory division of the bank in Mumbai to lead the park, with a brief from Vaghul that if she did not make it 'cash positive' in two years, ICICI would shut it down.

Naturally, Kulkarni was in a hurry in Bengaluru. The Indian Administrative Service (IAS) officer created two 'high-powered groups', cleverly put them in the state budget, and got approval from the Karnataka government. That was no ordinary group; it had powers of the government and Kulkarni had brought Infosys co-founder N.R. Narayana Murthy and Kiran to chair the information technology committee and biotechnology Vision Group respectively.

'To my mind that was the first time anywhere in the country, and probably the last time, that a group of professionals had the powers of the government,' remembers Kulkarni. He never took his files to the finance department or any other department for approval. The Millennium Policy had vested executive powers in groups with busy leaders like Murthy and Azim Premji devoting long hours to meetings, after which decisions were taken. The IT captains batted for good roads, hotels, airports, schools for employees' children, even altering the curriculum in engineering colleges so that more students were trained in computer science – all in the name of making 'Bengaluru a more welcoming place for customers'. Biotech benefited too.

'I was able to move very fast,' says Kulkarni. Fast indeed, since the state left New Delhi behind in articulating clear policies for those two technology sectors.

By the time Karnataka's biotech policy was formulated, Kulkarni had a replicable model in front of him. 'We said the IT industry had a state policy, an apex training institute, and an annual event in IT.Com; we would do the same for biotech,' he says.

IN IT's FOOTSTEPS

The formation document of the Indian Institute of Information Technology became a near-carbon-copy template for the Institute of Bioinformatics and Applied Biotechnology (IBAB). Gayatri Saberwal was the state department's first 'biotech' hire. When she was completing her Ph.D at the Centre of Cellular and Molecular Biology in Hyderabad, Sharat Chandra was the director, and he pulled her into the Vision Group activities in late 2000 when he himself got inducted. Incidentally, his request for land for a human genetics centre was long pending before the government. Saberwal would become the cultural touch point for rallying academics, industry and government.

Like the information technology institute, the biotech institute too received some land and seed money towards infrastructure. But it was an 'instant noodle recipe for an institution', for which Kiran would provide some fast-food ingredients, for several years. While the project manager at Biocon, Madhav Raj Sirsi, designed the labs, Saberwal had to shop for expensive equipment. She suggested they take the help of a purchase officer at the National Centre for Biological Sciences; she did not know about Kiran's reputation for tight-fistedness. 'She decided to show us what bargaining was. We got a $100,000 sequencer for 30 per cent of the price. She probably knew the dynamics of the market,' Saberwal says.

Kiran's earlier association with ICICI Bank also came in handy. Kulkarni struck a deal with the bank, which was already an investor in the Hyderabad cluster, for an interest-free loan of ₹5 crore, which, after a ten-year moratorium, would be payable in ten equal instalments. The government agreed to provide an equal amount. Aspirations soared. The state government sent officials to Singapore to study the design and operations of Biopolis, a biotech cluster that the nation state was then building. Kulkarni placed an advertisement in an international journal for the director's post at the Bengaluru institute. 'I was surprised to see that the government was willing to pay American salaries,' says Sharat Chandra, sounding amused even more than a decade later.

Kulkarni's advertisement did not elicit any suitable response; the institute was an experiment after all – a high-risk venture that few academics were willing to stake their reputation at. As chairman of the governing board, Chandra was finally able to lure away Manju Bansal on loan for three years from the Indian Institute of Science. But the real problem started afterwards. As an autonomous body and a non-profit society, not associated with any of the top-notch science or biotech funding agencies, the institute could not attract the right faculty for many years; in fact, eight of the first eleven faculty are no longer with the institute today. A sticky situation that also riled S. Sadagopan, founding director at the Indian Institute of Information Technology, in the neighbourhood, for many years. (The word 'Indian' was later replaced with 'International' but that hardly resolved the issue.)

Out of the cosy, close-knit consultations between industry, government and academe, the Institute of Bioinformatics and Applied Biotechnology was born, virtually a tabula rasa for the Vision Group and the faculty. So when the first batch of students arrived, Saberwal and a few others could not fully understand why they had joined. She circulated a questionnaire. Most of the students said they had been attracted by the governing body – a stellar group that comprised heads of institutions in Bengaluru, including the Indian Institute of Management, and, of course, Kiran.

As chairperson of the Vision Group, she had begun to own the task. One Friday evening in April 2001, she called Sircar from the intellectual property division, just as he was leaving for home. 'Tomorrow, Bengaluru BIO is starting. You all have to attend. By the way, you are the compère because we haven't found one yet. You have to be there all day, there's no breakout session, and yes, wear a suit,' she instructed. Sircar managed somehow. The following year, conference organizers had found a compère, so Sircar strolled in on the last day. To his amazement, he found Kiran behind the lectern, compèring throughout the afternoon, 'stepping up and down the stage tirelessly'.

'The compère had fallen sick on the last day but she did not call me; she chose to do it herself,' Sircar remembers.

Kulkarni and others had modelled the biotech event after BangaloreIT.com which, since 1998, had become a go-to event for the technology industry. A few years later, Hyderabad followed suit and started BIO Asia. To fragment it further, US BIO organized three events in India, beginning 2008. It was not funny that event organizers for an industry worth less than $3 billion were stretching it in just three southern states which the rest of the country watched from a distance. In the US, the biotech industry was $22.3 billion in size at that time, but there was just one event, US BIO, for which the organizers moved from city to city every year.

As the biotech event gathered visibility, funds for the biotech park – Bangalore Helix – and the institute dried up. Drought had hit north Karnataka, Chief Minister S.M. Krishna called for early elections and a pall of gloom fell on biotech and IT activities. The dry spell reached Hyderabad too, when Naidu's political career took a turn and he was voted out of power in 2004.

An engineer and a Wharton graduate who wanted to elevate

Bengaluru on the biotech map as fast as possible, Kulkarni left the government in 2004 to become an entrepreneur. The institute was left high and dry in the expensive technology park in Whitefield and the new director, N. Yathindra – who had joined from University of Madras when Bansal went back to Indian Institute of Science – often had to make panic calls to Kiran. She would then direct him to a minister or a bureaucrat, and the financial situation would ease temporarily. Sometimes, the stop-gap financing would come from her as well.

For the faculty, public–private partnership for running an educational centre was a new idea, but making it work was not easy since nobody knew where the next cheque would come from. 'We used to wring our hands; ₹5 crore is in the bank but what do we do? Kiran would say, "First prove yourself, then the money will come,"' says Saberwal.

In Hyderabad, Genome Valley and the Knowledge Park were only slightly better off. Four years after they started, the inadequacies began to irk entrepreneurs. In 2003, Varaprasad Reddy told Pharmabiz: 'The government has allocated 200 acres for the Biotech Park, but making it work is an altogether different game. For international investors, the park needs infrastructure of international standards and hassle-free clearances. The international conferences get attractive captions in the newspapers and the delegates enjoy Hyderabadi hospitality. At the end, what comes out of such meetings? The incentive packages seem to be applicable only to new investors. What about the existing units? Industrialists are unable to meet the Chief Minister though he says he is industry-friendly.'

*

The political crisis hardly eased in Karnataka, and Bangalore Helix was caught in a taciturn tangle of land and funds; it would be a decade before the place would be actually ready to house and serve start-ups, even though successive bureaucrats supported biotech.

Aside from these extramural activities, something else was brewing in Kiran's head.

Between a successful IT industry, which had Nasscom by its side, and a growing pharmaceutical industry, which leaned on the Indian Pharmaceutical Association, Kiran felt biotech was without a chaperone. She was also somewhat miffed with the pharma body.

When the drug makers formed the Indian Pharmaceutical Association, she had not been invited. Since the alliance was formed by invitation and she had a 'good equation' with Cipla's Yusuf Hamied and Ranbaxy's Singh, she was a little upset about being left out of it. It fell upon Raizada to tell her that the membership was decided based on the size of the company. The alliance wanted ten core members and the biggest companies by revenue were invited. 'When Piramal Healthcare and Cipla fell out with the Association, new members were again decided by the size of the company,' said Raizada. The other industry groups, CII and FICCI, were too big to bother about biotech since it had unique regulatory and funding requirements.

In July 2001, at the breakfast table at Mayfair Hotel in Washington, Kulkarni, Kiran and a few others who were attending US BIO, pulled out some paper napkins and wrote a plan to set up an industry body for biotech – the Association of Biotechnology Led Enterprises (ABLE). The following April, at the biotech event inauguration, Kiran delivered a fiery speech, recalls Anand Kumar, the former head of Astra Research Foundation. She outlined what biotech, backed by a professional body like ABLE, would do. Then she concluded, 'I really thank Vijay Chandru and Ravikumar for accepting to be the secretary and the joint secretary of the Association.' The two men were startled; she had not asked them formally but had only texted to be present at the inauguration. She also did not ask anyone before giving her house in Koramangala as the rent-free office for some years.

In the following years, ABLE tried copying Nasscom in being the voice of the industry, though not reducing itself to 'lobbying for sales tax reduction'. 'In terms of scale, we are where Nasscom was under Dewang Mehta,' says its president, Panchapagesa Murali.

With an institute, an event, a trade publication and an industry body in place, biotech in Bengaluru was ready to roll. International magazines and journals were feeding the frenzy. In April 2000, the weekly magazine *Newsweek* splashed bioinformatics on its cover. Earlier, in 1996, the American journal *Science*, as part of its 'Next Wave' series, wrote: *Bioinformatics: New Frontier Calls Young Scientists*. Two years later, before the draft sequences were published, project leader Francis S. Collins and members of the United States Department of Energy and the National Institutes of Health Planning Group wrote in *Science*: 'Programs must be developed that will encourage training of both biological and non-biological scientists for careers in genomics. Especially critical is the shortage of individuals trained in bioinformatics.'

At the IISc from where Sharat Chandra was retiring in 2000, he saw that Ph.D students who could do bioinformatics were easily getting jobs paying $70,000 or more per year in the US whereas the rest of the Indian Ph.Ds had to settle for half that salary.

Of Exact IT and Approximate BT

In fields such as engineering, information and communication technology, when a new product idea arises, little doubt exists that it can be created; the uncertainty lies in predicting its cost, customer acceptance and pricing. In biotechnology, most of the products exist in nature – hormones, proteins, blood factors, etc. So the need is known as is the fact that someone will pay for the product, if priced reasonably. What is not known is how to make it.

At the Indian Institute of Science, Brahmachari took to bioinformatics early because of the foreign exchange crunch of 1995 when, with skyrocketing import duties, research grants were effectively losing a third of their buying power. The IISc had reasonably good computation facilities and here over the next few years, he would try to marry the two disciplines. In addition, in his interactions with Cantor, he had learnt that IT and biology had remained separate in American research institutions and universities and this had slowed data interpretation. (Charles DeLisi would introduce America's first Ph.D programme in bioinformatics at Boston University as late as in 1999.)

After settling down at the Institute of Genomics and Integrative Biology in Delhi, Brahmachari forged a deal with Aptech, the software training institute in Delhi, to train students in bioinformatics. He had convinced The Chatterjee Group in Kolkata to fund a fellowship – and later with some consultancy money from Nicholas Piramal – Brahmachari trained over 500 students in five years. He had a stroke of luck in September 2001 when, in the post 9/11 turmoil, many students could not report for work in the US and a bunch of fourteen graduates from IIT Kanpur joined him for projects. 'We couldn't buy multiprocessor machines. [Craig] Venter [at Celera Genomics] was using sixty-four processor machines and all we had were two Silicon Graphics dual-processor machines. We connected them and got the fresh graduates to write the software. All early analysis of our genomic data was done by those kids,' he remembers.

Still, Brahmachari could sense the vacuum in informatics skills in the country. He flew down to Bengaluru to meet N.R. Narayana Murthy at Infosys to convince him to invest in bioinformatics. 'He asked me if I would publish papers in *Nature* out of this work. I felt I was defeated. I was saying I want to build capacity; Infosys would have a lead one day. That was the time when I had to teach everyone what biology could do in future,' recollects Brahmachari. Murthy wasn't convinced and said, 'When you are ready with a *Nature* paper, come to us.' (Brahmachari did go back to Murthy, ten years later, when he created the Open Source Drug Discovery portal. Infosys helped, free of charge, to create a professional portal for high-volume interactive use and later maintained the portal at a discounted fee.)

All big IT services companies had created a life sciences practice around that time. But the only company which really believed in it was Tata Consultancy Services (TCS). In 2000, M. Vidyasagar, director of the Centre for Artificial Intelligence and Robotics in Bengaluru, decided to leave the defence laboratory. A.P.J. Abdul Kalam had retired from the Defence Research Development Organization and Vidyasagar did not want to continue under the new leadership. He wrote to Subramaniam Ramadorai at TCS, asking if the chief executive had 'anything' for him. 'Ramadorai called back immediately saying, "When are you starting,"' Vidyasagar recalls.

After joining the Tatas in April 2000, Vidyasagar started the Advanced Technology Centre in Hyderabad to incubate five different research groups, two of them in life sciences. He hired a few Ph.Ds along with thirty other biologists; it was the kind of investment no other IT company would have made. They intended to use statistical and IT-based methods on public data to predict which drugs were likely to work for which patients and then verify them in clinical settings. The company also got into a large collaborative agreement with the Berkeley Institute of Genomic Variation for some discovery research in figuring out how one person's genome varies with another.

In the government, at CSIR, Mashelkar was aspiring for any of his labs to take the lead in Bio-IT. Under the New Millennium Indian Technology Leadership Initiative he sanctioned a project, later called BioSuite, to develop a comprehensive set of seventy-nine programmes that covered most of the bioinformatics applications in life sciences. Tata Consultancy Services, which got a soft loan of ₹7.5 crore, was the primary coding partner along with scientists from eighteen institutions. Brahmachari coordinated the project in the hope that TCS would install it in all colleges (at ₹50,000 each), leading to a surge in trained professionals. '[TCS] commercialized it but the return on investment was less; they never upgraded the software even in the few institutions they installed [it in]. How could we create human resources around it? If Microsoft had not given its software free to NIIT [National Institute of Information Technology], do you think Rajendra Pawar [co-founder of NIIT] could have trained half a million kids? I felt CSIR was cheated,' Brahmachari notes.

In Bengaluru, Vijay Chandru at the Indian Institute of Science was thinking along similar lines. He and his colleagues at the computer science and automation department were running workshops in computational biology. But in 1998, they got a real opportunity to apply their theoretical learning. Mike Pellini of Genomics Collaborative in Boston got in touch with Chandru, who, after a Ph.D from MIT, had continued to hook into the high-wire Cambridge network. Pellini's company was building a repository of genomes and tissues and needed informatics backing to process and organize the data. 'We thought it was a great opportunity. It started with the laboratory information management system, inventory tracking and all that, but eventually, it got us thinking about sequencing and related technologies,' recalls Chandru. He took it up as a consultancy project while working at the Indian Institute of Science. This, and a few other projects, subsidized the development of a hand-held computer, Simputer, that he and his other colleagues were building in the lab.

By 1999, this group of four academics was ready to use the taboo word on campus – entrepreneurship. Computer scientist Swami Manohar started the process with the institute administration while Chandru wrote to Kiran that he wanted to 'make the leap'. She wrote back, echoing Vaghul's plea that India needed more scientist entrepreneurs: 'I've been telling you for years. Come, we'll discuss.' Around the same time, Ratan Tata had 'chastised' the institute's scientists for not spinning off technologies in the private sector. (The institute did spin off technologies but to the public sector; they were willing to put their academic agenda on hold and take a reputational risk, but taking financial risk to start a company was still verboten.)

Chandru met Kiran and her senior management at Biocon. She said they would find some way to work together. At Syngene, Das was already looking at companies which were using modelling and computational techniques to predict drug-like properties of compounds. He was trying to partner with the small, privately held Camitro Corporation, which had different models for absorption, distribution and metabolism of compounds. (Camitro was acquired by drug discovery company ArQule in 2001). 'Wouldn't it be neat if you guys got together and built a virtual model of a mouse?' she had asked Chandru and Das.

Chandru was trying to muster enough courage to start Strand Genomics (later renamed as Strand Life Sciences). Kiran and he had been family friends and she was the only person he knew 'who had done anything like this'. 'She was always open to talking to investors on our behalf,' said Chandru. Later, when WestBridge Capital invested $5 million in 2002, it was Kiran who served as a reference.

At the same time, more by chance than in any step-by-step march of the competing cities, Anuradha Acharya landed in Hyderabad from California to build a business in bioinformatics. While doing her master's at Illinois in management information systems, she had identified outsourced genomics services to dig into, but when she advertised for a position in Hyderabad, she received 2,000 résumés, of which only one had something to do with bioinformatics. At that hiring rate, Ocimum Biosolutions would never build the sequence analysis product that it planned to build. She then struck a deal with Michigan Tech to train a few batches. Meanwhile, the bioinformatics bubble was forming; Hyderabad's newspapers were flooded with advertisements of centres offering such courses. 'It was strange; we were part of the bubble and yet out of it,' Acharya says.

Ocimum partnered with virtually all large IT services companies trying to develop 'applications that would solve some problem at a sufficiently large scale to be worth their while'. 'A few companies hired some people but they would get lost in other verticals. It had to be more entrepreneurial, a small team funded to try out a few things, do some research and allowed to make some mistakes. That did not happen. Patience was missing,' she says.

Strand and Ocimum worked with Infosys, Wipro and others for some time, even made a few customer pitches, but they were often being pitted against companies like Accenture which had 'things to show' whereas Indian partners would land up with 'only PowerPoints'.

'We all started life sciences thinking we would look at advances from genomics. But we did not have credibility with customers; we did not speak their language. They also realized that we would bring better value to them if we built the IT infrastructure. That's what happened with most of us,' Narayana Murthy recalled in 2015.

A few years later, in 2004, Syngene and Strand worked together to design and build compounds with drug-like properties for a Japanese customer. By then, Clinigene had taken off and Atignal wanted to predict the high risk of renal problems in diabetics using the diabetes registry and put them on additional renal care. 'There were no molecular measurements on the samples; they only had serological measurements, so our predictive power was limited because the descriptors were limited. We got reasonable results, though. By using biomarkers on serologics, we could predict about 20 per cent of the high-risk patients,' Chandru recounts. They filed for a joint patent, would flash it as 'IP' later on, but neither commercialized it.

For that, the next step was to use the samples to get more detailed molecular information with deeper data mining. Kiran's idea was to get a third partner, a protein expert from the Indian Institute of Science, who could do mass spectrometry on the samples. But the academic association did not work out with Utpal Tatu. Meanwhile, Strand continued to test toxicity for contract research organizations and a few other companies like Unilever. Genomics was clearly becoming strategic; Syngene's Chinese competitor WuXi had invested in multimillion dollar Illumina sequencers. Kiran could see which way the wind was blowing and suggested 'merging Syngene and Strand' but nobody else was enthused by the idea of a merger.

In Hyderabad, Vidyasagar retired from TCS in 2009, went back to academics in the US for five years, and now consults for a few start-ups. He believes the market for bioinformatics, which was very small those days, remains tiny even today. Worldwide, the software industry is seven to eight times the size of the pharmaceutical industry. And only about 15 per cent of the pharma market is the drug discovery budget, a lot of which goes towards clinical trials. So the actual addressable market for IT-based discovery services is not more than 5 per cent of the total pharmaceutical market, he says.

Nandan Nilekani, who was then the chief executive at Infosys, thinks the bioinformatics buzz was 'ahead of its time'. Fifteen years later, life sciences and healthcare make the smallest revenue segment of the top three IT services companies – TCS, Infosys and Wipro – but it's showing the highest growth, with highest or steady margins.

Back in 2000, Sylvia J. Spengler of the Centre for Bioinformatics and Computational Genomics at Berkeley gave an interesting, if somewhat unflattering, description of the discipline. She wrote in *Science*:

'There is a well-known story about the blind man examining the elephant: the part of the elephant examined determines his perception of the whole beast. Perhaps bioinformatics – the shotgun marriage between biology and mathematics, computer science and engineering – is like an elephant that occupies a large chair in the scientific living room. Given the demand for and shortage of researchers with the computer skills to handle large volumes of biological data, where exactly does the bioinformatics elephant sit? There are probably many biologists who feel that a major product of this bioinformatics elephant is large piles of waste material.'

In India, a waste pile built up in the education sector with training institutes popping up overnight knowing nothing about the shotgun marriage. Institutions started courses which offered a hotchpotch of computer science techniques for updating or accessing biological data. In most cases, students lost out on three years of college education. By the mid-2000s, it was apparent that the emperor had no clothes. By the turn of the decade, most such places had shuttered.

Like the East and West of Rudyard Kipling's 'Ballad', in India IT and BT never really met.

Fresh Impetus

In 2005, the new patent law put India's life sciences knowledge and practice to test. Thirty-five years of process engineering was giving way to a TRIPs-enabled product patent environment. Those with intellectual property would rule the market. At the Department of Biotechnology, Maharaj Kishan Bhan, a physician scientist from AIIMS, was taking on a massive experimentation of building knowledge networks, clusters as it were, across India. But first, taking a page out of the Karnataka playbook (as one Delhi official later confessed), a national strategy and policy framework was prepared, put out for public comments and finally released by the science and technology minister, Kapil Sibal, in August. The word 'industry' figured several times in the document and during its much publicized launch. (Once again, the document needlessly compared BT with IT.)

Bhan began to 'push' R&D in institutions and industry, building processes to connect them. He had spent some time studying the Banaras Hindu University. 'Malaviyaji understood clusters very well; they have to be functionally live ecosystems. What we have in the country today are good neighbourhoods, not clusters. A cluster has to have common governance; it has to be larger than the entities,' he had mused then, in the thick of his institution-building exercise. A self-confessed 'romantic and dreamer', Bhan matured as an intense paediatrician but evolved as a 'foolishly practical' administrator when he hard-landed as the biotech secretary and found most institutions to be 'silos'.

At the heart of most successful clusters is a large university but no city in India could boast of an anchor institution. Bhan and his colleagues then asked, 'What is a translational institute?' There were not too many examples, though. Stanford does it very well but it is a university. Officials finally settled for a large number of programmatic centres – for clinical studies; bio-design for devices, implants and imaging; technology platforms, and a host of other specialities. Apart from seven autonomous research and development institutions, Bhan created new models of governance in existing institutions across the country, particularly for new products because 'translational science was not acceptable to most basic scientists'. A soft-spoken Kashmiri who still reminisces and reminds others of the Sufi culture of the troubled region, Bhan seizes opportunities which often come veiled, in the unlikeliest of places. At a hotel in San Francisco, he bumped into Stanford bioengineer Paul Yock. The latter asked him: 'Are innovators born or are they created?' 'I said, "They can be created; genomics is all rubbish." Yock chuckled: "You are my man."' In less than a week, Yock was in Delhi signing a bio-design pact between Stanford and AIIMS.

Around the same time, in 2008, at a conference at the International Centre for Genetic Engineering and Biotechnology in Delhi, a dehydrated Bhan reached for the same glass of wine as the Wellcome Trust director Mark Walport. Once again Bhan was asked: 'What do you think of the Wellcome Trust fellowship in India?' A mark of excellence no doubt, the fellowships, but Bhan saw them as a mere drop in the ocean. 'India has 1.2 billion people and you offer six fellowships,' Bhan replied. Walport asked what he would do instead. 'I said, "I would fund at least a thousand people over the next three years. You should ask Dr Bhan what will be his response. Will he fund half of it? I think he would."' A month later, Bhan received an email from Walport. The Trust's board had approved a multimillion-pound programme to train hundreds of biologists in India. Today, the Department of Biotechnology is an equal partner in the £160 million alliance.

Before setting up the Biotechnology Industry Research Assistance Council (BIRAC), which would consolidate all industry-funding schemes, Bhan undertook a trip he called 'Bharat Bhraman'. He held discussions in one city after another; Kiran participated actively in some of them. She was no longer resistant to the idea of getting closer to Delhi.

In the late 1990s, the Mashelkar Committee was set up to frame rules and guidelines for pharma research and development. Kiran was a member, and when Ranbaxy's Singh died, Raizada was inducted into it. Raizada recalled, 'She would often say, "I don't need anything from the government." All she'd want is to be left alone. Swati [Piramal] was also a member. These women loved the sound of their own voices, but Swati would have a list of things she wanted whereas Kiran would not have any demands; she'd choose to comment on what others said. She wanted Biocon to be at arm's length from the government.'

That reticence receded to some extent when Bhan came to the helm. He wanted to build a new biotech strategy based on the 'conviction that research for *public good* and research *for profit* should reinvigorate the innovation system'.

'Initially, [Bhan] had a bit of disdain for the industry; he would say, "*Aap log bahut baat karte hain; aapke paas itna* paisa *hai, aap log kya karte hain* research *ke liye.*" I would tell him, "You must understand that industry will not do something for charity. It will invest in something that would give it returns. You have to make it attractive for us. Why do we go running after some labs overseas? Government has a wrong notion that industry has to support government institutions or labs,"' recalls Kiran.

For Bhan, over time, conversations with Kiran became mutually 'reinforcing'. For funding schemes of BIRAC, cabinet approval was very generous, but it was her influence that rationalized it. 'She would say that the department should not give easy money but reward people who take up challenges; that entrepreneurs must get support which would give them money at low interest rates rather than market rates,' Bhan says. He saw a certain spark and the courage of entrepreneurship in her. 'There are many who often look to the government for soft support but she is really into challenges. She discusses matters like an industry partner.'

In the eight years that Bhan rode the roller coaster, Kiran drew his attention to biosimilars guidelines and manufacturing. In the government, he admitted, 'We always value innovation but she made me realize, without saying so directly and by showing the way she herself was going, that the nation had to be a powerful manufacturing centre for innovation to thrive and get absorbed.' This was timely because Bhan was then studying South Korea and how the country was boosting its manufacturing capability and process innovation. That led him to pay more attention to the skills of medium-size companies. One of his favourite programmes, a bio-design initiative between Stanford University and AIIMS, had run into a rough patch when the prototypes developed during those fellowships could not be produced because industry was 'not ready to run with it'.

After that experience, the biotech department selected a few companies with international connections, mainly to agencies like the Bill & Melinda Gates Foundation, the World Health Organization and the Wellcome Trust for manufacturing oversight. This 'hugely augmented' the capabilities of the vaccine industry. The vaccine regulatory system now meets the standards in Canada and the United States, though the same cannot be said about pharma and other biotech products.

In early 2015, a child died in a rotavirus vaccine trial at Serum Institute after which the Delhi government intervened and stopped the trial. Even though the department had not invested 'a penny in that vaccine, it brought all the stakeholders together and got the vaccine trial on track'. 'This was the collective influence of Kiran and Bala [Manian] who had convinced us about why the department should empower entrepreneurs, not entitle them. I would say it's the finest example of good governance, of supporting a local manufacturer of a product,' Bhan says.

REGULATORY OVERHANG

The same 'good governance' did not apply to other parts of biotechnology, however. Public interest litigations continued to roil.

In May 2007, the Supreme Court heard the Aruna Rodrigues case on genetically modified (GM) crops. The three-judge bench headed by Justice K.G. Balakrishnan, the Chief Justice of India (CJI), was going to overrule the moratorium imposed earlier on open field trials of these crops. Rodrigues's case was against the Genetic Engineering Approval Committee (GEAC) of the Ministry of Environment and Forests (MoEF) and it listed a set of complaints to which the government had to respond. The first generation of genetically modified seeds, Bollgard-1 was in the market, the next-generation Bollgard-2 was nearly ready to be released, and a few field trials were on. Indolent and casual, the Committee did not take the 2005 PIL seriously. It never appeared in court, whereas the activists' group would regularly present themselves for hearings. After several adjournments, when the court threatened to issue an ex-parte decision for a blanket ban on field trials of these crops, the government woke up.

On 8 May, when lunchtime was about to get over, the judge took up the matter. He had studied the case, which he thought was very technical and which the court was not competent to sit in judgement on. Now that the opposite party was represented, he said, he was lifting the ban. He ordered setting up a Technical Expert Committee which would examine the matter and advise the court.

Soon after this, the government parties – the Genetic Engineering Approval Committee, seed companies and representatives of the Department of Biotechnology – rushed out. They apparently had a limited goal – to get permission for the field trials and sale of Bt cotton. Agriculture scientist K.K. Narayanan was in the court room and saw the act unfold. Justice Balakrishnan wanted the court master to write a ruling and asked what the two parties wanted. Petitioner's counsel Prashant Bhushan shouted, 'We want some conditions before the trials are conducted. We must have a detectable limit of 0.01 per cent.'

'I don't understand what you are saying; please talk to the court master,' the chief justice said, pointing to the man sitting in the corner. Bhushan dictated 200 metres as the minimum isolation distance and a level of detection which was ten times stricter than what even the European Union, averse to the idea of genetically modified crop, follows. In April 2008, the court ruled that 'all concerned were directed to comply' with these specific conditions.

Narayanan was fretting and fuming in the visitors' gallery where no one is allowed to talk. The two highly restrictive, somewhat unscientific, orders were imposed on the agriculture biotech community by screaming to the court master. Isolation distance is crop-specific – it can be much more than 200 metres, 1,600 metres for cauliflower, for instance, or much less, 3 metres for groundnut and 50 metres for cotton.

Many seed companies saw a black comedy unfold. In late 1999, when Bt cotton field trials were in full force, Narayanan would often visit Delhi as a senior scientist from Monsanto Research Centre giving scientific inputs to the government. He found a certain acceptance and optimism in the capital. By 2001, when he left Monsanto, the genomics hype was at its peak, but he was convinced he could bear his learning to 'do smaller things' relevant for India. Their net present value might not be in billions like Monsanto's research, but they could garner millions, he thought. He and his colleague Gautam Nadig set out to found Metahelix to develop transgenic and other agriproducts. By 2005, their Cry1C Bt cotton – different from Monsanto's – was undergoing field trial, but the complementary part of Cry1Ac gene (the two-gene approach is better than single-gene approach in fighting pests) got stuck when the Rodrigues- and Bhushan-led campaign choked the regulatory system. His Bt rice seeds remained waiting in the fields.

The delay came from all directions. One cycle of 0.01 per cent detection of transgenic contamination would take up to a year to get approval. In some of the accredited labs, companies had to do the field trials themselves and get a certificate. Paralysis struck the GEAC, which found a lack of accredited labs as an excuse to not take any decision at all.

By early 2010, the Bt brinjal spectacle broke out – a two-year moratorium on commercial sale of a non-Monsanto crop, unlike Bt cotton, which most Indian seed companies have licensed from Monsanto – that turned into an indefinite ban, smothering development of all genetically modified crops in the country. Approval powers were withdrawn from the GEAC and it became an 'Appraisal' agency.

Narayanan survived because he had not put 'all eggs in a transgenic basket', but much of government-funded transgenic research languished. 'At least half a dozen genetically modified crops were ready, each with a specific benefit. For instance, GM potato was developed with at least 30 per cent higher protein content, GM tomato had a much longer shelf life,' said Manju Sharma, a former biotech secretary, who often received baskets of potato dumped by Greenpeace outside her residence. All the field trial data lay at the GEAC table, but 'nothing happened' before Bt brinjal happened.

Cut to July 2015 – there was an action replay. Yet another public interest litigation case; and once again Prashant Bhushan was crusading on behalf of a paediatrician from Delhi. The case in Delhi High Court was filed to stop Phase IV study of the rotavirus vaccine which was launched earlier in the year. The argument Bhushan made was that complete and segregated data for all trial centres be made public before the vaccine was administered to 1,00,000 babies because the side effects – intussusceptions – reported in one centre were much higher than in other centres.

As industry partner, Bharat Biotech's Ella was stumped. It was an unusual request because, considering all scientific facts, disclosure of this data, even according to the April 2015 WHO guideline, would not alter the existing understanding of the vaccine and its effects. A larger study was needed anyway. More fundamentally, the existing vaccines, from multinational companies, have shown lesser efficacy in developing countries because babies in these regions are exposed to multiple pathogens which lead to a condition called 'environmental enteropathy'.

So, here was a vaccine, developed using a local strain isolated by Bhan in 1986 when he found babies infected by this virus showed strong immunity from subsequent infections. Over twenty-five years, sixty-five researchers from Bharat Biotech, Stanford University School of Medicine, National Institutes of Health, Centers for Disease Control and Prevention in Atlanta and the non-governmental organization PATH developed it. The Department of Biotechnology and the Bill & Melinda Gates Foundation funded it, with the latter pioneering a new model in India, of directly funding the trial centres rather than the vaccine manufacturer. As for the side effects, none emerged within one month of all three doses, effectively showing that the vaccine, Rotavac, caused no intussusceptions. In terms of science, this vaccine also challenged a prevailing dogma. 'We have shown that unlike other vaccines which are suspended in buffer solution, Rotavac does not require a buffer. So, as opposed to 2 ml, a smaller dose of 0.5 ml is sufficient, which effectively translates into five drops. It is easy to deliver, just like [two drops of] polio vaccine,' Ella said.

Activists kept the vaccine in the eye of a public storm until mid-October when the Delhi High Court dismissed the case as not being worthy of a hearing.

Even without the surgical vigour of activism, regulatory torpor has been all too evident.

In April 2000, Ramachandran was preparing to retire from Astra Research Centre; in two months, he would turn sixty-five. He had no specific plans for a post-retirement life, until one night when he watched an old BBC documentary, *The Virus That Cures*, on television. It was late in the night, but he called his colleague Anand Kumar and asked him to watch the rerun at 2 a.m.

During his sixteen years at Astra, Ramachandran had learnt a lot about infection and he was convinced that the traditional approach to antibiotics – small molecule anti-infectives – would not work. 'Because in the overuse of antibiotics, we have selected the most robust pathogens which were not only growing faster but stronger because companies are exiting infectious diseases and going to chronic diseases where the money lies,' he thought. (Astra, which worked on infectious diseases at its Bengaluru centre, closed its operations in early 2014.)

From that documentary and subsequent research, Ramachandran got solid scientific proof of a belief most Indians held – that water from the River Ganga had some secret curative powers. He looked up the history of phage therapy and one of its early discoveries made in India in 1896 when an English scientist, M.E. Hankin, found that Ganga's water 'contained an antiseptic that had a powerful bactericidal action on the cholera germ'. The Ganga water when mixed with cholera germs in a test tube killed the germs in just three hours, the scientist showed. Ramachandran decided to set up Gangagen (from Ganga Genesis). Unlike other biotech ideas, he would not have to spend time figuring out if the concept would work, he thought. If he could get the right phage – virus that kills bacteria – to the pathogen, it would be effective.

Ramachandran plunked his savings down in Gangagen. He had made 'a few bucks' when Elan Corporation acquired Neurex in 1998 for $700 million; he had planned to run Gangagen on that money. Then the IT bust of 2001–02 happened.

'I was busy running the start-up in Bengaluru, and Schwabb [in the US] sold all my stocks at ridiculously low prices. I lost my shirt,' he said. Mashelkar was impressed with the phage therapy idea, and wanted to fund it under the New Millennium Indian Technology Leadership Initiative. He formed a committee chaired by Nirmal Kumar Ganguly, director general of the Indian Council of Medical Research, to evaluate it. Ramachandran was called to present his idea at the Central Drug Research Institute in Lucknow, but Ganguly was not convinced. (However, the Council bulletin later carried an exhaustive review paper on phage therapy.) But Ramachandran hit his stride when ICF Ventures accidentally met him while evaluating another start-up in the same building. Norman Prouty and Vijay Angadi were so fascinated with phage therapy that they came the next day and expressed interest in investing $2 million. They had a condition, though. Gangagen would also have to be incorporated in the US for their American investors to receive their returns. Ramachandran had already pledged his Bengaluru house for a bank loan; he accepted Prouty's condition. Later, he even had a celebrity investor in Gangagen – Nobel laureate and co-discoverer of DNA's double-helix structure,

James Watson. (He later kicked up controversies by making some racist remarks and selling his Nobel medal in 2014.)

In 2005, Ramachandran once again tried to raise money in India. This time, he also made presentations at Biocon; however, deep inside, he wished the company could license his molecule. Biocon was not ready to venture into a new therapeutic area and as an investor, Kiran had not taken her first steps yet. 'It was an American company and the valuation was very high. I was not ready to invest so much,' she said. A year later, when the recombinant protein was ready for human trials, Ramachandran went to the drug controller in Delhi. The drug controller's office put up every regulatory hurdle they could find. India had not done a Phase I study of a new molecule until then, and it wasn't willing to change.

'I did not start this company to make money,' says Ramachandran. 'It would have been a matter of pride for the drug controller to take an Indian molecule, based on an Indian concept and discovered and developed in India. India had never done a Phase 1 trial but here was an occasion to do it.'

A year later, the drug controller would get another occasion.

The avian influenza virus was causing bird flu outbreaks in many parts of the country. The World Health Organization (WHO) had issued a stage-three alert. At Indus Biotech in Pune, Sunil Bhaskaran had a drug derived from cinnamon in preliminary stages, developed according to botanical drug guidelines of the US FDA. He rushed to the drug controller in Delhi with bagfuls of documents and data. The Investigational New Drug Committee met him and said, 'Sorry'. They said Bhaskaran would have to file a fresh application for a new chemical entity, never mind if the molecule was derived from the food chain and was not a chemical.

Unlike the small-molecule drugs, for a botanical drug, the American regulator requires toxicity studies to be done only in rodents, waiving off non-rodent studies (usually done in beagles). 'We met all the committee members separately, some of whom were convinced. It was the first time a botanical drug application was on their table, but they refused. At the end of the day, they are guided by the rule book,' said Bhaskaran. Politician Maneka Gandhi's animal welfare movement has ensured that no drug company can do non-rodent animal studies in India. The generics industry did not need it, but the biotech industry does. The rule books regulate even the funding agencies, not just the regulatory watchdogs; even the academics, not just the industry. There's little room for flexibility.

In 2001, Avadhesha Surolia found a new chemical, Triclosan, which showed promising results in inhibiting the malaria bug *Plasmodium falciparum*. He published his work in *Nature Medicine* and a while later, licensed it to Shantha in Hyderabad. Surolia had a set of discoveries that would lead to a new anti-malaria drug, but further research showed that the drug was toxic, and it was abandoned. A few years later, when Surolia had moved from the Indian Institute of Science to the National Institute of Immunology in Delhi as its director, with support from the biotech department, he found a non-toxic substitute. By the time he secured a fresh patent, he had retired. In 2012, he returned to his parent institution in Bengaluru and continued research as a Bhatnagar fellow. The intellectual property on the anti-malaria molecule lies with the National Institute of Immunology, but not the responsibility of its human use. In the following months, the biotech department would often inquire about the progress, but did not agree to transfer the intellectual property or pin the accountability to him. Tired with his hands tied, Surolia closed his application by signing off: 'Principal investigator retired'. Often, science projects become like monkeys, constantly jumping around.

Straws that Break

Meanwhile in Hyderabad, Varaprasad Reddy's dilemma was deepening. He had brought Interferon to the market at one-sixth the price of the multinationals' and wanted to get into monoclonal antibodies. Shantha needed to hire some experienced people and invest heavily in research and development because product patent was now applicable in India, and reverse engineering would no longer work.

By now, in 2006, Reddy's Omani investors wanted an exit. They were encouraging him to go public, but the entrepreneur knew it was a business with long lead times, so he did not want to 'take on quarterly pressures'. The Omanis suggested he find a strategic investor who would give him technology, market access and funds. When Merieux Alliance came along, as did the Omanis, many other investors exited. But the French investor (Merieux) did not agree to invest in monoclonal antibodies for which Shantha had set up a unit in San Diego, to avoid the hassles of sourcing reagents and other consumables.

Soon Reddy got frustrated. He confronted Merieux with his problem: as a majority equity holder, it had brought no value – be it new technology, funds, or even marketing. The chairman of the family holding company, Alain Merieux, then revealed that he had bought equity in Shantha to fulfil the last wishes of his son who had tragically passed away that year at age thirty-nine. A medical doctor who distributed medicines in Africa and was looking for a low-cost source of medicines, Christophe Merieux told his father that he had identified Shantha as a low-cost supplier. Father and son had agreed to invest in any company that would assist him in his philanthropic work. Soon after that, he went for a swim and died of a cardiac arrest in the pool. The father continued with the investment to honour his son's last words but after speaking with Reddy, understood that Shantha didn't need them; it needed a strategic investor. He proposed engaging with GlaxoSmithKline and Sanofi.

Reddy, at least mentally, ruled out GlaxoSmithKline because the two were competitors and the latter, claims Reddy, 'had run a vilification campaign against Shantha, calling it a roadside company'. Still, both Glaxo and Sanofi Aventis visited the Hyderabad biotech and Reddy finally chose to sell to the latter's vaccine division, Sanofi Pasteur. At that time, he held 17 per cent of the shares.

Merieux had stayed on for three-and-a-half years without adding any value to the company, but when it exited in 2009, it kicked the valuation higher than Reddy had imagined – to $850 million. Shantha had done well during 2006 and 2009 and had received a whopping $350 million order from the United Nations Children's Fund (UNICEF) that would double its revenue in that financial year. Sanofi paid $784 million to acquire majority shares in the company and spent ₹78 crore buying employees' shares. Reddy had given stock options to all 870 employees, including the janitor and his two drivers.

On the day of the news break in 2009, in a rare show of frankness, Reddy said that 100 per cent foreign direct investment in biotech would 'kill the local industry'. Kiran, tough as usual, has favoured foreign investment but lashed out at 'lack of investment and risk capital, tax credits, and the lopsided policy of the National Pharmaceutical Pricing Authority, which favours imported drugs of multinational firms and forces domestic players to a price level 25 to 30 per cent lower than that of foreign competition.'

(In a related event, Harish Iyer, who left Biocon to pursue a leadership role at public-health-oriented Shantha, quit in August 2015 when the French parent Sanofi restructured its business to plug the Indian unit more closely into its global manufacturing ambition. Iyer moved to the Bill & Melinda Gates Foundation. In a way, Reddy's fears turned out to be more than a founder's sentimental outburst.)

What also shattered Shantha's spirit before the sale was the near-absent bridge between the more established pharmaceutical industry and the nascent biotech business in India. Of the few who tried to build this bridge, some got bruised, others lost patience.

In Singh's time, Ranbaxy made some serious attempts to get into biotech. Then, around 2006, it made a second stab and invested in three start-ups – Zenotech Laboratories, Jupiter Bioscience and Krebs Biochemicals. It even built a large research and development team at its Gurgaon facility but the biologics initiative was a mishmash of misplaced ambition amidst little-understood complexities.

In 2007, Ranbaxy upped its stake in Zenotech to nearly 45 per cent based on the assessment done by Daiichi. The Japanese pharma company was looking to invest in Indian assets where it wanted to shift its Japanese biotech and oncology capabilities, away from tsunami-prone areas. Unfortunately, Jayaram Chigurupati, founder of Zenotech, 'did not let that happen', said Raizada, who, from Ranbaxy's side, ran Zenotech for two years. The investors, which included the Technology Development Board of India, inducted Raizada 'into the system to get Chigurupati out' but by that time, Daiichi had already taken a decision to set up a greenfield facility in Thailand and their biotech focus shifted away from India.

'If Zenotech had worked out correctly, Daiichi would be producing everything in Hyderabad,' Raizada rued in December 2014. 'Between them, Ranbaxy and Daiichi had invested ₹360 crore in Zenotech, which included repayment of loans. But the bottom line was, Chigurupati would not let anyone from these two companies step into his facility. He did not allow annual general meetings of the company to take place for two years.'

When Sun Pharmaceutical bought Ranbaxy in 2014, the latter, along with Daiichi, owned 64 per cent in Zenotech. Sun would later pay nearly ₹20 crore for Ranbaxy's 28 per cent in the controversial biotech, a mammoth crash from its heydays when the Hyderabad company claimed to have a bunch of biosimilars in its labs.

A similarly disappointing story unfolded at Cipla, which partnered with Avesthagen for development of biopharmaceuticals. Avesthagen was one of the few biotechs to be phenomenally successful in raising venture money, about $50 million since it was founded in 1998. But it expanded too rapidly into too many fields, and by early 2012, it was in financial free fall and fighting court cases with its former employees and Cipla. Since the matter was subjudice, chairman Yusuf Hamied was curt, but enraged: 'Our relationship with Avesthagen has been a disaster, scientifically and businesswise. I am fighting the case because I want my money back.' Founder Villoo Morawala-Patell, an agriculture scientist who took to entrepreneurship after her Ph.D from Pasteur Institute, put up a brave front in mid-2015 and said she had restructured Avesthagen into a holding company, spun off businesses in agriculture and pharmaceuticals, and was back in 'licensing mode'.

For various reasons, even promising biotechs shrunk their goals. The community at large got a blow in 2013 when Intas Biopharmaceuticals, even though vertically integrated, merged with its parent pharma company, Intas Pharmaceuticals. The Ahmedabad biotech was the first Indian company to sell a biosimilar in the European market in 2007, following which it brought a number of such drugs into the Indian market. But soon the promoters had a change of heart and they merged the two companies. Why? 'Because biologics are expensive, long-gestation products.'

The pharmaceutical industry which was expected to lift biotech spirits, took a swallow dive itself.

Network Effect

One day in 2013, Subramani Ramachandrappa came to tell Kiran he had successfully made recombinant trypsin, an enzyme used to convert insulin precursors into insulin. Without asking any questions, she said, 'Speak to Abhijit and supply.'

Trypsin was a strategic product for Biocon which it had been buying for long from a Swiss company at $600 per gram for some products; for the rest, it used animal-origin enzyme. Between

Barve and Bamzai, Ramachandrappa got the Biocon deal, but 'he got hammered on the price'. Even though Bamzai was leaving the company, he made sure that the start-up, Richcore Lifesciences, supplied at the lowest price. The Malaysia insulin plant would compensate on volumes in a few years, Bamzai convinced him.

Subbu, as Ramachandrappa is popularly called, was beginning to understand what the 'big word', entrepreneurship, meant. For a few years after leaving Biocon in 2000, he had 'bought and sold and thrived on arbitrage'. When he went to the Indian School of Business (ISB) in Hyderabad in 2005, he had 'heard the term entrepreneurship for the first time', even though his father ran his own business. At ISB, he played around with biotech – he would make different kinds of flowers and participate in a dozen-odd global competitions, earning nearly $100,000 in runner-up prizes. Eventually, he raised his first round of venture capital money in 2008.

'Biocon was not in the game of comparing. That's what I learnt. I don't have to be a big shot, I would do what I had to do,' Subbu says, with the air of a sure-footed entrepreneur. 'I found everyone was copying, poaching employees, and going to the same customer in the industry.' Subbu is among the select few who have a verbal no-poaching understanding with Biocon and a few patents under his belt. In 2015, he licensed his technology for animal-origin-free recombinant products to Merck.

More than a dozen Biocon employees left to strike out on their own. Most of them did what they had done at Biocon. Maybe faster, even bigger – enzyme formulation, trading in bulk drug substances, research and clinical services – though Kiran would have told them 'to do different things, not just do things differently', her well-worn starting-up advice.

One day, when she saw Madhav Raj Sirsi managing an art show, she said, 'If you had to do this, why did you leave Biocon?' He had left in 2007 after thirteen years of project management in building specialized labs, to start a design consultancy. He named it creatively – Strokes of Imagination – but did not do much beyond organizing art shows. When Kiran met him that day, she gave him a mouthful and an idea – 'Why don't you identify a gap and provide the full gamut of services, from design to construction? Get into a niche. You are a go-getter, do something that culminates in a bigger idea, but remember it takes a long time.'

Sirsi soon renamed his company SOI Design Consultancy, and today, counts clients from Haryana to Africa on its roster. Indeed, he had spotted a niche. 'When we go for tenders, often no one else turns up because it is so specialized, but I am willing to wait it out.'

The information technology services industry grew rapidly because newcomers 'learnt' from the older companies, often by 'imitation and movement of people rather than direct interaction'. Biotech cannot grow big by imitation. Even the large generics makers are learning this the hard way.

In 2010, Strides Arcolab bought controlling stakes of 70 per cent in InBiopro, a biotech that Millipore's Sohang Chatterjee and his colleagues started in 2007. For ₹65 crore, Strides founder Arun Kumar landed up with eight biosimilars whose full-scale manufacturing processes were developed at Syngene and transferred to the pharma company which wanted to market the products by 2013. Two years later, it had not commercialized any product from that basket. Once the two-year lock-in period was over, Chatterjee and his co-founder Kavita Rodrigues moved out of InBiopro.

By then, Chatterjee had earned his spurs and learnt a few things: 'Indian pharma is struggling [in biosimilars] because of its mindset.' So when he started Theramyt with Rodrigues in 2013, he decided he would develop products for the global market. Their yeast display and fucose-knockout technology platforms – which improve the discovery and optimization of monoclonal antibodies and their mechanism of cancer cell destruction, respectively –

could virtually turn out to be rapid prototyping of next-generation antibodies.

Chatterjee seems to have seen through the haze. After a few years at Millipore, he was sure he would start a company of his own. 'Doing this kind of science is very close to what my students would be doing if I were at the university. I also thought that the management style in India is very poor, I can do better than that,' he says. Some thirty-five employees at Theramyt are fined for odd breaches – for calling someone sir or madam, coming late for or think-tank meetings, or not showing up for common lunch and tea breaks. The money collected goes for fun outdoor activities.

If Chatterjee wields brushes, Shiladitya Sengupta looks at 'pharmacology as a painting'. Right from his medical pharmacology days at AIIMS in New Delhi in 2000, he has been able to spot 'patterns'. Over the years, he has moved to bioengineering but continues to see patterns where biology and chemistry meet and is dogmatic about building a life sciences business on them while being based out of India.

In 2007, Mallik Sundaram came to him in Cambridge, Massachusetts, where Sengupta had founded Cerulean Pharma to commercialize his multilayered nanoparticle technology that could deliver multiple drugs to cancer tumours. Sundaram's earlier company had listed on the Nasdaq; he had taken a management study break and was now raring to go for another drug discovery start-up. This time, he wanted to do something in India. Sengupta told him that nobody would give him money in India; instead, he suggested a services model in cancer diagnostics and connected him to Pradip Majumder at MIT who also wanted to move back to India. Mitra Biotech got incorporated at Cambridge but grew in Bengaluru. At MIT, Majumder knew Cooney; so when he moved to Bengaluru, he requested him to be on his board. Cooney later joked, 'First I used to come for Astra, then for Biocon, and now for Mitra.'

Slowly, Sengupta moved into new terrain. From services, he went into dermatology where most products are decades old. At Cambridge, at one of the biosciences events, he met Rajesh Gokhale, director of the Institute of Genomics and Integrative Biology (IGIB). The two found their interests and science converging in skin products. Together, they set up Vyome Biosciences where Sengupta found a pattern among resistant bugs and existing molecules which have never been used in dermatology. Ideas come to Sengupta faster than he can articulate. Between his three start-ups, he has raised more than $25 million. 'Getting money is easier than doing good science. Position the science like you show or see a diamond; it's about figuring out what society needs. That appeals to investors too. Just make sure you also show them why your science is not risky,' he says.

A few perceptive investors are now willing to grasp – and put their money where their understanding is – that the risk in science is after all a risk to be managed, but the industry is yet to see the real network effect of a cluster. That perhaps explains why Indian biotech has remained a start-up industry, almost trapped in a revenue range of $10–50 million. No epic wins have come its way. Like the army on the field, the industry has moved according to the slowest formation.

9

PUBLIC LIFE

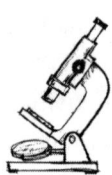

LET'S BE FRANK

'Did you know current government rules don't permit more than one R&D centre within a hospital? Crazy logic which must be questioned n debunked', Kiran tweeted in early February 2015. By the middle of the month, she had been sent an invitation by the Prime Minister's Office. Principal Secretary Nripendra Mishra wanted to know why she was so critical of the government. She replied, 'I really like your rhetoric – Make in India, Minimum Government Maximum Governance, Ease of Doing Business, Digital India, Skill India, and so on. But as someone who runs a business, let me tell you it's not been easy and it's not getting easier. Nobody is taking action on how to bring back clinical trials to India, the trial rules are absurd … If you are doing something, it's opaque because I don't see anything translating into action on the ground.'

Mishra sought an example. She had one ready. The Mazumdar-Shaw Translational Research Centre at the cancer hospital in her name at Narayana Health City was seeking certification from the Department of Scientific and Industrial Research, which would allow it to get tax exemption and apply for government grants. A year ago, the department had inspected but refused certification because the rules, it said, required that the research and development centre be housed outside the hospital. The purpose of a translational centre is to be inside the hospital so that the research gets 'translated' for patients, she explained.

Mishra agreed that it made sense. When a technocrat had earlier intervened on her behalf, the department had said, 'Change the address. Many hospitals – Apollo, Max, Arvind Eye Hospital and others – have done this.' She had raised a stink then. 'I am not going to change the address. Tomorrow if you inspect, you will book me under fraud.' She asked to see the rule in case they were misinterpreting it, but they seemed reluctant to show it to her. Eventually, she did see it and as it turned out, it was a misinterpretation; the directive was about a clear separation between a non-profit centre and a commercial entity in operations, not in physical location.

She also criticised the endless toing and froing of approvals between state and Central drug regulators, even for something as small as a manufacturing site change of an existing product. Mishra could not disagree. And so the officials in Delhi got an earful from an entrepreneur who uses every means of communication to add new levels of urgency to issues on the table.

A few months later, in May 2015, she took to Twitter again: 'Make in India needs to make new policies to make it easy and expeditious to set up manufacturing projects; approvals alone take >365 days.'

Most corporate leaders believe expressions of resentment are at best a distraction which takes them nowhere, but Kiran resents relentlessly.

The non-profit translational centre finally received the

certification; the Department of Scientific and Industrial Research realized its mistake. Her consistently assertive push for an abbreviated regulatory path was also approved by the drug controller in August and later notified in November, reducing the approval time by a third – a long overdue rapprochement.

But the real-time platform, Twitter, also lands her in a real-time public image crises. In November 2014, a casual tweet about a massive meta-analysis on genetically modified crops published in the *Economist*, which referred to 'widespread benefits', whipped up a storm on social media. High-profile opponent of such crops, Nassim Nicholas Taleb at New York University, author of the *The Black Swan: The Impact of the Highly Improbable*, was brought into the debate. After some hours, the social exchange got acrimonious, even personal. Several hours later, she signed off saying 'I am putting this to an end,' but she was angry that enough agriculture scientists and biotech entrepreneurs – who had their skin in the debate – had not joined in, and so she called up a few. The Twitter spat desperately needed bolstering from some facts and reasoning.

'I was not on Twitter but I opened an account as soon as I heard about it and joined the debate, rebutting Taleb, but by then it was dying,' says K.K. Narayanan. 'Kiran is brave. If she believes something is right, she will stand up for it. She understands the crux of the issue. One does not have to be a scientist to understand this.' Taleb has written extensively on the subject and believes that genetically modified organisms represent a 'public risk of global harm'. 'I have a problem with that assumption,' said Narayanan. 'If a GM crop runs amok will it exterminate life? Taleb defends himself by saying the absence of evidence is not evidence of absence. How can you have evidence of absence when it is actually absent scientifically? He thinks these crops will cause 'ecocide'. A gene is not so promiscuous – which is why we have brinjal as brinjal, and not as orange. We have been eating rice for so many years. Do we have green shoots coming out of our heads?'

Some promiscuous tweets, though, do get her cornered. In 2013, when the Congress government in Karnataka appointed sixty-five-year-old S.R. Patil as the minister for Information Technology and Biotechnology, Kiran and Mohandas Pai, chairman of Manipal Global Education, expressed their misgivings. She tweeted: 'Patil has a good reputation. I look forward to his support for IT and BT, but [I am] surprised that [a] younger tech-savvy person [was] not picked.' A year later, soon after a board meeting at Infosys, she tweeted that she was 'most impressed by Rohan Murthy's brilliant tech-loaded presentation which will enormously benefit Infosys.' Rohan, who is 'like her godson', had joined N.R. Narayana Murthy as executive assistant when the latter returned to Infosys as chairman in 2013.

In both instances, she apologized; even dusted off the tweets from her mental timeline as it were, because in January 2015, she was back engaging with Taleb. 'Whilst I don't agree with my Twitter rival @nntaleb's comments on GMO n Big Data, I do agree with his views on economics especially SMEs.' (She was referring to Taleb's new book *Antifragile* in which he says an economy of small and medium enterprises is 'antifragile', one that grows stronger with uncertainty.)

In all walks of business, engagement is her principal tool. At the India–US CEO dinner in January 2015 during President Barack Obama's second visit to India, she sought a meeting with Michael Froman. As United States Trade Representative, Froman is Obama's principal advisor, negotiator and spokesperson on international trade and investment issues. It is his office that prepares the 'Special 301 Report' and puts India on their 'Priority Watch List' every now and then, a list that is meant for countries with a poor intellectual property regime. (Since Prime Minister Modi's US visit in September 2014, India's intellectual property policy has been a sticky issue which a think tank has been deliberating on.)

With Froman she argued that India fully complied with TRIPs, and as far as the thorny compulsory licensing was concerned, India had only issued one; the patent office had denied many. 'So, I don't think you should hold it against us. You have done many more.' Talking of Novartis's anti-cancer drug, Glivec which, was denied a patent in India due to 'incremental innovation', Froman said, 'If there is a drug that works six times a day and then someone makes a formulation that requires one dose a day, is that not patentable?'

'But that is a process patent,' she told him. 'A company cannot get patent extension based on a new formulation, the formulation will be protected as a process patent but it cannot squat on its once-a-day formulation as a product patent. That is what multinationals try to do,' she said to him.

She was stepping up to a national issue because in the past she had been critical of companies seeking, and the government granting compulsory licences, calling the latter's move as 'abdicating India's responsibility to have a national healthcare system'. Her blunt remarks peeved many pharmaceutical executives. So, when Hetero Pharma director Srinivas Reddy took a stand that was contrarian to the generics industry – 'India has lost nearly $10 billion worth of investment by not respecting intellectual property, and the compulsory licence we issued [on Bayer's sorafenib] did more harm to our image than actually helped patients' – Kiran remarked, 'That's my language.'

By mid-2015, a new intellectual property policy was in the works which, among other things, would spell out what India would allow under Section 3(d) of the Indian Patent Act (1970), a provision that is meant to stop the prickly evergreening of patents.

Sometimes invited, sometimes uninvited, Kiran assumes public roles which perhaps have a genesis in her upbringing, when as a nine-year-old, she and her friends had knit socks for soldiers on the border during the Indo-China war.

CHANGE MY CITY

One day in 1981, when Kiran's childhood friend Pratima Rao went to the General Post Office (GPO), which was temporarily operating from a site next to the Bangalore International Hotel, she found the staff had their nose covered. Rotting food dumped by the hotel created an unbearable stink. She returned to the Biocon office on Palace Cross Road where she was helping Kiran manage the Biocon business for some time. When Kiran heard about the filth, she called the hotel and asked for the manager. No one connected the line. She called the second time and said it was the health minister speaking. The manager promptly came on the phone. 'I am the health minister. Why are you are creating such a stink in your neighbourhood? I am going to cancel your licence if you don't clean it up,' she pronounced majestically.

Two days later, when Rao visited the post office, it was no longer smelly. Miraculously, the staff said, the hotel had cleaned the place overnight. Rao was not surprised. Kiran's obsession with cleanliness and waste disposal always found room for new expression. Once, fed up with piling garbage in Koramangala in south Bengaluru where she lived, she circulated a note among residents asking them to bring their stuffed garbage bags to the Bangalore City Corporation (now Bruhat Bengaluru Mahanagara Palike) head office. Then she called the industries director and told him of her plan. Again, overnight, the corporation cleaned up. At other times, she collected money from neighbours, sought donations from corporate and rich residents towards placing large bins for segregated garbage. When a cow once got stuck in the bin trying to eat the wet waste, a local newspaper splashed the picture next day with the Biocon logo alongside.

She was game, even when the police, probably impressed by her active citizenry over driving offences, gave her a challan book to note vehicle numbers and offences of erring drivers.

By the late 1990s, many technocrats from Bengaluru had shot into fame. In 1999, Chief Minister S.M. Krishna, through his son-in-law and founder owner of Cafe Coffee Day, V.G. Siddhartha, sent an invitation to Nandan Nilekani at Infosys to chair a committee to 'get Bengaluru on track'. Chandrababu Naidu in Hyderabad was stealing the Bengaluru tech circle's thunder. Nilekani set up the Bangalore Agenda Task Force where he brought many professionals and raised philanthropic capital, including a personal contribution of ₹8 crore to resolve the city's infrastructure and governance challenges. Kiran went for the dross, contributing ₹50 lakh for garbage management.

Once again, in 2012, when the city began drowning in garbage, with dengue and chikungunya outbreaks peaking, one night, while returning from a wedding, Kiran and Mohandas Pai, former chief financial officer of Infosys, decided it was time for yet another civic movement in the city. They committed some philanthropic money to what became the third version of civic engagement – after Nilekani's task force of 1999 and Rajeev Chandrashekar's Agenda for Bengaluru Infrastructure Development Task Force of 2009 – but Kiran understood it needed a brand. She called Tania Khosla. 'You took a year to do the Biocon logo, this time you have five days,' she told her. 'We want people to take us seriously. We want to give it a proper identity, with a long-term goal and agenda.'

Pai, Kiran and others since then, have been in constant recruitment mode for the Bangalore Political Action Committee (B.PAC). At the Bangalore Literature Fest in January 2013, Pai met Revathy Ashok, a contemporary chief financial officer and director on the boards of many companies, who gradually warmed up to the idea and agreed to be the chief executive officer. A month later, N.R. Narayana Murthy, then chairman emeritus of Infosys, launched the charter and agenda of the 'apolitical' body. 'I don't see the same kind of helplessness that I saw when I was in my twenties. Therefore, I believe this is the right time to wake up, build an aspirational dream and an action plan,' he said.

Since then, B.PAC has launched and catalysed programmes on women and child safety, cleaning and greening the environment; created a baseline pool of civic and political leaders. But it was during the explosive debate of candidates before the parliamentary elections in the summer of 2014 that the rubber met the road. Kiran was moderating a two-hour debate among four candidates, but the supporters of BJP candidate Ananth Kumar stormed the stage when she intervened to remind Kumar that the debate was about the city and not national politics. Earlier, Congress candidate Nilekani was heckled for not speaking in the local language, Kannada. Kiran looked 'helpless and angry as she was escorted out of the venue' after forty-five minutes. The debate got nastier on Twitter with incessant trolls but she put up a spirited fight.

During and after elections, B.PAC was accused by political parties, as was Kiran, of being partisan but Revathy Ashok says the reputation has stabilized since. Pai and Kiran bear the operational expenses of a lean set-up but for various other activities, the committee is raising money and an unexpected supporter group has emerged among the real estate companies. On the day of its launch, Kiran had ambitiously said, 'A lot of the problems happen because we as citizens are apathetic. Starting from Bengaluru, we want to hold a candle for the rest of the country.' After two years, Ashok says, citizen groups from Patna to Pune want to emulate B.PAC.

Accidental Investor

While she is deeply invested in the city, the same cannot be said about Bengaluru's booming start-up enterprise.

In late May 2005, Kiran's assistant Susan Kumar called former colleague Ravikumar for a meeting. The next day, he was still at the door when she came out of her room and blasted off: 'What the hell are you doing? You have the best science company I thought I knew. Just because some jerk sits in your company, you cannot run it? If you cannot get him out, why did you start on your own? You should have stayed in Astra.'

Tears started brimming in Ravikumar's eyes; everyone around, including visitors from the Irish consulate in the adjoining room, stood up and watched in consternation.

'Can I come in?' Ravikumar mumbled. She calmed down a bit. 'Sorry about this, have some coffee,' she said, sliding a cup towards him.

A year earlier, Ravikumar had invited an investor with British roots to his company. The investor, a pure contract research manufacturing company, wanted to build a biotech story around itself. They invested only a quarter of the promised money and when Ravikumar inquired, they said they had borrowed money from Temasek, which had put a freeze on further investments. Since a large number of shares had been allotted, Ravikumar was stuck with this non-performing investor. He vented his frustration in the biotech community, bits of which reached Kiran's ears.

On hearing him out, she said, 'So you need money and legal help to get out of this.' She then called Chinappa, Biocon's deputy finance head. 'Nail the investor and bail him out,' she said, before rushing out.

Over a month, Chinappa set up several meetings and finally found an auditor with expertise in contractual agreements. At last, when the investors were willing to negotiate, Kiran advised, 'Negotiate them down, they have to take some beating.' Ravikumar took Kumud Sampath, former operations head at Astra, who 'bargained like hell'. Almost dramatically, the investors immediately accepted the lowest price. It was Wednesday and they wanted to close the deal by Monday. Ravikumar lost his nerve. Kiran was travelling to London as part of the prime minister's delegation but she had left her UK number with Susan, in case he needed to call her.

'I have left instructions with Chinappa. Do well, but your bargaining powers disappoint me. I thought you would do better,' she said on the phone. Chinappa had two signed, blank cheques with him. 'Who are you? Kiran left so many instructions for this to happen and you say this was finalized only yesterday? How did she know? I have never seen her paying so much attention to anything like this before, she makes us work for ourselves,' he said.

'I don't know,' Ravikumar said solemnly. 'I am a religious man, and I believe God comes in different forms.' When he later went to check the terms of share allotment for the ₹1.2 crore she had loaned him, she said she would take shares for only half the amount whenever the next investor came. As for the interest, she said, 'You have to promise that next time you do well and when another Ravikumar comes along, you have to fund double the amount.'

It was never her philosophy to invest in businesses; only assets in manufacturing or intellectual property interested her. That did not change even when she became wealthy.

'Historically, she never expressed any interest in being involved in start-ups. I never ask her for investment now that I spend most of my time helping early-stage companies. She's been largely focused on Biocon,' says Gordon Ringold, who is now a senior advisor at Mavericks Capital Partners in California.

She did not get involved, financially or otherwise, when she sprung entrepreneurship on her mother. 'Bhawna is coming from London; she is going to start a business and you are her partner,' she announced one day in 1999. Yamini Mazumdar was sixty-eight, widowed for six years, and enjoyed growing herbs and salad leaves on the vacant land in the Biocon campus. What's more, she had borrowed ₹24 lakh from the State Bank of India to start a laundry business.

For many years, most financial outflows were philanthropic donations which she organized under Biocon Foundation after the company went public. When Rani Desai, an advertising professional who had drifted into a cancer hospice, joined the Foundation, she recognized that 'Kiran doesn't believe in giving anything free, she likes to help people who help themselves'. So she began creating programmes that were sustainable in the community, particularly in healthcare and early detection and prevention of chronic diseases. For many years, Desai struggled with the micro-insurance programme because villagers did not trust it. Later, as the state government provided populist, free insurance schemes, the Foundation evolved its healthcare programmes into primary care and screening clinics.

By then, her longtime friend Nilima Rovshen was diagnosed with cancer. Kiran watched in anguish as she moved from city to city, Mumbai to New York to Maryland, in search of good doctors and right therapies. 'By any standard, Nilima was an affluent, single person. I would want to help her but she would say, "I do not have a family and I don't have to bequeath anything to anybody; so let me use the money I have earned to spend on myself." But I saw how expensive it was and what pain she went through. There was only the Health Care Global [cancer] hospital in Bengaluru,' Kiran said. She then began pondering a world-class cancer centre in Bengaluru.

Down Hosur Road, three kilometres from her office, was Dr Devi Shetty, a 'charismatic' doctor who had built an image of a compassionate capitalist getting economies of scale to beat down cardiac care costs. The two had met at meetings of the Electronics City Industries Association in the early years of the millennium where Shetty would often be a quiet observer and Kiran a passionate speaker on civic issues. 'I used to be amazed at how much clarity she had about improving civic amenities,' recalled Shetty. One day, she said casually, 'Devi, why don't you start a cancer hospital?' He did not have expertise in cancer care but said that if she was serious, the two should build it together. 'She offered to invest and I suggested an amount. Before I could think about it seriously, she sent the money, a huge amount. No document was ready but she said, "Let's start the work, documents will come later,"' Shetty said. Her speed and ambition surprised him – he wanted to start with 100 beds but she suggested 1,000.

For that Shetty needed a 'creative' solution. So in 2008, he sent a two-way ticket to Paul C. Salins in Qatar. The cranio-facial surgeon had graduated from the same college as Shetty in Mangaluru, so the two knew each other, but Salins was surprised at the open-ended invitation to Bengaluru. When he arrived, Shetty showed him around, explained how 'they had brought down the cost of cardiac care' and then asked if he would come back to build a cancer hospital. Later in the afternoon, they met Kiran.

Hers is a corporate office unlike most. Framed canvases add life to each wall, hallways give space for artistic expression. Kiran spoke about her long-term vision of a cancer hospital, showing Salins what she was doing at Biocon in pharmaceuticals. 'She actually impressed me,' Salins recalls. He was not particularly interested in cardiac care. 'It is modular, you can apply processes to improve services; it is a precise thing which you can industrialize. Eighty per cent of procedures are of one type. You can get an army of doctors and you will never fall short of revenue; the business model is very different,' he notes. With cancer, we come to a different world. Temperamentally too, Salins inhabits a different world. An artist himself, he believes that 'if you have gusto, only then you can be a real philanthropist'.

'Meeting Kiran, I could sense she wanted some truly new development to come out of India. If we come out with something novel, we can find a number of ways to reduce cost. I thought it was worthwhile investing my time in a new hospital,' Salins says. (When asked how severe a cut in pay he settled for, he says, 'If you force me into telling you, it will send me into depression.')

Over a year later, Mazumdar-Shaw Cancer Centre opened for patients. By then, Kiran had had yet another encounter with cancer – Shaw was diagnosed with kidney cancer in 2007. During the surgery in London, she stayed with him in the ward, nursing him and learning about cancer care. (Atignal, who had gone as a family physician, came back after the surgery and Kiran stayed on for a few months, managing the business from London: 'I would not even hazard a guess if any Indian businessman would stay in a hospital for so long had anything happened to his wife.')

Once the Cancer Centre was functional, she began ploughing in philanthropic money, through a newly set up Mazumdar-Shaw Medical Foundation, for more facilities, an advanced bone marrow transplant, cancer wards, and more importantly, a translational centre. The initial investment in the hospital, which later got converted into equity in Narayana Health, represents 20 per cent of her philanthropic contributions to the hospital.

Just when she was formulating her Medical Foundation strategy, with Salins as the medical director, Chandru, at Strand Life Sciences, made a pivot – from a technology company to a clinical company. When he showed her the cancer panels Strand had built – a set of mutations against which to test a patient's tumour for deciding the treatment strategy – she pinpointed the price. 'Her market sense was that if we could bring the test cost down to ₹10,000, the mass market would open. That number probably came by benchmarking with other tests like PET or MRI scan,' says Chandru now. Kiran supported a Strand lab at her translational centre with nearly $1 million.

'I'll help you bring down the cost to ₹10,000 and then you don't need my support,' she said. Two years later, Strand developed a diagnostic kit that for ₹15,000, one-fourth the current cost of similar procedures in the market, can assess the likely occurrence of cancer. (In 2015, when Strand was raising growth capital, Kiran made a strategic investment in the company. Strand's focus on cancer genomics could gain from and benefit her cancer hospital.)

Essentially, it is on the eighth floor, on 25,000 sq. ft of translational research space, that Salins and Kiran are pinning their hopes for a purposeful change. Oral cancer is dominant in India not just because of high tobacco use, but maybe because of a virus. Tobacco-related cancers are coming down and cancers without cause are going up in young people. 'Somebody had to understand the trend,' said Salins. In the study of head and neck cancer, he has linked clinicians with strong research and believes that the hospital has the 'best outcomes in the world'. Using a mobile phone platform for oral cancer screening, Oncogrid, remotely monitored by an oral cancer specialist, researchers could detect 90 per cent cases (in a sample of 3,500) of pre-malignant lesions or carcinoma.

Early detection, all practitioners agree, will be the sole driver of cost reduction in the long run in India.

In cancer, Kiran's philanthropy converges with personal interest. Just before Christmas in 2012, she was leaving for London when her mother was diagnosed with breast cancer. She booked an additional ticket and began making arrangements for surgery in London when her mother remarked, 'You have built a cancer hospital here. If you take your mother to the UK, what message will you give to the world?' (The senior Mazumdar probably understood branding as well as Anand Mahindra, who always rides Mahindra & Mahindra vehicles, very often even outside India.) After the surgery, Salins recalls, when she was coming out of anaesthesia, she found Kiran by her bed and mildly chided: 'What are you doing here? Get back to work.' Family friend Sudha Murty stepped in for the day instead.

If at Biocon, a made-in-India drug for the global market is her Pole Star, at the hospital, it's the incremental improvement in treatment outcomes. At the translational centre, chief scientific officer Aditya Chaubey has one objective – every bit of research has to keep the patient in mind. And with Bala Manian's start-up ReaMetrix next door, Chaubey, a bioengineer from Cincinnati University, makes sure technology doesn't intimidate clinicians. At ReaMetrix, a few years ago, Manian had developed the first ever dry reagent which was temperature-stable and did not require the cold chain. He had wanted to supply the reagent to India's AIDS control programme for HIV diagnosis but when, once again, government tendering smothered affordable innovation, he sold that part of the business to BeckmanCoulter. Now he is back to applying his reagent technologies to the age-old microscopy for better detection of tuberculosis. However, it is not just reagent this time. He is building a device as well – from the point of sputum up to detection and disposal.

It's a tiny, cross-fertilized world of research and medicine that the patron and the practitioners are building. Kiran's global network helps – she is on the board of Koch Institute of Integrative Cancer Research and supports a few postdoctoral fellows at MIT as Mazumdar-Shaw Oncology Fellows – as does Salins's creativity. He is trying to tie in doctors with resident Ph.D programmes, a master's in technology in association with Vellore Institute of Technology and a likely programme in humanities with Harvard University for creating 'physician humanists'.

Five years after starting it, Shetty is somewhat stunned at what has happened. 'I build according to demand,' she says build the infrastructure, demand will come. I would never build a hospital that she has built – like a Taj Mahal. She has guts to invest.' Then he added, softly: 'I am very cautious, I am a surgeon. My boss at Guys Hospital [in London] taught me that a surgeon has to be like a thief – to keep the back door open, always.'

SMART CAPITAL

Kiran's back door is of another kind. A few years ago, Sudha Murty, chairperson of Infosys Foundation, was writing an endowment cheque for a few chairs at the International Institute of Information Technology in Bengaluru. Kiran was around and she suggested Murty endow a chair at IBAB as well – the former's loss was the latter's gain as it bagged ₹2.5 crore in a blink. Kiran supports a chair too – and a lecture series – but the money comes every year, not as an endowment. At the cancer hospital, she has invested ₹100 crore and she spends about ₹15 crore every year, running it and augmenting the facilities, but there's no endowment anywhere other than the free pharmacy to which she has given ₹5 crore for compassionate treatment. (It is rare for a corporate hospital to run a free pharmacy which cuts into the margins.)

When the Indian government began discussing a mandatory 2 per cent spend of profits on corporate social responsibility, Kiran looked at it strategically. Bradbury had joined the Biocon board and since he was also on the board of Keck Graduate Institute in California, Kiran thought of a certificate programme in biosciences, because the California institute is the only college supplying junior-level professionals to the life sciences industry in the United States. 'I started the academy because of the shrinking talent pool; everybody was poaching from each other. You need better-skilled people or else how are we going to sustain?' she says. It started with a course in manufacturing but is now expanding into the 'business of biotech', finance and others, and will start costing Biocon ₹10 crore annually.

Some viewed the natural advantage of this expansion as competing with the state-run Biotech Finishing Schools because it charged a fee. Biocon, though, provides up to 75 per cent scholarship. Such talk of competition hardly distracts her. 'The government does not have the kind of focus we have. We are taking the Keck curriculum, I can't prescribe a course to the government school here,' she says.

In September 2015, she deviated from her norm and invested in a niche venture capital fund – Saha Fund – that provides risk capital to women entrepreneurs. Back in the 1980s, as a neophyte entrepreneur, she set up the Association for Women Entrepreneurs along with Madhura Chatrapathy. 'Through the Association we managed to get a lot of concession for women entrepreneurs, though most of them stuck to the cottage industry. Over the years, many women used to approach me for funding but I could not possibly help all, nor did I have the time to invest. So when Ankita [Vashistha of Saha Fund] came to me, I found her serious in getting a return on investment and thought it'd be easier for me to invest in her fund and then ask her to look at certain businesses in life sciences and healthcare,' Kiran says.

Around the same time, she contributed to the ₹100 crore resource pool of the Independent Public-Spirited Media Foundation, led by two of Bengaluru's ace philanthropists, Rohini Nilekani and Azim Premji. Nilekani is known to have supported numerous independent media outfits, but how was Kiran convinced? 'The kind of journalism that we see today is very poorly reported and written. Anything goes ... if by encouraging good media start-ups this Foundation can help create journalism that people can trust, we'll see transformation,' she said. As one of the most media-friendly corporate leaders, she knows, or at least has a sense of, how newsrooms work and how countervailing narratives are formed.

Being chatty and accessible may be middlebrow for some – 'Do you smoke, Ma'am,' someone tweeted to her. 'No, I kicked the habit twenty-five years ago,' she tweeted back – but her public profile is getting larger with time. In 1982, it was the National Institute of Marketing Management which awarded her for the first time, the title of Best Woman Entrepreneur. Scores of awards, prizes and rankings on sundry global power lists have followed since then. It's hard to tell if she is a bigger brand or Biocon.

'If today Kiran chooses to say "enough of industry leadership" and steps back, there is nobody to talk to the government on behalf of Indian biotech,' says Krishnan of Novozymes.

10

THE ROAD AHEAD

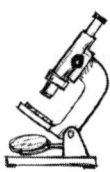

THE DISTANCE RUNNER

For the inaugural address at the annual Biotech Entrepreneurship Students' Contest in 2011, Nandita Chandavarkar, then director at ABLE, sent an email to Kiran stating the topic of her talk: 'My takeaways from my entrepreneurial journey'. Within minutes, Kiran responded with an edit: 'My *learnings* from my entrepreneurial journey *thus far.*'

Five years later, the journey is far from over. In July 2015, it reached yet another milestone when Syngene listed on the Bombay Stock Exchange. As much as it gave the company a life of its own, the public offering marked a turning point in Biocon's corporate strategy – it cleared the mixed messaging. Was Biocon an in-licensing company or a clinical development company; a service company or a commercial generics company that wanted to build the best Asian biotech sales force? There was a little too much of too many different things. Merging Syngene and Clinigene and spinning it off as a public company made the focus clear.

Biocon has at least five molecules in advanced clinical testing. It is a matter of pride; very few pharmaceutical companies anywhere have so many biosimilars in advanced stages. But it is also a matter of shrewd planning and extreme caution because the company will need a steady infusion of capital for a few years to take these drugs to the market. 'We have always been a debt-free company' is Kiran's preferred refrain and if she wants to continue to be so in future, she will have to find some more creative ways to generate funds. Biocon still holds 74.5 per cent of Syngene and the subsidiary could be demerged in a few years when some of the biosimilars start generating revenues and, more importantly, profits.

There are a few more rods in the fire. Biocon has a small stake in Vaccinex, the Rochester-based clinical-stage company which is ready for a public offering in the near future. Then, its own novel molecules could pack a bigger punch if hived off to raise money. In recent times, big pharma companies have been doing that to mimic small biotech – Baxter spun off Baxalta in 2015; earlier still, Abbott hived off Abbvie. Finally, Biocon could also seek a listing on the stock exchange in the United States for better access to the world's largest pharmaceutical market.

Ducks in a Row

In his best-seller *Good to Great*, author Jim Collins says companies which make the transition understand the tremendous power that exists in 'continued improvement and the delivery of results'. However incremental, if the results fit into the context of an overall concept that will work, people will line up with enthusiasm. He calls this the 'flywheel effect'. Biocon has been preparing well for its flywheel effect.

For a long time, innovator biotech companies waged a patent war, saying no generics maker could get an equivalent product, exact replicas so to say, because biologics are not manufactured by machines. It took years for a definition of biosimilars, at least a reasonable definition, to emerge. Consequently, biotech pioneers like Amgen, Genentech, Biogen and others maintained their lead for years. Entry to this coveted league is now more difficult as there is no standardized way of manufacturing these drugs. For a small biotech or generics company to invest substantially in biologics manufacturing and then not have the pricing of innovator drugs to garner big margins have been the biggest challenges. Even large companies which entered the field, thinking all they had to do was to show their product was bio-equivalent, were shocked to see 60–80 per cent, sometimes even 100 per cent of their R&D budget taken up by development costs of these products. Add to that the cost of dealing with the FDA and getting regulatory approvals. No wonder drug makers are getting cold feet. In 2013, for instance, the Swiss contract manufacturer Lonza abandoned its biosimilars agreement with Teva for these reasons.

In addition, after decades of pricing freedom, pharmaceutical companies in the US are now under pressure as insurers and payers are getting impatient. For the first time, innovator companies are making copies – biosimilars, that is – and they are likely to continue doing so. Many of them have large plants; they are rebuilding them, amortizing the cost because it is the economics of healthcare that trumps everything. Hospira's biosimilar of Merck's best-selling arthritis drug Remicade bagged a public contract in France at a price that is nearly half the innovator's price, whereas Novartis's biosimilar of Amgens's Neupogen was launched in the US at just 15 per cent discount.

As biosimilars bag approvals around the world, it is not clear to what extent prices will erode – 15 per cent or 50 per cent, or even more. It certainly won't be like small molecules, where a plethora of companies compete for a plethora of molecules. There are less than twenty biotech molecules and a handful of people are trying to make money off these molecules. Analysts have predicted a transfer of at least $100 billion (by value) from innovator companies to copycat drug makers in the next decade.

Biocon, with its partner Mylan, is one among them. It's low-cost quality manufacturing – it has not had any major quality issues with the US regulatory agency so far – and five monoclonal antibodies and recombinant proteins in advanced stages in clinics, make it fit for the 'flywheel effect'. Its challenge, though, will be to remain as precise while entering every market; some of these drugs are not for the universal set of patients. If Novartis entered the biosimilar market with a copy of Neupogen, it is because cancer is a segment that the Swiss company understands very well.

Equally vital is the quality of the molecule, not just the speed to market. 'Quality matters in the most exceptional manner. I cannot cite you a chapter where a company is better and does very well but I can certainly cite you a chapter where the quality is bad and the company fails. Everybody has the example of Genzyme in mind as they get into biologics,' says Biocon's board member Jeremy Levin, who as chief executive of Ovid Therapeutics, a neurology-focused biopharma company, closed $75 million funding in 2015.

(In 2009, Genzyme, maker of highly expensive, life-saving medicines for rare genetic disorders, had a viral contamination in its plant which led to a temporary shutdown, shipment delays and prolonged regulatory supervision that depressed its stock price to such an extent that Sanofi grabbed it in 2011 for $20.1 billion.)

Quality, with its associated cost and skill, is also the reason why Indian generic makers like Dr Reddy's, which was the first Indian company to launch a biosimilar in India in 2002, and Lupin, which made a big biotech push around 2005, do not have biosimilar baskets to match their early leads. They have been making amends, though. In 2012, Dr Reddy's entered into a partnership with Merck Serono to jointly develop a set of biosimilars; three years later, it inked a pact with Amgen to distribute and market three products. In 2014, Lupin capitalized on its long presence in Japan to set up a joint venture with Yoshindo Inc. to develop and commercialize biosimilars.

Clearly, it's a frenetic time worldwide for bio-partnering. However, with the oldest biosimilar, recombinant human insulin, the dynamics is different because just a handful of innovators dominate the market.

In 2008, after selling her enzyme business to the Novo Group, Kiran was in Copenhagen for a conference where she met Lars Sorensen, chief executive of Novo Nordisk. He invited her for dinner. She recalls the conversation vividly:

"'I must say you are very ambitious about insulin,' he told me. I said, "The market is big enough for everybody; even if all of us make insulin we will not be able to cater to the world market. It is a very difficult market but I am selling in India and I am doing very well.

"'Yes, but selling in India is different from selling in other parts,' he added.

'I said, "I know that and I'll figure it out." I told him about our oral insulin and he said, "It's a holy grail and you will never be able to do that." "We haven't been able to do it, how can you develop it?" he asked me. I told him, "I am taking it up as a challenge."'

The truth is, insulin is not just a challenging product technically; it is also a highly political product. At one end is the recombinant human insulin whose price has been falling – the tender pricing is one-tenth of what it was in the 2000s – and at the other end are expensive analogues whose biosimilars have not yet kicked in. Then there is the long-acting glargine, a biosimilar of Sanofi's Lantus, which makes up 15 per cent of the Indian insulin market where even traditionally, non-insulin companies like Lupin are selling by forging distribution alliances.

The troika of Novo Nordisk, Eli Lilly and Sanofi dominate the Indian market with more than 80 per cent share. Sanofi had earlier ignored human insulin, but is now promoting it aggressively with locally manufactured pens. It is also ring-fencing itself by investing in diabetes care, pumping ₹90 crore into Apollo Sugar Clinics for a 20 per cent stake.

In clinics, innovators are weaning doctors away from human insulin. They may want to do to human insulin what they did to animal-origin insulin in the early years of the century – replace them with analogues which are priced higher. That leaves the bottom of the pyramid for companies like Biocon, Wockhardt and a few others, where the government's generic-generic ploy might shift the game from doctors to retailers. Companies which until now gave iPhones and iPads to doctors to prescribe their drugs will now give the gadgets to retailers and ask them to substitute. Retailers do not fall under the Medical Council of India's code of conduct.

Biocon took ten years to become the largest Indian insulin brand but still has only 6.5 per cent share in the overall insulins market and 10 per cent in the represented market. It isn't going to get any easier. At a recent cardiac and diabetes conference in Mumbai, a doctor was speaking about insulin, and his first slide had Novo Nordisk's ultra-long-acting insulin Tresiba. 'The PowerPoint slide with the branded pen was on view for five minutes. The doctor should have used the generic name, degludec. Some of us were ashamed; it would never have happened at any conference in the US,' said a doctor who was present in the audience.

Big pharma companies are pushing newer diabetes drugs, oral as well as insulin, even though in many cases, the older ones work just as well. 'All companies are pushing DPP-4 inhibitors, which are ten times more expensive than metformin. Even with insulins, older versions, which are a fourth or fifth of the price of newer analogues, are pretty effective. There is no difference between Tresiba and glargine but the company is promoting the [former] aggressively,' said Anoop Misra, chairman of the Fortis Diabetes and Metabolic Diseases Centre in New Delhi. (Misra has convened a programme with all diabetes associations in India to develop a treatment protocol so that diabetes cost in India is contained.)

Regulation is consistently evolving in developed markets. And it is really the emerging markets which could prove the saviour in the immediate future. Governments in some of these countries are beginning to consider diabetes as a public health challenge and are floating tenders. (In tender markets, the price is low but so is the marketing cost.) In places like Japan, China, Russia and South Korea, Biocon is conducting clinical trials with local partners; after all, there are not many generic insulin makers that operate at a global scale. Because of this, in Malaysia, Biocon is harmonizing the regulatory requirements of both Europe and the US. Once the Malaysia plant starts commercial manufacturing, biotech's revenue trajectory would be very different as would the profit margins of the fourth-largest insulin manufacturer in the world.

What Still Rankles

As for the rest of the industry, it's a mixed bag.

'We have confused the whole world – we told the investors they can come in, invest; but we offered them no exit policy, no IPO scope, as loss-making companies cannot list in the early years. It was a complete antithesis of what biotech was in the traditional sense,' says Murali, ABLE president who runs the Indian arm of Swiss biotech Evolva. 'The Indian government never gave global investors and companies confidence that would let them invest, repatriate and take it forward. You can't have the Johns, the Jacobs or the Davids to run businesses here, whereas they can do it in Singapore or Brazil.'

In a June 1982 meeting at the New York University, when Ivan Ostholm asked why investing in India would make sense for Astra, S. Anand Kumar hauled out a stack of journals from under his desk and showed a large number of papers in modern biology that had Indian authors or co-authors. He argued that many of those authors would want to return to India and 'be with their family' if they got an opportunity to work on new technologies in biology. In the days that followed, Astra did attract many such scientists from overseas to its Bengaluru centre but the overall pie never grew big enough to repatriate talent in droves, like it has happened in IT.

'What we have done in the last fifteen to twenty years is get people from the best labs in the world [to India] who train people to go to the best labs in the world. That is a horrible cycle,' said K. VijayRaghavan, secretary of the Department of Biotechnology. The cycle is broken, only partially though, through some fellowships that fund 're-entry' of scientists from overseas. Unlike the elite programmes of the West which fund excellence, the fellowships in India fund capacity building, excellence and societal development. 'We have a mix, not bad scientifically, but not great either.'

The scientific enterprise is linked to the business enterprise, which in turn is linked to the regulatory sort of non-enterprise. The bill for an independent Biotech Regulatory Authority of India has lapsed in political limbo of recent years. India is a country that has a France and a Germany mixed with a sub-Saharan Africa, and it saw its bureaucrats making decisions for the former. Genetically modified crops and clinical research are just two examples. In the absence of this authority, and in the now-yes-now-no-now-I don't-care decision-making style of the Genetic Engineering Appraisal Committee, agriculture scientists and regulators did little to get rid of Monsanto from the genetic modification debate in India. When I asked former secretary Manju Sharma if activists had hijacked the subject in India, she said, 'No, the media just gave them undue publicity, like everywhere else in the world.'

Incidentally, it was the media again, *The Times of India* specifically, which 'discovered' in June 2015 that Monsanto had never patented the Bt gene Cry1Ac in India but had still collected high royalties all these years. Several Bt cotton hybrids developed at the University of Agricultural Sciences in Dharwad and the Central Institute for Cotton Research in Nagpur were left gathering dust on laboratory shelves and unsold because the patent on the gene they had used supposedly rested with Monsanto.

Not just crops, those who ventured into fuel did not race it to the automobile tanks, either. In the late 1980s, the time when Vaghul at ICICI was searching for technology evangelists, a young IIT graduate came to him with an incineration technology. The young aspiring technologist wanted to set up a pilot plant to demonstrate it. '"How much do you need?" I asked. He said ₹65 lakh. It was a lot of money so I asked him how much would he invest. He said he was just out of the institute and had no money,' recalled Vaghul. 'I thought for a while, let him interact with others in my office, and then gave him the money.'

The engineering graduate was Pramod Chaudhari and ICICI gave the risk capital to develop vinasse incineration technology which further evolved into front-end distillery processes and equipment. In nearly three decades, Chaudhari's Praj Industries has moved on to second-generation cellulosic biofuel technology, but a policy that, on paper required 20 per cent ethanol blend by 2017, did not lead to even 5 per cent blending by late 2015.

However, of the blend in IT and BT, academics and technology companies face a gaping divide today. Human resources that Brahmachari wanted to train fifteen years ago are still missing. VijayRaghavan is a concerned technocrat because 'there is no conversation' between engineers and biologists in Indian institutions. 'Using biology as a fulcrum, we need to train people across the spectrum. My fear is, do we have the capacity as a nation to do this?' he says.

Maybe not, but those who are long invested in it are figuring a way out. The first generation of bioinformatics and genomics start-ups began by serving the research market and had their fortunes tied to an inherently small business. More than a decade later, Genotypic, Strand and others are correcting it by addressing the real market – clinical services. At Syngene, Kiran admits, it is the 'missing piece'. 'At least Syngene has now started data management. You need a champion, I can't do everything,' she says. Acharya of Ocimum even floated a separate company, MapMyGenome, to provide genetic tests for disease and wellness management, a segment that is fast getting crowded.

And this time, academics are diving into the stream.

After retiring as director general of the Council of Scientific and Industrial Research, Brahmachari became an advisor to Genotypic; soon after, he became a stakeholder in its spin-off, Dhiti Omics. 'We want to create India's largest generics diagnostics industry,' he says. 'In the TRIPs agreement, provision 27(b) says diagnostics are not patentable in India; the kit is. We have to build a process model here,' he says. Plainly speaking, the existing tests have to be standardized with respect to the Indian population. A lot of companies in India today use Western markers for diagnosing diseases, which may not be directly applicable in India. 'A marker may be rare in the United States but may be common in India. We will find our own markers,' says Brahmachari.

In Hyderabad, Lalji Singh is taking a different tack. His earlier research had reliably shown that genetically, India is not one, or a few, but more than four thousand populations. With the present trend of genetic diagnostics, especially in urban India, he believes over time 'we will create two different Indias – the population will become so different that they will look like they are coming from two different countries'. Rural India will become riddled with genetic diseases and exploited by quacks whereas urban India will be genetically screened and better off.

It was in July 2015, when he received a rude, casual administrative notice that he had turned sixty-eight and was no longer part of the Centre for Cellular and Molecular Biology, that Singh revived the non-profit Genome Foundation he had set up ten years ago. He already had a handsome grant from the Department of Science and Technology, which he used to set up a genetic testing and research lab. An in vitro fertility centre in Hyderabad, Prasad Hospital, offered him free space for a few years, though the state government has given him five acres for the purpose. Presently screening rural populations in Andhra Pradesh and Telangana, he says: 'Once we demonstrate our capability, we will appeal to every Indian to donate. Even one rupee per person can go a long way.'

Not far from Singh, in Genome Valley, Bharat Biotech's Krishna M. Ella has also done some course correction and the move is more attitudinal. For the first time, he is selling a brand new vaccine, pricing it the multinational way. 'I realized nobody wants to believe in science. Then I figured doctors were making money on the mark-up price. I began selling at a higher mark-up. Quality is nothing but price. If you give it cheap, people think you are giving them a low-quality product,' he says.

In 2003, Bharat Biotech made a typhoid vaccine but could not sell it. Ella met 'all the big guns', who asked him to sell for ₹5 a dose; he was willing to come down to ₹25. Still unable to sell, he decided to do more science and developed a conjugate vaccine which turned out to be the first commercial conjugate typhoid vaccine in the world. 'In India, when breastfeeding stops, children get contamination through their liquid diet and develop fever. So babies under five are getting typhoid and paratyphoid, but the first line of therapy given is antibiotics. This vaccine is not in demand because multinationals don't sell it,' Ella says. Indian drug companies do not do concept selling, often because they sell me-too products. For his vaccine brochures, Ella borrowed images of the housefly from the filmmaker of the popular Telugu film *Eega* (remade in several other languages) as if to say, 'Houseflies spread typhoid.'

It took Ella more than a decade and a few failures to understand marketing. But Shiladitya Sengupta at Invictus Oncology has a penchant for it, at least for scientific marketing. 'To mitigate risk, we are moving everything out of India,' he says. He is filing two Investigational New Drug applications – a molecule from Vyome Biosciences for antibiotics resistant acne and a platinum drug conjugate from Invictus for treating triple-negative breast cancer which has hardly any drug treatment today. For the latter, Invictus has even chosen a European contract manufacturer for the clinical-stage manufacturing because the regulatory snag in shipping platinum-based experimental drugs is even higher.

Following the same principle, at Theramyt, Sohang Chatterjee has parked its intellectual property abroad and is now moving part of his research and business development to the Boston region. His investors are worried about the legal system in India and are not confident that he 'can defend or have good penetration of his patents'. He has raised $11.5 million so far, but by 2017, when he will need to raise the next round of $30–50 million, he probably will not find an investor that big in India. 'If you are a taxi aggregator, maybe you can, but not in life sciences,' he says.

The calculus of whether companies are doing good science or not is hard to crack for most investors in India, whether private or public. Which makes calculating the worth of the business very like a juggler's performance – a few elements are always up in the air.

Whither Valuation?

'Have you taken your research and development to their natural conclusion? Why are you wasting money? It is a big risk. Why don't you do what other pharma companies have done, or to monetize manufacturing why don't you become a preferred partner like Samsung?' tweeted an analyst to Kiran after the quarterly results announcements in early 2015.

'In exams it's the marks that count, for good behaviour you only get a star' – that was the cheeky response of another when she said Biocon had a good track record in regulatory compliance.

'This is the attack I get every day. How come those who get [FDA] warning letters have higher valuations? Is there any logic? That means it's all gamed. Just because I don't play the stock market game …' she says, frustration creeping into her voice.

In the eleven years since Biocon went public, it has not vaulted into the large market cap that many had thought it would. It had a stellar listing, crossing $1.1 billion valuation on the first day in 2004. A company that gave private investors dream returns soon realized that public investors were more demanding, and perhaps less understanding. They lump Biocon with pharma companies – Lupin's market cap grew more than twentyfold, Dr Reddy's more than tenfold, and Biocon's grew twice in the same period – because it has some product overlaps. But it is difficult to compare its share value and progress with generic companies.

'Biocon, in some ways,' says former Bristol-Myers Squibb executive Howson, 'has the same personality as Actavis. I was on the board of Actavis, it took a while for the world to realize what the company was.'

On the day Syngene went public and listed at 18 per cent premium, Biocon shares were down by about 1 per cent. Once again, the bourses showed they understood a services model better than a complex generics and discovery model. In the following months, Biocon's value sans Syngene remained ridiculously low. Its value in Indian investors' eyes pales in comparison with the multi-billion dollar valuation of the Samsung Bioepis and Merck biosimilars pipeline which is no bigger than Biocon-Mylan's. Samsung Bioepis plans to raise $1.3 billion from Nasdaq for developing its molecules.

That hurts. As Silicon Valley tech seer and venture capitalist Mark Andreessen once said, everything is connected to the stock price. 'Employee morale, ability to recruit new employees, ability to retain employees, ability to sign customer contracts, ability to raise debt financing, ability to deal with regulators. Every single part of your business ends up being connected and it ends up being tied back to your stock price.'

It is not just Biocon. Unless a few other biotech companies work out, people will not have confidence in the industry. 'In e-commerce, people are paying for future potential and they can see a few companies at number one, two and three, where earnings have caught up with valuation. In technology, people see it again and again, but it is yet to happen in biotech,' says Parag Saxena, founding general partner of New Silk Route, who has a history of investing in biotech in the United States.

Since the start of the second decade of the millennium, biotech in the United States has seen an upswing not seen in over a decade – stock prices are high, drug approvals are swift, and public offerings have been as regular as Friday movie releases. In 2014, one in four initial public offerings in America was in biotech. The ripples reached the UK too, making 2014 a record year that grossed more than two-fifths of all money raised in the country in biotech public offerings over the past decade.

Against this, right valuations seem to elude life sciences businesses in India. When Vijay Chandru at Strand Life Sciences needed to raise $20 million and more for expansion in the US, he was as dissuaded by Biocon's chronic struggle in the public market as he was dispirited by the private equity grasp of his business in clinical genomics. In January 2016 he chose to go to Nasdaq, albeit through a shorter route of reverse merger with Venaxis, a diagnostics company which traded as a penny stock but had $20 million in cash, the precise growth capital that Strand was seeking.

'None of the Big Four [professional services firms] have the capability to evaluate intellectual property or value life sciences start-ups. As soon as you ask them, they begin to write down your valuation substantially by saying it is loss-making. When I raise my fund and make, say, six investments, and all of them get written down, my investors will jump at me. These big companies only know how to value on price-earnings multiple or Ebitda multiple,' says a venture capital investor in Mumbai.

It's not just money, investment bankers in India even fail to find the right partnership deals for start-ups. At Kotak Private Equity in Mumbai, chief executive Nitin Deshmukh has learnt to go to investment bankers overseas. For valuations of companies he has invested in, he goes to American Appraisal. But this is not an option for most small companies.

THE ANCHOR

If not much has changed in the last ten years, indications are that the next ten years might look decidedly different. The self-comforting or self-deprecating line that biotech entrepreneurs use – India is the only country with a federal biotech agency – may now take on a new meaning. After the department consolidated its industry funding under BIRAC, the latter has emerged as the biggest source of early-stage funding for wannabe or existing entrepreneurs. The BIRAC has supported over 100 entrepreneurs, close to 300 companies and strengthened 150 small and medium enterprises. The fifteen bio-incubators it has supported in different institutions, with at least ₹100 crore in investment, are meant to promote 'bio-entrepreneurship' and 'biology-inspired research and innovation'.

Bengaluru scores once again with two incubators competing and complementing each other – if the Centre for Cellular and Molecular Platforms in the north provides high-end technologies as fee for service, a unique offering in the country, the Bangalore Bio-innovation Centre (deliberately branded as BBC) at the Institute of Bioinformatics and Applied Biotechnology boasts of its 60,000 sq. ft of plug-and-play space. The IBAB has been offering incubation space since 2009, and sees a visible uptick. 'Earlier, we could give two lab benches easily; then we had to ration it to half a bench, and now we have to turn entrepreneurs away,' says Gayatri Saberwal. In a first such survey – which will become a longitudinal study – Saberwal looked for start-ups which are less than five years old and surveyed fifty of the ninety she found. 'Each one had something new to offer,' she says. With financial stability, and alumni numbering over 500, the bench-to-market in biotech is a hard question that can now appear to be easy even to an academic administrator like Bhan.

As if to cap his years of relentless makeover of Indian bioscience, he has registered a start-up, KNIT. The acronym stands for Knowledge Integration and Transfer – it sounds more like a benign plea than a business-minded start-up – which intends to 'transform secondary care in district hospitals in the states'. Having worked with the Bill & Melinda Gates Foundation for long, in 2015 Bhan wrote them a brief note on his idea, admitting that he was 'too old to write a full proposal'. Bill Gates did not think so. The Foundation has granted him $1 million, offering to review KNIT after a year.

In Hyderabad, at the ICICI Knowledge Park, Deepanwita Chattopadhyay has supported 175 companies in fifteen years. During and after her Ph.D days at IIT Delhi, she had an almost fantasist desire to build a hands-on science museum which, of course, she could never pursue, not least because of a lack of funds. As she is expanding in Bengaluru, she hopes part of her earlier ambition will be fulfilled through the makerspace, IKP-EDEN – a hardware do-it-yourself incubator and accelerator which allows members can rent a desk or a corner to build their devices or their subsystems.

For all such focused labours, Kotak's Nitin Deshmukh has a rush of longing. He has funded more than forty life sciences companies in his career but for the first time, he notices high-quality ideas taking shape, particularly in medical devices, diagnostics and bioinformatics. 'I wish I had a fund from which I could back twenty to thirty of these to take them to the next level,' he says.

(BIRAC announced an equity fund, AcE, in March 2015 but until January 2016 it had not received any money.)

In his tenure, as Bhan watched some of the bio-design ideas become prototypes, a high point in a low era, he had said, 'By the time I retire, I will make sure bio-design becomes a movement in the country'. The Stanford-India bio-design programme trained twenty fellows and transferred seven technologies. Bhan retired in 2013, and bio-design hasn't become a movement yet. Most companies are still assembling med-tech devices in India, using imported components. Bhan argues that a new inter-institutional centre involving the IIT and AIIMS in Delhi, a Translational Health Science and Technology Institute in Faridabad, the proposal for which is lying with the Union cabinet, and a new multimillion-dollar fund from the World Bank for product development, will prove in time that bio-design was not a wrong-footed initiative.

In February 2016, in the thick of the global Zika virus scare, one of Bhan's vaccine partners, Bharat Biotech, stunned the world when it said it has two vaccine candidates for the virus. Krishna M. Ella had filed for patents a year ago, not caring when his science would be distilled into usable technology. It was a moment of glory for the industry even though the regulatory clearance around the import of Zika virus for research was mired in controversy.

There's definitely something up ahead for the bioscience enterprise. Many first-generation biotech entrepreneurs built companies for science, technology or themselves; the second generation is building for exits, some confident enough to buy back assets from multinationals. Chandrashekaran Siddamadappa was the fourth employee of Bangalore Genei when Padmanabhan Babu started it at the Astra Centre. Its ownership changed a few times in twenty-eight years but its last owner, German Merck KGaA, chose to shut down the biological reagents and tools company in mid-2015. Siddamadappa, who had founded two companies, and sold one since leaving Bangalore Genei, bought the assets from Merck in 2016 to revive the Indian brand. 'We will hire most of the [laid-off] fifty employees and rebuild Bangalore Genei into a global brand. Why can't we have a billion-dollar Indian company in this space,' he says.

It's still a bit of a conundrum as to where many of the BIRAC-supported entrepreneurs will get their next round of funding from, and how the grossly undersized local healthcare market will absorb their technologies, but it appears that a serious push to a 'bio-economy' is under way. A twentyfold increase in revenue by 2025 is what industry body ABLE has set itself up for. If each state strives to put in a few billion, if a fraction of the pending applications for seventy-odd new crops get approved, and if a handful of new molecules make it to the advanced licensing stage, $100 billion may not look like a pie in the sky. 'The differentiation must continue. We must not try to unify biotech in different regions – Chennai will never grow like Bengaluru, which will never be like Hyderabad, which will never be like Pune,' says P. Murali.

At Indus Biotech in Pune, which exports botanical ingredients for sports nutraceuticals to several pharmacy chains in the US, Sunil Bhaskaran for the first time finds that the top few Indian generics companies are not allergic to evaluating botanical drug candidates. True bio-partnering may not be illusory any more. It took fifteen years for Singapore's Biopolis to finally yield a clinical discovery – a new cancer molecule, in collaboration with Duke University. The second may not take that long. Every country is inspired by the United States where, since 1980, life sciences has played a commanding role in the country's 'strategies of economic and imperialist self-reinvention'. Since then, as Melinda Cooper writes in *Life as Surplus: Biotechnology and Capitalism in Neoliberal Era*, 'The US government has been at the centre of efforts to reorganize global trade rules and IP [Intellectual Property] laws along lines that would favour its own drug, agribusiness and biotech industries. Moreover, the unique position of the US itself in relationship to world financial flows has meant that even the most speculative of its life sciences enterprises has attracted a constant and incomparable flow of funds.'

In contrast, New Delhi never paid attention to generating

sufficient credible data for taking informed decisions – decisions that were not propped by industry data. Additionally, it has muddled its regulatory environment, which may have inadvertently created a monopoly that favours bigger companies against which activists and nationalists agitate. In agriculture, the inarguable truth is that big seed companies do not depend on Indian fields to test their new seeds or technology, but when they enter the Indian market, they do so in a flurry, leaving local or smaller companies gasping. Bt cotton is a fine example of this. Worse still, no one in the regulatory agencies is talking, at least publicly, about the new gene-editing tool – CRISPR-Cas9 – hitting the scientific labs, although this is unquestionably one of the biggest breakthroughs in genetics in recent decades. An affordable, simple-to-use tool for editing the letters of DNA, its methodology is akin to correcting typographical errors in a document by using the search-and-replace (or search-and-delete) function in a word processor. Agricultural labs across the world are already editing crop seeds like rice and potato. Creating new and better crops by editing genes may be less controversial than genetic modification, but treating human diseases should entail extensive public discussions, a practice Indian researchers shy away from.

Yet, what we are observing – a sense that everything has always been thus – is the lag phase of microbial culture, which in time gives way to the log phase of exponential growth. Indian biotech is at least past the lag midpoint.

'In our generics-oriented country, biotech, in the philosophical sense, has been an ancillary industry. Whereas, in an efficient regulatory environment, this industry can grow at 25–30 per cent without much effort,' says Murali.

EPILOGUE

A large, contemplative acrylic on canvas hangs near the entrance wall; it's a signature Hariraam. Inside the room, a Shuvaprasanna – 'it is an original, not a poster', Narendra Chirmule emphasizes – has recently replaced a Hussain. A set of tablas, flute and African drum djembe are neatly lined up in a corner; Chirmule has weekly jams in his cabin. Soaking in the arty ambience on a Tuesday morning, in pink linen shirt and sandals, he is at once at home and out of place at the Biocon Research Centre. It has been a few weeks since he joined and he is already talking of 'changing the culture of research and development'.

In March 2015, when Chirmule met Kiran over lunch, he was visiting India from Los Angeles in search of consulting opportunities. 'What is someone with your experience doing here,' she asked, adding, 'you could be of more help to Biocon if you join us.' A few weeks after he joined in May, Abhijit Barve called Chirmule to say he was leaving; he was relocating to the US for personal reasons. 'Congratulations, I want your job,' Chirmule told him. Suddenly, the next 'inflection point' floating in his head looked real, staring him in the face. It would come at one-fifth of his usual remuneration, though.

Twice in his career of twenty-eight years, Chirmule had

witnessed the field of science shift itself because of projects he was part of. First, at the University of Pennsylvania, where he worked in the team of the unfortunate pioneer of gene therapy, James Wilson. The death of a patient in a clinical trial had turned out to be a precipitating event for the therapy. Then, some years later, at Merck, where Chirumule worked as an immunologist. The project was the HIV vaccine. In a landmark test-of-concept clinical trial, called STEP, researchers found that instead of reducing the risk of getting AIDS, the vaccine candidate increased the risk of disease.

He left Merck to join Amgen where, for eight years, as executive director, he worked with the regulatory agencies. When he realized his 'learning curve was going flat', he jumped the ship. At fifty-four, Chirumule comes to Biocon when the company is about to enter an 'inflection point', his favourite two words.

Collectively, Biocon's biosimilars basket represents market opportunities exceeding $50 billion. Even if the Biocon-Mylan combine gets a fraction of that, it would change the course of biotech in Bengaluru. In getting there, biosimilars will lob off a disproportionate share of the research and development budget; therefore a strong pair of hands is needed to steer the team to deliver on the existing programmes, remain motivated on the novels and still be hungry for something new and untested. At Amgen, Chirmule was once part of organizing a symposium that discussed what the Thousand Oaks firm had learnt in thirty years of biotechnology. He probably also got insights into how to save R&D from the so-called 'tyranny of accountants'.

Certainly, research at Biocon needs a champion. By end-2015, oral insulin studies were on the expected course. The storied molecule now has an international non-proprietary name – Insulin Tregopil, an analogue which is the first drug in its class – and has an accompanying assay which can measure its precise impact, separate from the endogenous insulin in the body. Multiple early studies in the United States showed that oral delivery of insulin is feasible.

However, in early 2016, Biocon renegotiated its partnership with Bristol-Myers Squibb, which had divested its diabetes franchise to AstraZeneca three years earlier. The Bengaluru biotech will now carry out further clinical studies on its own. 'Big pharma is very slow. It took us more than three years to complete Phase I. This is one lesson we have learnt while working with big companies. We will drive further studies ourselves, even if we get partners along the way,' Kiran says. Once again, orphan indication – like gestational diabetes, which affects nearly a sixth of pregnant women worldwide – could provide the first user group.

Even if Tregopil tanks as a one-size-fits-all blockbuster, it will probably end up as a safe, cheap and convenient replacement for mealtime injection. Diabetes is a continuum of care. With so many people suffering from this disorder, Biocon has a great many opportunities to innovate because not many new drugs are being developed. Also, the new and stringent norms by the US FDA require drug makers to demonstrate there is no increase in cardiovascular events linked to the molecule.

Then there's oncology, where it will strive to grab more market share since it is not among the top four brands in the country. Biocon may add more products by licensing from innovator companies because its own antibody, BIOMAb, is a promising drug in head and neck cancer treatment but is now reaching a life-cycle plateau. Since Biocon has limited marketing rights on this molecule, the drug's expansion to other indications will be slow.

However, itolizumab's expansion is imminent. After five decades of Cold War enmity, Cuba and the US are normalizing relations. This will ease Biocon's conversations with potential partners because its Cuban origin has been a bottleneck so far. When Tamar Howson was at Bristol-Myers, she had tried 'very hard' to in-license the molecule but could not get over the American government's sanction rules. 'Earlier, Bristol-Myers Squibb managed to get the meningitis vaccine from Cuba because there was nothing else available, so the American government allowed the product to be used in the United States. But for competing products like monoclonal antibodies, we could not do it,' she said.

Itolizumab, which could either turn out to be the mother of all opportunities or remain a middling new molecule, has advanced Biocon's research capabilities to an extent that it can now in-license and develop a molecule on its own. Some of the technology lead that Biocon had in India has been bridged of late; the company now must jump from one lily pad to another. Through the Mazumdar-Shaw Cancer Hospital, Kiran is integrating into healthcare where the translational centre could possibly offer new commercialization opportunities. From a cancer genomics point of view, novel mutations could present as drug targets where a relationship with Strand may be useful.

Yet, this is also where Biocon is vulnerable. Kiran is the only one who can make gutsy bets, show a certain blindness to the odds that is necessary to drive innovation. In elevating Arun Chandavarkar as the chief executive, Biocon has brought a competent leader to replace a charismatic leader. 'Kiran has a certain celebrity profile and we leverage that. As long as Steve Jobs was there, nobody knew who Tim Cook was. Kiran and I may speak different languages but we say the same things,' Chandavarkar says. But it's true that they don't make the same bets.

Kiran is still heavily hands-on, though. She still believes she can do it all. Long-term board member Charles Cooney thinks it has to do with her self-confidence. 'If you are very self-confident, you can go beyond normal boundaries. I see this in many of my students [at MIT]. It's like athletes; what drives them to great heights is their supreme self-confidence.'

At sixty-three, Kiran remains the animating spirit of Biocon, travelling 40 per cent of the time, and still thinking 'what's new, what's next' for the company. In a few years, maybe, she would become an executive chairman, further strengthen Chandavarkar's hands with a few more capable leaders, and herself play a smarter and bigger role with her philanthropic donations. 'She is as much on the go as ever before,' says childhood friend and chairman of the United Breweries Group, Vijay Mallya. A few years younger than her, he tries to keep up with her energy to avoid being bullied. 'When I was six, she made me run around her house ten times, saying if I did that I would go to the moon. I merrily ran till I was rescued by her mother. She can still bully me,' he says.

In 1989, when Kiran was awarded the Padma Shri, she called a few among friends and family to say she was entering politics. This unnerved her younger brother in the US so much that he gave her a dose of wisdom on how politics was not for her. But it was a joke, just another April Fools' prank that she pulls on people every year, even today.

'I have a very non-partisan approach to politics,' she says. 'I engage with politicians on development and policies which have an apolitical hue. I would never be a good politician and clearly have no delusions to be one! My friend Nandan [Nilekani] has made me realize how we are just not politically savvy. So I have decided to engage with the political system as a citizens' pressure group through B.PAC. If at all one has to jump into politics, one must jump in by cutting one's corporate strings, and I have no such intentions.'

Still, four decades is a long innings in corporate life. What if a buyer comes with a hard-to-ignore valuation and a good set of hands to run the company? (Between Shaw and Kiran, they still own about 60 per cent of Biocon.)

'It's not for sale. Not in my lifetime,' she quips.

NOTES AND REFERENCES

1. Brewing a Business

The Reluctant Entrepreneur: Interviews with Leslie Auchincloss, Yamini Mazumdar, Ravi Mazumdar.

The Compulsive Entrepreneur: Interviews with Leslie Auchincloss, Colin Dowzer, Declan MacFadden, Joe Dunne, Ritchie Piggott.

Australia to Ireland: Interviews with Yamini Mazumdar, Ravi Mazumdar, Colin Dowzer, Parag Saxena.

Starting Up: Interviews with Yamini Mazumdar, Meeru Pai, Leslie Auchincloss, Pratima Rao, Murali Krishnan; also Dinesh C. Sharma, *The Long Revolution: The Birth and Growth of India's IT Industry*, HarperCollins.

The Core Team: Interviews with Murali Krishnan, Shrikumar Suryanarayanan, Leslie Auchincloss, Ajay Bharadwaj, Arun Chandavarkar, Mike Woulfe.

The Outlier: Interviews with Leslie Auchincloss, GS Krishnan, Murali Krishnan, Narayanan Vaghul.

Pangs & Perks of the First Plant: Interviews with Shrikumar Suryanarayanan, Ajay Bharadwaj, Leslie Auchincloss, Joe Dunne, Jyothi Kamath.

Growing the Pie: Interviews with Ajay Bharadwaj, Leslie Auchincloss, Shrikumar Suryanarayanan, Murali Krishnan; also, Stephen Budiansky,

Battle of Wits: The Complete Story of Code Breaking in World War II, pp. 172–173.

2. A Decade with Unilever

Cookie Crumbles in Cork: Interviews with Roland Cocker, Leslie Auchincloss, Declan MacFadden, Joe Dunne, Ritchie Piggott.

Bengaluru Bulks Up: Interviews with Jyothi Kamath, Roland Cocker, Auchincloss, Mike Woulfe.

New Beginnings, New Challenges: Interviews with Mike Powell, Ajay Bharadwaj, Joe Dunne, Declan MacFadden, Shrikumar Suryanarayanan, Murali Krishnan, Mike Woulfe.

Face-Off: Interviews with Ajay Bharadwaj, Leslie Auchincloss, Mike Powell, Declan MacFadden.

Cog in the Conglomerate: Interviews with Mike Woulfe, Roland Cocker, Murali Krishnan, Ajay Bharadwaj.

Building Platform Technologies: Interviews with Arun Chandavarkar, Roland Cocker, Rakesh Bamzai, Mark Emalfarb, Subramani Ramachandrappa, Shrikumar Suryanarayanan, Mike Powell, Declan MacFadden, Murali Krishnan, Nirupa Bareja.

Plafractor: Interviews with Shreehas Tambe, Shrikumar Surya Narayanan, Murali Krishnan, Anindya Sircar.

Learn, Earn, Burn: Interviews with Tara Jayaram, Nirupa Bareja, Shrikumar Suryanarayanan, Murali Krishnan, Ajay Bharadwaj.

Parting: Interviews with Joe Dunne, Kunal Kashyap, John Shaw, Leslie Auchincloss; also, John Thompson and Frank Martin, *Strategic Management: Awareness and Change*, 6th ed., p. 718.

Support System: Interviews with John Shaw, Yamini Mazumdar, Meeru Pai, Ravi Mazumdar, Pratima Rao.

3. Birth of a Cluster

Modern Biology – Lifting the In Vivo Veil: Interviews with Pushpa Mittra Bhargava, Govindarajan Padmanaban, Janaki Ramachandran, S. Anand

Kumar, Banda Venkata Ravikumar; also, 'Classical versus Modern Biology' http://www.laskerfoundation.org/awards/pdf/2012_s_maniatis.pdf. See also, Sally Smith Hughes, *Genentech: The Beginnings of Biotech*, University of Chicago Press; Ivan Ostholm (tr. by Indien Kallar) *India Calling*, Tre Bocker Forlag AB, Sweden; and Eric J. Vettel, *Biotech: The Countercultural Origins of an Industry*, University of Pennsylvania Press.

The Gospel of Biotechnology: Interviews with S Anand Kumar, Govindarajan Padmanaban, Janaki Ramachandran, Kumud Sampath, Charles Cooney, Samir K. Brahmachari, Sriram Padmanabhan, Goutam Das; also, Rishikesha T. Krishnan, 'Biotechnology & Bioinformatics: Can India Emulate the Software Success Story?', and G. Padmanaban, 'Application of Biotechnology to Medicine in India', *Current Science*, 25 March 1995, http://www.iimb.ernet.in/~rishi/biotech.pdf.

Spotlight on Biology, Finally: Interviews with Pushpa Mittra Bhargava, K. VijayRaghavan, H. Sharat Chandra, Lalji Singh, Govindarajan Padmanaban, his autobiography, *To Reach the Stars or Dig the Earth*, Vigyan Prasar; see also, Dinesh C. Sharma, *The Long Revolution: The Birth and Growth of India's IT Industry*, and Ivan Ostholm, *India Calling* by Ivan Ostholm; http://www.currentscience.ac.in/Downloads/article_id_068_06_0584_0585_0.pdf

The Clubby Environment: Interviews with Samir K. Brahmachari, Banda Venkata Ravikumar, Govindarajan Padmanaban, Janaki Ramachandran, Raghunath Mashelkar.

The First Recombinant Product: Interviews with K.I. Varaprasad Reddy, Pushpa Mittra Bhargava, G. Padmanaban, Raghunath Mashelkar, Manju Sharma.

The Story of Shantha Biotechnics Limited by Boston Consulting Group, August 1998.

Creating a Market: Interviews with K.I. Varaprasad Reddy, Krishna M. Ella, Manju Sharma, Maharaj Kishan Bhan, Govindarajan Padmanaban; also see, 'Price war to hit anti-hepatitis drive', http://articles.economictimes.indiatimes.com/2002-09-20/news/27345475_1_hepatitis-b-vaccine-bharat-biotech-uip; and Yennapu Madhavi,*Vaccine*

Policy in India, by Yennapu Madhavi, http://journals.plos.org/plosmedicine/article?id=10.1371/journal.pmed.0020127.

Hit and Miss Biology: Interviews with Samir K. Brahmachari, H. Sharat Chandra, Govindarajan Padmanaban, Manju Sharma, Raghunath Mashelkar, Lalji Singh, Girish Sahni.

4. Transformation – From Enzymes to Drugs

Chance Meeting: Interviews with Bimal K. Raizada, Shrikumar Suryanarayanan, Ajay Bharadwaj, Rakesh Bamzai; see also, William Shurtleff and Akiko Aoyagi, 'A Brief History of Fermentation, East and West', http://www.soyinfocenter.com/HSS/fermentation.php.

Statins and Cash Flow: Interviews with Anand Khedkar, Shrikumar Suryanarayanan, Ravindra K.C., Ajay Bharadwaj, Rakesh Bamzai, Sandeep Rao, Tara Jayaram, Nirupa Bareja.

Real Pharma Flavour: Interviews with Shrikumar Suryanarayanan, Arun Chandavarkar, B.S.V. Prasad, Bimal Raizada, Rakesh Bamzai, Anand Khedkar, Jyothi Kamath; see also, Directory of Pharmaceutical Manufacturing Units in India, NPPA India, http://www.nppaindia.nic.in/Directory-NPPA.pdf.

The Pivot: Interviews with Harish Iyer, Shrikumar Suryanarayanan, Arun Chandavarkar, K.I. Varaprasad Reddy, B.S.V Prasad; see also, 'Wockhardt buys out Rhein Biotech from Joint Venture', http://www.business-standard.com/article/companies/wockhardt-buys-out-rhein-biotech-from-joint-venture-102032701024_1.html.

Oral Insulin: Interviews with Shrikumar Suryanarayanan, Anand Khedkar, Christopher Price, Bala Manian, M. Chinappa; see also, 'Oral Insulin and Buccal Insulin: A Critical Reappraisal, Journal of Diabetes Science and Technology', http://www.ncbi.nlm.nih.gov/pmc/articles/PMC2769877/.

Into the Unknown: Anand Khedkar, Shrikumar Suryanarayanan, Harish Iyer, Christopher Price.

Cuba: Cigar, Coffee, Communism & Science: Interviews with Ajay Bharadwaj, Rakesh Bamzai, Patricia Sierra, John Shaw, Shrikumar

Suryanarayanan, Arun Chandavarkar, Anuj Goel; 'Biopharmaceutical Benchmarks 2010', *Nature Biotechnology*, Vol.28, No.9, 2010, pp. 917–924; and Lara Marks, 'A Healthcare Revolution in the Making, The Story of César Milstein and Monoclonal Antibodies', http://www.whatisbiotechnology.org/exhibitions/milstein.

5. Diversification – Closing The Life Sciences Loop

Sold on Services: Interviews with Janakiraman Ramachandran, Gordon Ringold, Goutam Das, Kumud Sampath, Ganesh Sambasivam, Balu N. Subramanian; see also, D.A. Pereira and J.A. Williams, 'Origin and Evolution of High Throughput Screening', http://www.ncbi.nlm.nih.gov/pmc/articles/PMC1978279/#bib20.

Enter Big Pharma: Interviews with Goutam Das, Balu N. Subramanian, Tamar Howson.

The Clinical Touch: Interviews with Arvind Atignal, Gordon Ringold, Bala Manian, Vijay Chandru, Goutam Das

Serendipity: Interviews with Gordon Ringold, Bala Manian, Goutam Das, Narayanan Vaghul, Arvind Atignal.

Quality Stamp: Interviews with Tamar Howson, Goutam Das, Balu N. Subramanian.

Syngene 2.0: Interviews with Tara Jayaram, M. Chinappa, Goutam Das, Kunal Kashyap, Peter Bains, Goutam Das, Manoj Nerurkar.

Ripe for Public Listing: Interviews with Kunal Kashyap, Carl Decicco, Goutam Das, Peter Bains.

Clinical Research Bubble: Interviews with Arvind Atignal, Abhijit Barve, Peter Bains, Manoj Nerurkar; see also, Archana Kalegaonkar, Richard Locke and Jonathan Lehrich, 'MIT-Sloan Case Study, Learning Edge: Biocon India Group'; also, Robert H. Carlson, *Biology is Technology: The Promise, Peril and New Business of Engineering Life*; also, 'Indian Labs Deleted Drug Test Results', http://www.bloomberg.com/news/articles/2014-12-03/indian-labs-deleted-drug-test-results-documents-show; also, 'GVK Biosciences: European Medicines Agency recommends

suspending medicines over flawed studies', http://www.ema.europa.
eu/ema/index.jsp?curl=pages/news_and_events/news/2015/01/
news_detail_002256.jsp&mid=WC0b01ac058004d5c1; also, Surinder
Singh, 'Clinical Trials New Horizon – India', http://www.who.int/
medicines/areas/quality_safety/regulation_legislation/icdra/1_India_
ClinicalTrialsNewHorizon.pdf; also, 'From tragedy to travesty: Drugs
tested on survivors of Bhopal', http://www.independent.co.uk/news/
world/asia/from-tragedy-to-travesty-drugs-tested-on-survivors-of-
bhopal-6262412.html, accessed on 2 June 2015; and 'Injury and death
in clinical trials and compensation: Rule 122DAB', http://www.ncbi.nlm.
nih.gov/pmc/articles/PMC3835962/

6. START-UP BECOMES A CORPORATE

The Trigger: Interviews with Kunal Kashyap, Nitin Deshmukh, Tania
Khosla, Murali Krishnan.

Governance in Place: Interviews with Suresh Talwar, Charles Cooney, Bala
Manian, Ajay Bharadwaj, Rakesh Bamzai, Ravi Mazumdar, Catherine
Rosenberg, Bala Manian, Narayanan Vaghul, Gordon Ringold.

The IPO: Kunal Kashyap, Murali Krishnan, John Shaw, N.R. Narayana
Murthy, Ajay Bharadwaj, Rakesh Bamzai, Meeru Pai, Nirupa Bareja,
Susan Kumar; see also, 'Biocon IPO oversubscribed by 33 times', http://
articles.economictimes.indiatimes.com/2004-03-20/news/27384953_1_
price-band-biocon-plans-post-issue-capital.

Battle for Insulin: Interviews with K.I. Varaprasad Reddy, Murali
Krishnan, Raghunath Mashelkar, Manju Sharma, Ajay Bharadwaj,
Abhijit Zutshi; see also, 'Centre admits deaths in clinical trials of GE
drugs', *The Hindu,* 22 August 2004, http://www.indiaresource.org/
news/2004/1039.html; also, 'Private Battles in Public Arena', http://
www.biospectrumindia.com/biospecindia/news/157113/private-battles-
public-arena; also, 'Wosulin: A Milestone for Wockhardt', http://articles.
economictimes.indiatimes.com/2003-08-04/news/27554197_1_insulin-
wockhardt-habil-khorakiwala; and 'State FDA pulls plug on Wockhardt
insulin drug', http://articles.economictimes.indiatimes.com/2006-11-28/
news/27461480_1_wosulin-human-insulin-fda-commissioner.

The Flashpoint: Interviews with Ajay Bharadwaj, Rakesh Bamzai, Nirupa Bareja, Shrikumar Suryanarayanan, Murali Krishnan, Harish Iyer, Arvind Atignal, Goutam Das, M. Chinappa, Suresh Talwar, Ganesh Sambasivam, Ravindra K.C., Bala Manian, G.S. Krishnan.

Celebrity Stardust on a Biologic: Interviews with Praveen Bose, Subir Basak, Arvind Atignal, Rakesh Bamzai, Ajay Bharadwaj.

Being Tactical was Hurting: Interviews with Sudhir Nayak, Rakesh Bamzai, Dan Bradbury, Anoop Misra, Harish Iyer, Arun Chandavarkar.

Power-packed Partnerships: Interviews with Robert Coury, Jeff Kindler, Patricia Sierra, Abhijit Zutshi, Bala Manian; see also, 'I-Bank Espirito Santo concerned at Biocon's accounting process', http://www.businessstandard.com/article/companies/i-bank-espirito-santo-concerned-at-biocon-s-accounting-processes-112052200042_1.html; and 'Cubist buys Trius, Optimer for New Hospital Antibiotics', http://www.bloomberg.com/news/articles/2013-07-30/antibiotic-maker-cubist-buys-trius-optimer-for-hospital-drugs.

Bets that Did Not Fly: Interviews with Bala Manian, Shrikumar Suryanarayanan, Harish Iyer, Anuj Goel, Christopher Price, Anindya Sircar, Arun Chandavarkar; see also, 'The Economics of Biosimilars', http://www.ncbi.nlm.nih.gov/pmc/articles/PMC4031732/; and 'Biocon divests stake in Axicorp', http://archive.indianexpress.com/news/biocon-divests-stake-in-axicorp/782788/.

The Shift: Interviews with Harish Iyer, K.I. Varaprasad Reddy, Abhijit Barve, Rakesh Bamzai, Sandeep Rao, Ravi Limaye, Arun Chandavarkar, Mahesh Gowrishankara, Dan Bradbury, Jeremy Levin, Vijay Kuchroo.

7. BIG, HAIRY BETS

The Pin-up Molecule: Interviews with Anand Khedkar, Harish Iyer, Maharaj Kishan Bhan, Bala Manian, Harold Lebovitz; see also, 'Clinical trials are not a slam dunk', http://timesofindia.indiatimes.com/business/india-business/Clinical-trials-are-not-a-slam-dunk-Biocon-CMD/articleshow/7329047.cms; and 'BMS and AstraZeneca to take control of Amylin', http://www.ft.com/cms/s/0/2422b508-c2b0-11e1-8d12-00144feabdc0.html#axzz3uxTwmzyo.

One in the Crowd: Interviews with Anand Khedkar, Harold Lebovitz; see also, 'Novo heralds promising phase III diabetes data for once-a-week semaglutide', http://www.fiercebiotech.com/story/novo-heralds-promising-phiii-diabetes-data-once-weekly-semaglutide/2015-07-10; and 'LifeSci Advisors', http://www.oramed.com/wp-content/uploads/2015/01/Oramed__LifeSci_Initiation_Report_3-19-14__clientinfo.pdf.

Itolizumab – The New Kid on the Block: Interviews with Enrique Montero, Patricia Sierra, Shri, Ramakrishnan Melarkode, Vijay Kuchroo, Bala Manian; see also, 'Reciprocal developmental pathways for the generation of pathogenic effector Th-17 and regulatory T cells', http://www.nature.com/nature/journal/v441/n7090/full/nature04753.html; and

'Autoimmune Disease', *Nature Biotechnology*, 2000, http://www.nature.com/nbt/journal/v18/n10s/full/nbt1000_IT7.html.

The Aha! Moment: Interviews with Ramakrishnan Melarkode, Vijay Kuchroo, Mahesh Gowrishankara.

The Cross Bearer: Interviews with Kiran Mazumdar-Shaw, Ramakrishnan Melarkode, Jeremy Levin, B.N. Manohar; see also, 'Reshaping the Legacy', http://www.drreddys.com/media/pdf/Reshaping-The-Legacy-FORTUNE-Jan-2014.pdf.

Upping the Ante: Antibodies to Nucleic Acid: Interviews with Daniel Zurr, Arvind Atignal; see also, 'Negotiating the RNAi patent thicket', *Nature Biotechnology*, March 2007, http://www.nature.com/nbt/journal/v25/n3/full/nbt0307-273.html; and 'Gene silencing drugs finally show promise', *Technology Review*, September 2014, http://www.technologyreview.com/featuredstory/530631/gene-silencing-drugs-finally-show-promise/.

Common Aspirations: Interviews with Daniel Zurr, Mugasimangalam Raja, Yusuf Hamied, Bala Manian, Vasan Sambandanamurthy, Arvind Atignal.

Vulnerabilities: Interviews with Vasan Sambandanamurthy, Daniel Zurr, Utpal Bhadra; see also, 'RNA-based therapeutics and vaccines', http://www.genengnews.com/insight-and-intelligence/rna-based-therapeutics-and-vaccines/77900520/.

8. The Start-up Industry

Risk of the Rhyme: Interviews with Vivek Kulkarni, Vijay Chandru, H. Sharat Chandra, Deepanwita Chattopadhayay, Krishna M. Ella; see also, Sally Smith Hughes, *Biomania, Genentech: The Beginnings of Biotech*; and 'The Millennium Biotech Policy of Karnataka', 2000, http://investkarnataka.gov.in/sites/default/files/The%20Millenium%20Biotech%20Policy.pdf

In IT's Footsteps: Interviews with Vivek Kulkarni, S. Sadagopan, H. Sharat Chandra, Gayatri Saberwal, Madhav Raj Sirsi, Anindya Sircar, Jagdish Patankar, N. Yathindra, K.I. Varaprasad Reddy, Krishna M. Ella, Bimal Raizada, Yusuf Hamied, Vijay Chandru, B.V. Ravikumar; see also, 'Bioinformatics: New Frontier Calls Young Scientists', https://www.sciencemag.org/content/273/5272/265.citation; and 'New Goals for the Human Genome Project, 1998–2003', http://www.sciencemag.org/content/282/5389/682.full?sid=54a0034e-60b7-4d74-bb42-cc92e0a4c482

Of Exact IT and Approximate BT: Interviews with Samir K. Brahmachari, Raghunath Mashelkar, N.R. Narayana Murthy, M. Vidyasagar, Vijay Chandru, Goutam Das, Anuradha Acharya, Gayatri Saberwal, H. Sharat Chandra, Nandan Nilekani; see also, 'Bioinformatics in the Information Age', *Science*, 18 February 2000, No. 287, pp. 1221–1223; also, Gordon Binder, Philip Bashe, *Science Lessons: What the Business of Biotech Taught Me About Management*, Harvard Business Press; 'Revenue, Biotechnology Industry Organization', 2001, quoting 13 US Patent and Trademark Office, http://www.currentscience.ac.in/Downloads/article_id_089_06_0915_0916_0.pdf, http://www.tcs.com/investors/Documents/Annual%20Reports/TCS_Annual_Report_2014-2015.pdf, http://www.infosys.com/investors/reports-filings/annual-report/annual/Documents/infosys-AR-15.pdf, http://www.iimb.ernet.in/~rishi/biotech.pdf, http://dst.gov.in/about_us/12th-plan/10-wg_dbt2905-report.pdf.

Fresh Impetus: Interviews with Maharaj Kishan Bhan, Renu Swarup, Manju Sharma, see also, 'TRIPs and Changes in Pharmaceutical Patent Regime in India', http://www.who.int/hiv/amds/IDA_India-Patent-amendments-Sudip.pdf.

Regulatory Overhang: Interviews with K.K. Narayanan, Manju Sharma, Krishna M. Ella, K VijayRaghavan, Janaki Ramachandran, S. Anand Kumar, Gordon Ringold, Raghunath Mashelkar, Sunil Bhaskaran, Avadhesha Surolia; see also, 'The Court dismisses rotavirus PIL', http://www.indiaenvironmentportal.org.in/files/rotavirus%20vaccine%20clinical%20trial%20High%20Court.pdf; also, Anna Kuchment, *The Forgotten Cure: The Past and Future of Phage Therapy*, Springer; and 'Triclosan offers protection against blood stages of malaria by inhibiting enoyl-ACP reductase of *Plasmodium falciparum*', *Nature Medicine*, 2001, http://www.nature.com/nm/journal/v7/n2/abs/nm0201_167.html; and 'The Role of Environmental Enteropathy', http://rstb.royalsocietypublishing.org/content/370/1671/20140143.

Straws that Break: Interviews with K.I. Varaprasad Reddy, Bimal Raizada, Yusuf Hamied, Villoo Morawala-Patell, Subir Basak.

Network Effect: Interviews with Subramani Ramachandrappa, Ajay Bharadwaj, Madhav Raj Sirsi, Sohang Chatterjee, Shiladitya Sengupta, Charles Cooney, Pradip Majumder; see also, 'Vyome raises Rs 18.5 cr', http://articles.economictimes.indiatimes.com/2012-09-14/news/33844136_1_vyome-biosciences-vyome-s-biosciences-indous-venture-partners; also, 'Vyome closes $8 million funding', http://articles.economictimes.indiatimes.com/2014-08-11/news/52687498_1_sabre-partners-spring-healthcare-indous-venture-partners.

9. PUBLIC LIFE

Let's be Frank: Interviews with K. VijayRaghavan, K.K. Narayanan, Rohan Murthy, Pratima Rao; see also, 'USTR Froman in New Delhi on U.S.-India Trade Relationship', http://iipdigital.usembassy.gov/st/english/texttrans/2014/11/20141124311422.html#ixzz3v207Zexi; also, 'Indian drug cos worried about patent regime changes', http://www.thehindubusinessline.com/companies/indian-drug-cos-worried-about-patent-regime-changes/article6871490.ece; and 'Compulsory licensing hit India's image: Hetero Pharma', http://articles.economictimes.indiatimes.com/2015-03-31/news/60682269_1_sofosbuvir-swine-flu-drug-kidney-cancer-drug-sorafenib.

Change my City: Interviews with Pratima Rao, Yamini Mazumdar, Nandan Nilekani, Tania Khosla, Revathy Ashok, N.R. Narayana Murthy; see also, 'Narayana Murthy, Kiran Mazumdar-Shaw form BPAC to improve quality of life in Bangalore', http://articles.economictimes.indiatimes.com/2013-02-04/news/36743130_1_kiran-mazumdar-shaw-mohandas-pai-nr-narayana-murthy.

Accidental Investor: Interviews with M. Chinappa, B.V. Ravikumar, Kunal Kashyap, Kumud Sampath, Susan Kumar, Gordon Ringold, Yamini Mazumdar, Rani Desai, Devi Shetty, Paul C. Salins, Vijay Chandru, Arvind Atignal, Aditya Chaubey, Bala Manian.

Smart Capital: Interviews with S. Sadagopan, N. Yathindra, Dan Bradbury.

10. THE ROAD AHEAD

The Distance Runner: Interviews with Nandita Chandavarkar, Bala Manian, Subramani Ramachandrappa; see also, 'Drugmaker Shire bids $30 billion for Baxter spinoff Baxalta', http://www.reuters.com/article/us-baxalta-m-a-shire-idUSKCN0Q918F20150804.

Ducks in a Row: Interviews with Robert Coury, Jeremy Levin, Sriram Padmanabhan, Subir Basak, Anoop Misra; see also, Jim Collins, *Good to Great*, pp. 174–177; also, 'Biosimilar marriage ends in divorce for Teva, Lonza', http://www.genengnews.com/gen-news-highlights/biosimilar-marriage-ends-in-divorce-for-teva-lonza/81248645/; also, 'Key dates in Genzyme manufacturing crisis', http://www.reuters.com/article/genzyme-idUSN1321252820100813; also, 'Dr Reddy's, Merck Serono in pact to develop biotech drugs', http://www.business-standard.com/article/companies/dr-reddy-s-merck-serono-in-pact-to-develop-biotech-drugs-112060700062_1.html; 'Insulins market share in India, IMS, MAT, TSA', June 2015; and 'Sanofi invests Rs 90 cr in Apollo Sugar Clinics', http://www.business-standard.com/content/b2b-pharma/sanofi-invests-rs-90-cr-in-apollo-sugar-clinics-115013100214_1.html.

What Still Rankles: Interviews with S. Anand Kumar, K. VijayRaghavan, P. Murali, Renu Swarup, Narayanan Vaghul, Pramod Chaudhari, Anuradha Acharya, Lalji Singh, Samir K. Brahmachari, Krishna M.

Ella, Shiladitya Sengupta, Sohang Chatterjee; see also, 'Seeds of doubt: Monsanto never had Bt cotton patent', http://timesofindia.indiatimes. com/india/Seeds-of-doubt-Monsanto-never-had-Bt-cotton-patent/articleshow/47578304.cms.

Whither Valuation: Interviews with Tamar Howson, Parag Saxena, Nitin Deshmukh; see also, 'Samsung Bioepis hires banks for planned Nasdaq IPO', http://www.reuters.com/article/us-samsung-bioepis-ipo-idUSKCN0QP08F20150820; and 'The IPO is Dying', http://www.vox.com/2014/6/26/5837638/the-ipo-is-dying-marc-andreessen-explains-why.

The Anchor: Interviews with K. VijayRaghavan, Renu Swarup, N. Yathindra, Gayatri Saberwal, Nitin Deshmukh, Rajiv Doshi, P. Murali, Sunil Bhaskaran, G. Padmanaban; see also, Melinda Cooper, *Life as Surplus: Biotechnology and Capitalism in Neoliberal Era*, In Vivo – A Mclellan Book; also 'The Gene Hackers', http://www.newyorker.com/magazine/2015/11/16/the-gene-hackers.

INDEX

Acharya, Anuradha, 241, 289
Affymax, 129-30, 132, 133, 136, 137, 139
Association of Biotechnology Led Enterprises, 236
Astra Centre, 76-81, 85-86, 130-31, 297
AstraZeneca, 66, 208, 209, 225, 302
Atignal, Arvind, 136, 137-39, 140, 152, 176, 182, 226, 242, 275
Auchincloss, Leslie, 1, 6-11, 16, 17, 18, 20, 21, 22, 24-25, 27, 28, 34-35, 36, 37, 38-41, 43, 67
autoimmune diseases, 211, 212, 213, 215
AxiCorp, 197

Babu, Padmanaban, 79, 87, 130, 297
Bains, Peter, 146-49, 156
Bamzai, Rakesh, 53-54, 104, 106, 107, 109, 110, 123, 124, 174, 175, 177, 178, 183, 184, 199, 259
Bareja, Nirupa, 63, 177
Barve, Abhijit, 152-54, 155, 156, 199, 259, 300-01
Basak, Subir, 181, 182-83
Bedi, Atul, 196-97
Bhan, Maharaj Kishan, 2, 94, 244-48, 251, 295, 296-97

Bharadwaj, Ajay, 24-25, 27, 32, 34, 35, 36, 44-45, 48, 49, 53-54, 55, 56, 64, 69, 106, 107, 116, 122-23, 170, 171, 173-74, 175, 176, 177-78, 179
Bhargava, Pushpa Mittra, 71, 72, 82, 84, 89, 95
biobetters, 194
BioChemizyme, 27, 30, 32, 33, 41, 45, 51, 52, 65
 will to succeed at, 32-34
Biocon Biopharmaceuticals Private Limited, 180, 188
Biocon Group, 40-41, 42-43, 44, 46-47, 48-50, 67, 147
Biocon India, 7, 8, 14, 27, 28, 29-32, 36, 41, 42, 43, 44, 47, 49, 50, 51, 52, 54, 56, 66, 69
 and Bristol-Myers Squibb, 143, 144, 150-52, 208, 302, 303
 and CIMAB, 124-26, 180, 188
 and Unilever, 41, 44, 47, 49, 50-52, 69
 clinical advisory board at, 185-86, 206, 218
 exodus of senior management, 178-80, 199
 partnership accounts of, 7-8, 112-

13, 118–19, 143–44, 150, 187–94, 195–96, 197, 208
public interest litigation, 172
public offering by, 2, 6, 145, 149, 150, 168–69, 170–71, 172, 281
stock options at, 169–70
secret of success at, 26–27, 36, 60–61, 62–64
Biocon Ireland, 10, 14, 16, 22, 23, 27, 38–40, 50
Biocon-Quest, 51–52
biological sciences, 72, 76, 230, 237
BIOMAb, 181, 182–83, 302
biosimilars, 127, 166, 187, 188, 189, 190, 191, 193, 194, 195, 247, 258, 259, 261, 282, 283–85, 293, 301
Biotechnology Industry Research Assistance Council (BIRAC), 246
Biswas, Nirmal, 15–16
B.PAC, 270–71, 304
Brahmachari, Samir K., 85, 94
Bristol-Myers Squibb, 133–34, 141–44, 200, 201, 207, 217–18
and Biocon, 143, 144, 150–52, 208, 302, 303
Buchanan, John (Horlicks), 8
Bush, George, 3, 230

Chand, Puran (Barmalt), 7–8
Chandavarkar, Arun, 25–27, 32–33, 52, 55, 56, 57, 58, 64, 81, 112, 114, 126, 142, 158, 178, 186, 198, 199–200, 281, 303, 304
Chandavarkar, Nandita, 281
Chandra, H. Sharat, 83–84, 232, 233, 237
Chandrashekar, H.N., 19–21, 270
Chandru, Vijay, 236, 240–41, 242, 276, 294

Chatterjee, Sohang, 261–62, 292
Chattopadhyay, Deepanwita, 231, 296
Chinappa, Muckatira Bhemaiah, 119, 145, 272
CIMAB, 124, 125
Cipla, 147, 171, 224, 236, 258–59
clinical research business, 94, 152–57, 288
Clinigene, 137, 138–39, 140, 141, 152, 153, 154, 155, 156, 157, 168, 182, 199, 221, 242, 281
cluster development, 4–5, 231, 233, 244–45, 263
Cocker, Roland, 38, 39, 42, 50
compensation in the clinical trial, 156
Council of Scientific and Industrial Research (CSIR), 71, 72, 97, 239–40
Coury, Robert, 187–88, 190, 191

Daiichi, 258
Dave, Nitesh, 120
Defence Research Development Organization (DRDO), 31
DeLisi, Charles 94, 238
Desiraju, Gautam, 2
diabetes, 117, 121, 136–37, 138–39, 140, 141, 174, 184, 185, 204–05, 206–07, 208, 209, 242, 285, 286–87, 302
Dowzer, Colin, 9, 11
Dunne, Joe, 10–11, 35, 40–41, 45, 64, 65

Ella, Krishna M., 93–94

Francis, Ann, 63

Gandhi, Indira, 80, 81, 142
Gandhi, Rajiv, 78, 82, 85, 95
Gangagen, 4, 253
Genentech, 73, 77–78, 79, 112, 122, 165, 202, 283
generic drugs, 2, 3, 93, 104, 106, 109–10, 112, 120, 127, 131, 132, 138, 146, 153, 157, 166, 185, 187, 191–92, 195, 198, 215, 216, 218, 255, 261, 268, 281, 282–83, 284, 286, 287, 290, 293, 298–99
Genome Valley, 231, 235, 291
Genpharm, 104, 105
glargine, 185, 189, 191, 203, 285, 286
glaucoma, 221, 228
GlaxoSmithKline, 116–17, 118, 122, 130, 133, 146, 147, 148, 202, 256
Gowrishankara, Mahesh, 200, 216
GVK Bio, 142, 146, 157

handwriting analysis in hiring, 11, 24–25
Heber Biotec, 123, 124
Helix, 56, 100, 131, 234, 235
hepatitis, 89, 90, 91, 92–93, 152
Hindustan Antibiotics Limited (HAL), 102
Horgan, Liam, 46
Howson, Tamar, 142–43, 293, 303

ICICI Bank, 30, 31, 91, 140, 167, 231, 233, 289, 296
ICICI Ventures, 31, 32, 161–62
Immunotherapy, 200, 211
Imperial Chemical Industries (ICI), 64–66, 124, 164
Institute of Bioinformatics and Applied Biotechnology (IBAB), 232–33, 278, 295
Insugen, 173–75, 182, 183–84, 197

Insulin
  human, 112–13, 115, 120, 121, 172, 173, 175, 285–86
  nasal spray, 115, 138
  oral, 115–21, 195–96, 204, 205, 207, 208, 209, 285, 302
ISRO, 31
itolizumab, 128, 200, 202–03, 210–18, 302–03
Iyer, Harish, 111–12, 115, 120, 121, 172, 173, 175, 185–86, 197, 198–99, 207, 211, 257

Jayaram, Tara, 62–63, 105, 145–46

Kalam, A.P.J. Abdul, 31, 239
Kamath, Jyothi, 41–42, 43, 59, 110–11
Kashyap, Kunal, 65–66, 146–47, 150, 161, 162, 163
Khedkar, Anand, 103, 107, 110, 115, 119, 205, 207
Khosla, Tania, 164, 270
Kindler, Jeff, 188–89
Krishnan, Murali, 21–22, 26, 29, 36, 56, 60–61, 64, 85, 93, 142, 175
Kuchroo, Vijay, 202–03, 212, 214–15
Kulkarni, Vivek, 230, 231–33, 234, 235, 236
Kumar, S. Anand, 73, 74, 75, 236, 252, 287

Lebovitz, Harold (clinical advisor to Biocon), 5, 121, 205, 206–07, 210
Lecchini, Sergio, 47, 56, 66
Levin, Jeremy, 201–02, 219, 284
Limaye, Ravi, 200, 203, 204
Lovastatin, 99–100, 103–04, 105, 107, 161, 176, 179

MacFadden, Declan, 10, 39, 45, 46, 47
Majumder, Pradip, 262
Manian, Bala, 119, 139–40, 167, 180, 193, 196, 201, 205, 207, 213, 225, 248, 277
Mashelkar, Raghunath A. (CSIR), 86–87, 97, 172, 239, 246, 253
Mazumdar, Rasendra (father), 7, 8, 21, 68
Mazumdar, Ravi (brother), 13, 14, 18, 69, 165, 166
Mazumdar, Yamini (mother), 7, 15–16, 18, 273, 277, 305
Mazumdar-Shaw Cancer Centre, 275
Mazumdar-Shaw Centre for Translational Research, 226, 264
Mazumdar-Shaw Medical Foundation, 276
Mazumdar-Shaw, Kiran
  aesthetics of, 159–60
  and John Shaw, 65, 66, 67–70, 133, 275
  as viewed by
    Auchincloss, 25
    brother, 13
    Dr Shetty, 278
    Maharaj Kishan Bhan, 247
    Narayana Murthy, 266
  education of, 6, 12
  fun quotient, 67–68
  labour trouble faced by, 29
  manages multiple risks, 2
  philanthropy of, 270–71, 273–76, 278–80
  principles of, 14–16, 16–17, 264–65
  strengths of, 26–27, 36, 46, 48–49, 57–58, 60–61, 62–64, 268–69

Melarkode, Ramakrishnan, 212, 213
Merck (MSD Pharmaceutical), 100, 138, 139, 158, 164, 176, 182, 184, 193, 216, 217, 260, 283, 284, 293, 297, 301
Montero, Enrique, 210–11, 212
Mukherji, Subodh, 17
Murthy, N.R. Narayana, 169–70, 231, 238, 242, 267, 270
Murty, Sudha, 277, 278
Mylan, 187–88, 191, 199, 284, 293, 301

NAION, 221, 226, 227, 228
National Biological Lab, 71, 82
National Biotechnology Board, 81
Nayak, Sudhir, 185
Nilekani, Nandan, 243, 269–71, 304
NIMHANS, 218
Nobex, 116, 117–20, 195–96

Ostholm, Ivan, 73–77, 78–79, 287
outsourcing business, 55, 81, 130, 131, 133, 134–35, 138, 139, 141–42, 154–55, 159, 241

Padmanaban, Govindarajan, 74–75, 76–77, 79, 82, 86, 87–88, 92
patents, 4, 43, 62, 87, 89, 97, 100, 104, 106, 107, 112, 113, 119, 123, 136, 143, 146, 168, 187, 195–96, 197, 200, 214, 225, 231, 242, 244, 255, 260, 267–68, 282, 288, 290, 292
Pfizer, 145, 188–90, 191, 193, 197, 207, 221, 227
Pharmaceutical Product Development Inc. (PPD), 140, 141, 190
Prasad, B.S.V., 108–09, 114

Price, Chris, 116
Prime Minister's Office, 82, 264
psoriasis, 211, 212, 213–14, 216, 217, 218
public interest litigations (PIL), 172, 248, 251

Quality Assurance, 23, 62
Quark Pharmaceuticals, 220, 221, 222–23, 224, 225, 227, 228

Raja, Mugasimangalam, 223–24, 226
Ramachandran, Janakiraman, 4, 77–78, 79, 80, 81, 86, 129–30, 131–32, 133, 152–54
Ramachandran, S., 76, 83, 94
Ramachandran, Subramaniam, 239
Ramachandrappa, Subramani, 259
Ramnath, Renuka, 162, 163, 171
Ranbaxy, 24, 99, 157, 236, 246, 257, 258
and Biocon, 99–103, 106–07
Rangarajan, P.N., 92
Rao, C.N.R., 30, 166
Rao, Naveen, 139, 160
Rao, Sandeep, 104, 105, 106, 139, 199
Rao, U.R., 31
Ravikumar, Banda Venkata, 78–79, 86–87, 236, 271–73
Ravindra K.C., 103, 106, 159, 179
Read, Ian, 190
Reddy, Varaprasad, K.I., 88–92, 93, 112–13, 198, 235, 255–57
Ringold, Gordon, 129–30, 133, 136, 137, 139–41, 273

Saberwal, Gayatri, 232–35, 295
Saha Fund, 279
Sambandanamurthy, Vasan, 225, 226

Sambasivam, Ganesh, 132, 135, 145, 178–79
Shanghvi, Dilip, 3, 5
Shantha Bio, 89, 91, 92, 112–13, 172, 198, 225, 255–57
Sharma, Gita, 89–90
Sharma, Manju, 96, 250, 288
Shaw, John, 65, 66, 69, 133
Shetty, Dr Devi, 274–75, 278
Siddiqi, Obaid, 83
Sierra, Patricia, 124–25, 128
Singh, Lalji, 84, 85, 290
Singh, Parvinder, 99
Sircar, Anindya, 61, 168, 196, 234
Sirsi, Madhav Raj, 232
Spengler, Sylvia J., 243–44
start-ups, 1, 81, 129, 154, 231, 235, 243, 257, 263, 273, 280, 289, 294, 295
statins, 55, 99, 100, 101, 103, 105, 106–08, 111, 126, 157–58, 161, 162, 174, 176
stem cells, 3–4, 72, 219, 230
Subramanian, Balu N., 133–35, 142, 143, 144, 239
Sun Pharma, 3, 182, 216, 217, 258
Sundaram, Mallik, 262
Surromed, 136, 137, 138, 139, 140, 141
Suryanarayanan, Shrikumar (Shri), 22–23, 25, 26, 27, 28, 32–33, 34, 45, 53, 55, 56, 58–60, 64, 100, 103, 107, 115, 119, 121, 125, 126, 165, 179, 180, 186, 194, 211
Syngene, 1, 4, 131–33, 134, 135–36, 137, 139–40, 142, 143, 144–46, 147–52, 155, 156, 157, 168, 177, 178–79, 201, 208, 221, 241, 242, 243, 261, 281, 282, 289, 293

Taleb, Nassim Nicholas, 266–67
Talwar, Suresh, 164–65, 176, 201
Tambe, Shreehas, 57–60, 159, 165
Technology Development Information Company of India (TDICI), 30, 31–32, 46, 161

Vaghul, Narayanan (ICICI Bank), 30–32, 91, 140, 167, 231, 240, 289

Vidyasagar, M., 239–40, 243
VijayRaghavan, K., 5, 288–89
Vyome Biosciences, 262, 291

Yathindra, N., 235

Zaheer, Syed Hussain, 71
Zurr, Daniel, 220–28

ACKNOWLEDGEMENTS

I would like to thank everyone quoted in the book for their time and willingness to share their perspective. Thanks, especially to a few people with whom I had multiple meetings – Shrikumar Suryanarayanan, Ajay Bharadwaj, Arun Chandavarkar, Shreehas Tambe and Janaki Ramachandran. Special thanks to Mike Powell for giving me a clear understanding of the multi-layered corporate structure at Unilever. I'm also grateful to those who have not been quoted – Rajiv Doshi, S. Sadagopan and Sriram Padmanabhan, and to Seema Ahuja for pointing me to the right people in the industry. At HarperCollins India, my sincerest thanks to publisher Karthika V.K. and associate editor Arcopol Chaudhuri; thanks also to my husband, Shashank, and our son, Kshitij, for putting up with the pre-publication jitters and general edginess of a first-time author.

ABOUT THE AUTHOR

In a journey spanning two decades in journalism, it was a year-long Knight fellowship at the Massachusetts Institute of Technology early on in Seema Singh's career that brought her the realization that science and its handmaiden, technology-driven stories are the coolest ones. Never mind if they often entail hard sell on both sides – to the editor and the source. She has written on science and technology and everything at their intersection for Indian publications like *The Times of India, Mint, Forbes* (India) and specialist ones like *IEEE-Spectrum, Cell, New Scientist*.

She can be found at www.seemasingh.in.